A Soldier's Soldier
A biography of Lieutenant-General Sir Thomas Daly

Lieutenant-General Sir Thomas Daly was a renowned soldier and one of the most important and influential figures in Australia's military history. As Chief of the General Staff during the Vietnam War, he oversaw a significant reorganisation of the army as he fought a war under political and resource restrictions. In this unique biography, Jeffrey Grey shows how Daly prepared himself for the challenges of command in a time of great turbulence and political upheaval.

A Soldier's Soldier examines Daly's career from his entry to Duntroon in the early 1930s until his retirement forty years later, covering the key issues in the development of the Australian Army along the way. Drawing on extensive interview transcripts, the book provides a compelling portrait of Sir Thomas Daly and his distinguished career.

Jeffrey Grey is Professor of History and founding director of the Australian Centre for the Study of Armed Conflict and Society at the University of New South Wales, Canberra. The author or editor of numerous books and articles, he has held the Major General Matthew C. Horner Chair in Military Theory at Marine Corps University, Quantico, and served as a trustee of the Society of Military History.

OTHER TITLES IN THE AUSTRALIAN ARMY HISTORY SERIES

Series editor
David Horner

Phillip Bradley *The Battle for Wau: New Guinea's Frontline 1942–1943*
Mark Johnston *The Proud 6th: An Illustrated History of the 6th Australian Division 1939–1946*
Garth Pratten *Australian Battalion Commanders in the Second World War*
Jean Bou *Light Horse: A History of Australia's Mounted Arm*
Phillip Bradley *To Salamaua*
Peter Dean *The Architect of Victory: The Military Career of Lieutenant-General Sir Frank Horton Berryman*
Allan Converse *Armies of Empire: The 9th Australian and 50th British Divisions in Battle 1939–1945*
John Connor *Anzac and Empire: George Foster Pearce and the Foundations of Australian Defence*
Peter Williams *The Kokoda Campaign 1942: Myth and Reality*
Karl James *The Hard Slog: Australians in the Bougainville Campaign, 1944–45*
Robert Stevenson *To Win the Battle: The 1st Australian Division in the Great War, 1914–1918*
Mark Johnston *Anzacs in the Middle East: Australian Soldiers, Their Allies and the Local People in World War II*

A Soldier's Soldier

A BIOGRAPHY OF
LIEUTENANT-GENERAL
SIR THOMAS DALY

JEFFREY GREY

CAMBRIDGE UNIVERSITY PRESS
Cambridge, New York, Melbourne, Madrid, Cape Town,
Singapore, São Paulo, Delhi, Mexico City

Cambridge University Press
477 Williamstown Road, Port Melbourne, VIC 3207, Australia

Published in the United States of America by Cambridge University Press, New York

www.cambridge.org
Information on this title: www.cambridge.org/9781107031272

© Jeffrey Grey 2013

This publication is in copyright. Subject to statutory exception
and to the provisions of relevant collective licensing agreements,
no reproduction of any part may take place without the written
permission of Cambridge University Press.

First published 2013

Cover design by Rob Cowpe
Typeset by Aptara Corp.
Printed in China by C & C Offset Printing Co. Ltd

A catalogue record for this publication is available from the British Library

*A Cataloguing-in-Publication entry is available from the catalogue
of the National Library of Australia at* www.nla.gov.au

ISBN 978-1-107-03127-2 Hardback

Reproduction and communication for educational purposes
The Australian *Copyright Act 1968* (the Act) allows a maximum of
one chapter or 10% of the pages of this work, whichever is the greater,
to be reproduced and/or communicated by any educational institution
for its educational purposes provided that the educational institution
(or the body that administers it) has given a remuneration notice to
Copyright Agency Limited (CAL) under the Act.

For details of the CAL licence for educational institutions contact:

Copyright Agency Limited
Level 15, 233 Castlereagh Street
Sydney NSW 2000
Telephone: (02) 9394 7600
Facsimile: (02) 9394 7601
E-mail: info@copyright.com.au

Reproduction and communication for other purposes
Except as permitted under the Act (for example a fair dealing for the
purposes of study, research, criticism or review) no part of this publication
may be reproduced, stored in a retrieval system, communicated or
transmitted in any form or by any means without prior written permission.
All inquiries should be made to the publisher at the address above.

Cambridge University Press has no responsibility for the persistence or
accuracy of URLs for external or third-party internet websites referred to
in this publication and does not guarantee that any content on such
websites is, or will remain, accurate or appropriate.

Contents

Illustrations	vii
Maps	ix
Tables and diagrams	x
Acknowledgements	xi
Abbreviations	xiii
1 Regimental soldiering	1
2 Balikpapan, 1945	37
3 'He could fill any appointment with distinction'	58
4 The challenges of senior rank	90
5 Chief of the General Staff	114
6 Daly, the army and the war in Vietnam, 1966–71	146
7 The civic action crisis, 1971	177
8 Epilogue	197
Notes	208
Sources and bibliography	236
Index	243

Illustrations

1	Baby Tom	3
2	Major T.J. Daly, Broadmeadows Camp, December 1911	5
3	Young Tom, aged three, 1916	6
4	Major T.J. Daly, Palestine, 1917	7
5	Tom Daly and Joe St Ellen winning the junior pairs, Xavier College, 1929	9
6	First Eleven, Royal Military College, 1932	10
7	Graduation portrait, Royal Military College, 1934	12
8	Lieutenant Daly, attached to 16th/5th Lancers, Risalpur, 1938	13
9	In bivouac, 1938	14
10	2/10th Battalion officers, 1939	16
11	Captain T.J. Daly, England, 1940	17
12	Officers' Mess, Headquarters, 18th Australian Infantry Brigade, Giarabub, Libya, 21 March 1941	20
13	The town of Giarabub from Ship Hill, March 1941	23
14	Major T.J. Daly, Giarabub, Libya, March 1941	25
15	Lieutenant-Colonel T.J. Daly addressing a parade of the 2/10th Battalion, Kairi, Queensland, October 1944	41
16	Daly and Brigadier Chilton inspecting a parade of the 2/10th Battalion	43
17	Assault barges at the beachhead, Balikpapan, 1 July 1945	47
18	Soldiers of the 2/10th Battalion moving along Vasey Highway towards Hill 87, Balikpapan, 1 July 1945	52
19	Wedding day	60
20	Lieutenant-Colonel T.J. Daly, Camberley, 1948	63

21	Colonel T.J. Daly is farewelled before departure for Korea, 1952	71
22	Brigadier Thomas Daly, DSO OBE, on a tour of the front line, Korea, c. 27 June 1952	76
23	Brigadier T.J. Daly talks to unidentified soldiers at a camp in Korea, September 1952	81
24	The 1956 course, Imperial Defence College, London	88
25	Chief of the General Staff	115
26	Military Board, 1966	117
27	Handover of Oakey facilities to the army, 1 July 1969	144
28	Lieutenant-General Sir Thomas Daly is greeted by Lieutenant-General Tran Ngoc Tam of the Army of the Republic of Vietnam	157
29	The CGS talks to a soldier from 6RAR manning the perimeter of Fire Support Base Discovery, November 1969	171
30	The CGS talks to soldiers from C Company, 7RAR at the Horseshoe, 1970	173
31	The CGS inspects a guard from the Grenadier Guards, Whitehall, 1970	184
32	Military Board, 1970	195
33	Chairman of the Board of Trustees escorts the Lord Mayor of London, Sir Murray Fox, on an official visit to the Australian War Memorial, September 1975	203
34	Sir Thomas is carried from the cathedral to the hearse on the way to his final resting place, 2004	205

Maps

1	Western Desert, 1941	19
2	Giarabub, March 1941	22
3	Siege of Tobruk, 1941	27
4a	Balikpapan, July 1945	49
4b	Balikpapan, July 1945 – detail	50
5	Area of operations, 1st Commonwealth Division, Korea, 1952–53	73
6	28th Commonwealth Brigade, Korea, 1952–53	74
7	Phuoc Tuy province, South Vietnam, 1966–71	149

Tables and diagrams

Table 4.1   Strength of the Australian Regular Army and Citizen Military Force, 1960–64 — 105

Figure 6.1   Build-up and relief patterns of Australian Force, Vietnam, 1967–69 — 155

Acknowledgements

As a young and impatient academic a long time ago, I used to wonder why productive historians in their seeming prime often appeared to drop away completely and write less just when one might think they had more in them. I know the answer now – it's called 'life', and it has a habit of getting in the way. I started work on this book fifteen years ago, and a lot of things have happened in the intervening period to explain why it has taken so long to reach fruition. On the one hand, it has travelled with me like the spectre at the feast, reproving me silently for its unfinished state and at the same time stopping me from moving on with anything new. On the other hand, biography is a difficult form of historical writing (which is why I think every serious historian should attempt one), and I think this one is a better book for being written by someone in his early fifties rather than, as might otherwise have been the case, appearing from the keyboard of an author in his late thirties. Readers will be the judge of that.

As with every book I have written, this one has accrued debts near and far, and it is a pleasure to acknowledge and thank those whose contribution was essential at some step along the way. The staff of various archives head the list: National Archives of Australia, Parkes (especially Tim Mifsud, who dealt with a barrage of access clearance requests quickly and efficiently) and Melbourne; Australian War Memorial, Canberra; and the National Archives, Kew (which must now be the best public archive in the English-speaking world in which to work). Roger Lee and his people in the Australian Army History Unit helped with access to records not yet transferred to archival custody and with photographs, production of the maps and the provision of transcripts of Bob Breen's series of interviews with Sir Thomas Daly, and supported the early research with an Army history research grant, for which I thank them. Dr Breen was kind enough to fill in some gaps in the transcripts as well. Dr Garth Pratten very generously gave me a copy of his own interview with Daly and notes on interviews with former soldiers of the 2/10th Battalion, and shared thoughts on the record of unit commanders in the latter years of the war. Tom Richardson kindly gave me a copy of his paper on Giarabub. David Nalson, Queen's Royal Lancers Museum, answered some queries about the regiment's service in India, and Colonel A.J. Lenard, Chief of Staff, Royal College of Defence Studies, London, provided photos from the 1956 course together with a class list for that year. Yasmin Tadich of the Army Production Learning Centre kindly transferred two interviews with Daly to DVD and forwarded them to me. I also benefited from correspondence and the provision of papers from Brigadier John Salmon, Colonel Derek Sharp and Colonel Stan Maizey, and from Monsignor Eugene Harley.

I had the advantage of several extended conversations with my subject before his death in 2004, greatly to my benefit. I think Daly was slightly bemused by the idea of a biography, although he recognised a certain inevitability in the process given his long and distinguished public career. I have also had considerable assistance from the Daly family and especially his oldest daughter, Betty-Ann, or BA, as she is generally known. I was generously given the run of the family photo albums, and BA has dealt with my intrusions into the details of family life and lore with good humour and patience; I am very grateful for her efforts. The editor of the Army History Series, David Horner, read the manuscript with his usual gimlet eye. Isabella Mead at Cambridge University Press smoothed the submission process of the manuscript, and she and the staff at CUP Melbourne have my thanks. My editor, Cathryn Game, imposed order, discipline and readability on me.

The book is dedicated to the memory of my mother, and to my small son, Sebastian. My mother used to ask periodically, 'How's Tom going?' I regret that she did not live to see its publication. She never met Sebastian, either, although I am sure she would have approved of him. He is, as yet, too young to understand what Dadda does for long periods in his study, which perhaps is just as well.

Abbreviations

AAF	Australian Army Force
AATTV	Australian Army Training Team Vietnam
ACAU	Australian Civil Affairs Unit
ADC	aide-de-camp
AFV	Australian Force Vietnam
AG	Adjutant-General
AHQ	Army Headquarters
AHU	Army History Unit
A&I	Administrative and Instructional
AIF	Australian Imperial Force
ALH	Australian Light Horse
ALSG	Australian Logistic Support Group
AMF	Australian Military Forces; official name of the army of Australia, 1916–80, encompassing both full-time and part-time forces
ARA	Australian Regular Army
ARVN	Army of the Republic of Vietnam
ATF	Australian Task Force
ATIS	Allied Translator and Interpreter Section
CAS	Chief of the Air Staff
CGS	Chief of the General Staff
CIGS	Chief of the Imperial General Staff
CMF	Citizen Military Forces
CNS	Chief of Naval Staff
CO	Commanding Officer
COMAFV	Commander, Australian Forces Vietnam
COMUSMACV	Commander, United States Military Assistance Command Vietnam
COSC	Chiefs of Staff Committee
DCGS	Deputy Chief of the General Staff
FARELF	Far East Land Forces

GOC	General Officer Commanding
GSO	General Staff Officer
GVN	Government of [South] Vietnam
JIO	Joint Intelligence Organisation
LST	Landing Ship Tank
MA	military assistant
MGO	Master-General of the Ordnance
MM	Military Medal
NCO	Non-Commissioned Officer
OCS	Officer Cadet School, Portsea
PIR	Pacific Islands Regiment
PMF	Permanent Military Forces
PNGVR	Papua New Guinea Volunteer Rifles
QMG	Quartermaster General
RAAOC	Royal Australian Army Ordnance Corps
RAEME	Royal Australian Electrical and Mechanical Engineers
RAR	Royal Australian Regiment
RF/PF	Regional Forces/Popular Forces
RMC	Royal Military College
RNSWR	Royal New South Wales Regiment
RQR	Royal Queensland Regiment
RSM	regimental sergeant major
RVNAF	Republic of Vietnam Armed Forces
RWAR	Royal Western Australian Regiment
SAS	Special Air Service
VC	Victoria Cross; Viet Cong
WRAAC	Women's Royal Australian Army Corps

CHAPTER 1

REGIMENTAL SOLDIERING

Armies are living entities, human organisations that develop their own cultures and characteristics over time. Some armies have commonalities, but no two national armies are the same, although they might, on occasions, be alike. Field Marshal Lord Carver, a senior soldier and noted scholar of his institution, wrote of the British Army as possessing seven 'ages', periods associated with an individual such as Marlborough, Wellington or Montgomery, who dominated or typified a period in the life of the institution.[1] The Australian Army was, and is, a 'British-pattern' army; it has many things in common with its British counterpart, but is not the same institution. It lacks, for example, a tradition of 'great captains', which provided Carver with a useful organising device around which to structure his account of the British Army's history. The Australian Army's development nonetheless can be organised around a 'generational' perspective, one that helps to identify both the continuities and distinct differences in different periods of its existence.[2]

The army emerged from the tangle of confusions that accompanied Federation, the establishment of the Commonwealth of Australia and the gradual development of centralised government at the federal level. The first generation of the army came of age during the Great War and reached its culminating point in 1918, both on the Western Front and in Palestine (the latter often being overlooked). Thereafter it entered a period of neglect and decline that saw the Regular Army, at least, attenuated almost out of existence by the early 1930s. The growing threat of war in Europe and Asia led to the renewal of the army and arguably to its greatest achievements during the latter half of the Second World War, during which its senior leadership functioned at the strategic level for the first time.[3] As with the generation following the Great War, this army was quickly broken up and the organisation 'forgot' much of what it had learned at such expense during the Pacific War. However, unlike the 1920s, the army's leadership was able to take the organisation forward into a new generation of development and activity, made possible both by the very different strategic circumstances that confronted the nation after 1945 and, ironically perhaps, by a shared memory of the consequences of decisions made by an earlier generation of political leadership.

The third-generation army was characterised by the creation of a regular standing field force in peacetime and the extensive use of that force on operations in Asia between 1946 and 1972. The army developed and extended a professional ethos, one that stood it in good stead during the twenty-five years that followed the withdrawal from Vietnam – during which the army was attenuated once again, if not quite on this occasion to the point of non-existence then, certainly, to a position where its ability to respond effectively had it been called on must be very severely doubted.[4] The intervention in East Timor in the second half of 1999 marked the emergence of the current generation of the Australian Army, one that again has been more or less continuously deployed on operations in various parts of the world simultaneously, and whose foundations were laid by far-sighted senior leadership in the mid-1990s, against the political trend of the previous two decades. The generations of the army have thus occupied a 'boom and bust' cycle familiar to students of Western armies elsewhere in the course of the twentieth century.

Thomas Joseph Daly joined the Australian Army towards the end of its first generation, gained his experience of the craft of soldiering during its second, and had a sizeable influence upon its development during its third, during which time he came to its head as Chief of the General Staff (CGS). A few of the things he put in train during that period – especially the development of army aviation and the acquisition of helicopter capabilities – have stood it in good stead subsequently, but the army that deployed in Afghanistan or Timor Leste bears few similarities to that in which he spent his entire adult life. Armies, after all, are living entities.

Photo 1 Baby Tom. (Daly family)

Daly was born on 19 March 1913 in Ballarat, Victoria. His Majesty George V was King-Emperor; his viceregal representative, Viscount Denman, the fifth Governor-General since Federation, exercised a broadly supervisory role over the Labor government of Andrew Fisher (and, after Labor's defeat in the federal election in June, the Liberal government of Joseph Cook). The first Australian postage stamps were issued that year, as were the first national banknotes. Eastern Suburbs won the 1913 rugby league premiership (there was no grand final; the minor premiers were considered league champions by dint of topping the competition table against their seven rival sides that season). Posinatus won the Melbourne Cup; the site of the new national capital, Canberra, was dedicated by Lady Denman; and the flagship of the new Australian squadron, HMAS *Australia*, sailed from Portsmouth upon commissioning. In rugby, Australia toured New Zealand for only the second time, losing five of its nine matches, although it scored 118 points with only 114 scored against, and beat the All Blacks in the third test 16–5.

The population of Australia, as reflected in the census of 1911, stood at 4 455 005; unemployment nationally was a little over 5.5 per cent, while the average weekly wage varied between trades and location: electrical fitters earned 66s a week in Sydney but 72s in Perth; the weekly rate for a shoeing smith in Melbourne was 57s 6d in Melbourne but only 45s in Brisbane. Cellarmen in a brewery could expect between 48s and 60s, but milliners earned just 15s in Hobart and 22s 6d in Melbourne. Pastoral workers were, likewise, relatively poorly paid; shearers when in work, on the other hand, earned 24–25s a day. The United Kingdom provided the major market for Australian exports, was the overwhelming source of investment capital and was the source of more than 50 per cent of Australian imports, both material and population. Primary industries dominated the economy.

As their name would suggest, the Daly family was of Irish extraction: Thomas Joseph Daly arrived in the Australian colonies in 1878 from a small village in County Clare. Daly's own father, also Thomas Joseph and born in Coburg in 1884, was a bank manager with the State Savings Bank in rural Murtoa in the Wimmera district and at equally rural Maffra in Gippsland. His mother, Eileen Mary, was a native of Ballarat, and the two married in 1912. The family was Catholic, and lived the comfortable life of the professional middle class of the time. Daly senior had completed matriculation at Marist Brothers, Melbourne, in 1899 and successfully sat the Civil Service examination. He was a dedicated citizen soldier, joining the 4th Battalion in 1901 before transferring to the light horse, in which he held various appointments in several different units over the next decade or more.[5]

The Australia into which the young Daly was born, and in which his family lived an ordered and predictable existence, was largely to disappear during his childhood as a consequence of the Great War. The most immediate impact for Daly was his father's enlistment, with his peacetime rank of major, on 21 October 1914 in the 9th Light Horse, part of the 3rd Light Horse Brigade. One squadron of the 9th was drawn from Victoria, the rest from South Australia. The first commanding officer was a South Australian militia officer, Lieutenant-Colonel Albert Miell, a veteran of the South African War and peacetime commanding officer of the 24th Light Horse, Citizen Military Forces.[6] Initial induction took place at Morphettville in South Australia, and the men then entrained for Broadmeadows Camp, near Melbourne, where the Victorian A Squadron, under Daly's command, joined them to complete the unit's establishment. With his father's enlistment the family moved to new lodgings at Albert Park;

Photo 2 Major T.J. Daly, Broadmeadows Camp, December 1911. (Daly family)

families often moved closer to relatives or amenities upon the enlistment of the head of the household, and perhaps Daly's wife and very young son went to be closer to him during the work-up period since they lived there for a while with young Daly's paternal grandmother. In any case, they subsequently returned to Ballarat and lived with Eileen's three unmarried sisters.[7]

Daly's father had both a good and a fortunate war, not least through contracting pneumonia in Egypt. He thus missed the Gallipoli campaign; most of the regiment's officers who sailed from Australia and landed at the Dardanelles were killed, wounded or evacuated due to sickness. Daly rejoined in Egypt after the evacuation as second-in-command under Major (subsequently Lieutenant-Colonel) W.H. Scott and spent most of the rest of the war in that role.[8] He commanded the 9th Australian Light Horse in the CO's absence on several occasions, and on one such in July 1918 was injured while making a forward reconnaissance by motor vehicle when the car rolled, trapping him beneath it. Several months of convalescence followed. Daly saw action with the 9th Australian Light Horse

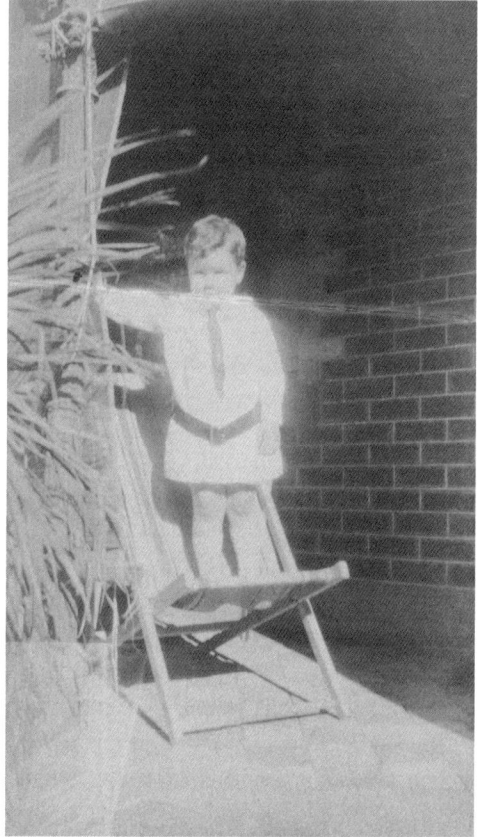

Photo 3 Young Tom, aged three, 1916. (Daly family)

in all the major actions of the Sinai and Palestine campaigns: Romani, Maghdaba, Rafa, First and Second Gaza, Beersheba (or Third Gaza), the capture of Jerusalem, Es Salt, and the operations in 1918 in the Jordan Valley and Syria. He led his regiment in a mounted charge on 2 October 1918 ('the last light horse engagement in the campaign', according to the official history), and in a spirited action captured a Turkish column of around 1500 Turks, eight Germans, three artillery pieces and twenty-six machine-guns as well as the regimental standard of the Ottoman 46th Infantry Regiment.[9] He was awarded the Distinguished Service Order 'for distinguished service in connection with operations in Egypt', was twice

Photo 4 Major T.J. Daly, Palestine, 1917.
(Daly family)

mentioned in despatches, and was judged 'an all-round good officer thoroughly competent to command a regiment' by Major-General Granville Ryrie, commander of the Australian Mounted Division, at the end of the war.

He returned to Australia in July 1919, and young Daly, aged six, and his mother were at Port Melbourne to welcome him home. 'He came striding along Station Pier swinging his cane; somehow I knew it was he and I ran to meet him', his son wrote many decades after.[10] Daly's father continued his service in the citizen forces after the war and his repatriation, commanding the 13th and 4th Light Horse Regiments. He transferred to the Unattached List in 1924, and to the Reserve of Officers in 1929. Like many of his generation, he re-entered service at the outbreak of the Second World War, in his case on the staff of the Chief Censor (then a military office), only finally being placed on the Retired List in December 1944.

With his father's return the family moved to Elwood, a seaside suburb of Melbourne, where Daly senior taught his young son to swim ('every morning down to the beach irrespective of weather') until a transfer to Koroit, in the Western District, in 1921 where Daly's father opened a new branch of the bank and young Daly went to a convent school staffed by Irish nuns. Another transfer by the bank took the family to Sale in east Gippsland. A sister, Margaret, was born in 1920, a post-war service baby, and her arrival completed the family. Like his father, Daly was educated by the Marist Brothers, in his case at St Patrick's College, Sale. Daly was bright, and his progression through school was accelerated to the extent that he first attempted his Intermediate certificate at the age of 12, although he failed it on that occasion, resitting it the following year. He was also a keen and talented sportsman and especially good at cricket, talents undoubtedly inherited from his gregarious father whose taste for and skill in cricket and golf passed to his son. Daly completed his Leaving certificate at the age of 15, and the question of a future career now beckoned, although not urgently, given his relatively tender years. His father's intention was that he study medicine, but this would require a scholarship to support his residence at the University of Melbourne and one was not available. Instead he was sent to do a final year of secondary education as a boarder at Xavier College, Melbourne, during which he undertook Leaving Honours. A personal connection with General Sir Harry Chauvel, whose own sons were then at the Royal Military College, Duntroon, appears to have settled Daly's future.

Daly entered RMC at the beginning of 1930, as the Depression began to bite – the following year there would be no Fourth Class entry at all as an economy measure, while the college closed altogether at Duntroon and moved to Victoria Barracks, Sydney. He was not yet 17. Duntroon was a very monastic and isolated environment, nestled into a Canberra that had a population of fewer than 5000. The classes of the Depression era were small and got smaller, while the army generally underwent a period of retrenchment occasioned by the global economic situation and a then orthodox federal response that saw budget outlays cut rather than enhanced.

Daly recalled enjoying RMC, having been through a stint at a Jesuit boarding school; the physical abuse of the entry class – known more recently as bastardisation and in his time as 'Fourth Class training' – did not worry him unduly, either. 'There were one or two sadists round

Photo 5 Tom Daly and Joe St Ellen winning the junior pairs, Xavier College, 1929. (Daly family)

about the place. There always are, I suppose... and they made life miserable for anybody they could get their hands on.'[11] The leading historian of the college has shown that harassment of the entry class intensified significantly in the early and mid-1920s, and was clearly well established by the time Daly entered.[12] The first year emphasised civilian academic subjects, drill and loads of sport, with formal military instruction largely relegated to the later years, peaking in the final year known, confusingly (to outsiders), as First Class. For what it was worth, given that his entering class had numbered just twelve, Daly was listed as one of the three most academically distinguished in his year.[13]

Duntroon was 'a monastic institution' and 'a little inbred', in Daly's own words, populated by 'rather narrow, restricted little boys'.[14] The move to Victoria Barracks, Sydney, brought a very different, and much improved, environment.[15] As part of the economy measures, many of the directing and administrative staff held dual appointments: the Commandant, Brigadier F.B. Heritage, for example, was also commanding the 2nd Military District. Daly's results were solid, if unspectacular, and he graduated fourth in a class of just nine.[16] As noted, the emphasis in instruction swung heavily towards tactics, weapon training, military history, law and administration, although in Daly's case he maintained study

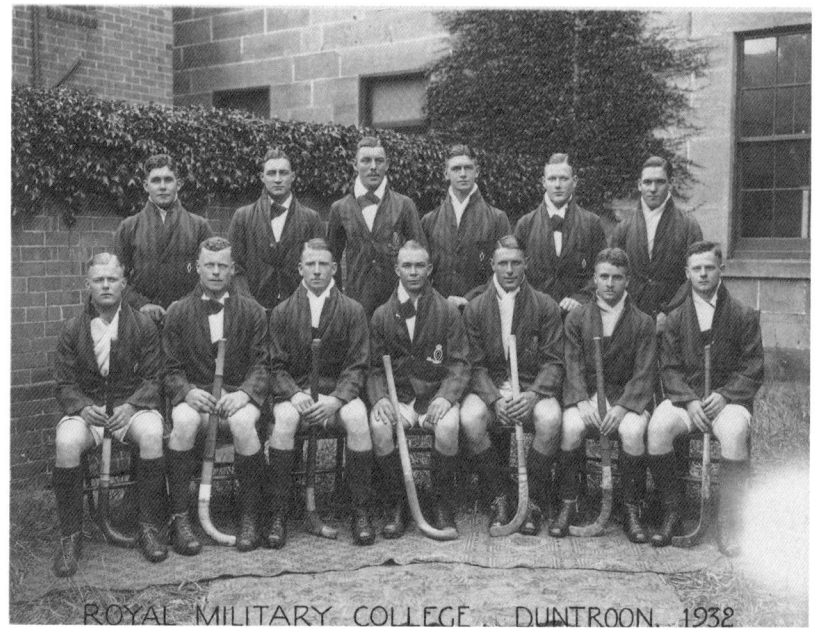

Photo 6 First Eleven, Royal Military College, 1932. Daly second from left, standing. (Daly family)

in Japanese at a respectable level across the full four years.[17] He played a lot of sport – as they all did: hockey (of which he was captain), tennis, rugby and becoming 'a most consistent batsman' and bowling well 'at times'.[18] He also wrote for publication in-house, usually humorous or whimsical pieces and some poetry.

Opportunities were narrowing as the Depression worsened and, like others around him, Daly wondered whether he had made a sound decision by opting for the army. His father counselled patience, and in truth he probably had little choice but to see it through; attendance at university was not an option, and few others beckoned. At the beginning of the college year in 1931 there were just thirty-one cadets, all classes; some graduates in these years transferred to the British and Indian armies while a few exercised the right to transfer to the public service and others still, destined for service in the RAAF, were transferred early to their parent service. At the beginning of his final year he was appointed corps sergeant major (equivalent to the more familiar battalion sergeant major, but so called because the Corps of Staff Cadets was now so small that it could no longer be sensibly described as a 'battalion'). He was stripped of the rank in April, however, at the direction of the Commandant, by now the formidable Colonel J.D. Lavarack, for 'neglect to the prejudice of good order and military discipline – not taking steps to prevent improper procedure at a meal'; in plain English this meant that he had not reacted sufficiently firmly to an outbreak of fourth-class training.[19] Reinstated to the rank before the end of the year, on graduation he was awarded the Sword of Honour.

The final year involved exposure to the wider army, such as it was in 1933. The whole class completed a six-week course at the Small Arms School (precursor of the later Infantry Centre), then conveniently located at Randwick. In April, Daly and another classmate were attached to the 16th Light Horse, a militia unit, during its annual camp at Muswellbrook. Daly was given a troop command and impressed all around with his power of command, ability as an instructor and horsemanship, all of which were rated as 'very good'.[20] Looking back, he remembered it as a 'tremendous experience' and one 'of enormous value' after he graduated. The reduction in rank early in the year had done little to mar the regard in which he was held; Lavarack wrote in his graduation report that he possessed 'good general ability, has earned the confidence and respect of both his seniors and his juniors, and has all the makings of a fine officer... tactful, modest and unassuming in his manner... he is keen and possesses a receptive and practical mind... In short, a very suitable type of young officer, best suited for employment with cavalry.'[21] The real army now awaited him.

His first posting was as assistant adjutant to the 4th Light Horse Regiment, based at Warrnambool near the district he had lived in as a boy. His riding skills and background made him a good fit for a mounted unit in country (or, as we would now call it, 'regional') Australia, and he enjoyed his surroundings enormously. After about six months, he was posted as adjutant and quartermaster to the 3rd Light Horse, with its headquarters in Mount Gambier, South Australia. In his annual report for 1934, his commanding officer noted his 'decision, self-reliance' and that he was 'tactful and commands respect', while the brigade commander thought that he 'should prove successful as a LH adjutant'.[22] Rurally based militia units faced challenges and provided opportunities not always shared by their urban counterparts, although the militia generally was starved of funds, personnel and equipment through most of the 1930s. The regiment's troops and squadrons were scattered across South Australia while it formed part of the 2nd Cavalry Division with headquarters in Melbourne. Both the commanding officer and the brigade major lived

Photo 7 Graduation portrait, Royal Military College, 1934. (Daly family)

and worked in Adelaide, and in a very real sense, therefore, Daly ran the regiment on a day-to-day basis for most of the four years he was in the position; he recalled that he saw the CO only during the annual camp.[23] Comfortable in a country environment, Daly enjoyed the social and recreational opportunities that came his way while the responsibilities he inherited certainly did him much good in professional terms.

His predecessor had been Captain Ragnar Garrett, an RMC graduate of the class of 1921 who had spent ten years in appointments with militia units together with a two-year attachment to a British heavy cavalry regiment in India in 1923–25. A shortage of professional opportunities was married to reduced pay – a Depression-era measure that affected all federal government employees and not just the army. Daly again wondered about his prospects, and again his father counselled patience and this, together with a lack of realistic opportunities elsewhere plus the fulfilment he enjoyed from his semi-independent role in Mount Gambier, persuaded him to stay on. Nor were his qualities and abilities unappreciated. His annual reports all spoke of his keen and zealous approach

Photo 8 Lieutenant Daly, attached to 16th/5th Lancers, Risalpur, 1938. (Daly family)

to his duties, his smart turnout, tact, sound judgement and powers of command.[24]

In September 1938 Daly embarked for India and service at Risalpur (near Peshawar in modern Pakistan) with a British light cavalry regiment, the 16th/5th Lancers (a regiment combined from the former 16th (Queen's) and 5th (Royal Irish) Lancers in the reductions and amalgamations that followed the end of the Great War). Attachments to the British and Indian armies were designed to broaden the viewpoint and range of experiences available to young regular officers serving in the tiny peacetime establishment; they also brought encounters of a new and occasionally unsettling kind. The social relationships within the officers' mess and between commissioned and enlisted ranks were very different from those pertaining in an Australian militia unit. Daly held a range of positions within the lancers: troop commander, squadron second-in-command, squadron commander, even quartermaster (in which his previous experience stood him in excellent stead). Although the regiment mounted a column to the North West Frontier during his time with them, Daly saw no action. He impressed his British superiors markedly. 'A

Photo 9 In bivouac, 1938. (Daly family)

very strong, active, cheerful and energetic officer', wrote his commanding officer, Lieutenant-Colonel Nicholson; 'tactically sound in the field he is also a good organiser. Has a good brain and is well above the average in ability.' Although still only a lieutenant, he was judged 'a very suitable candidate for the Staff College', and Nicholson noted that should he wish to transfer to the British service 'he should be most definitely accepted... for any regiment would be lucky to get him'.[25] Views as to his suitability for Staff College were shared in Australia, and in February 1939 his name was placed on the list of officers judged 'qualified and selected' for attendance at Staff College in due course, Daly himself being judged 'in every way suitable for special training as a Staff Officer'.[26]

Before his period in India was up, Daly was sent by the military authorities in Melbourne on a further attachment, to the 3rd Carbineers, a heavy cavalry regiment undergoing mechanisation, as horsed cavalry was in most Western armies in the late 1930s. The Australian Army had begun thinking about armour and mechanisation in the late 1920s, but the financial restrictions of the 1930s largely frustrated such modernising intentions.[27] Other than learning to drive the Vickers Mark VI tank, his exposure to mechanisation was probably fairly superficial, although he also completed the regimental wireless course.[28] Australian Army authorities realised that they needed to catch up on a decade of inaction in this area, reflected by the appointment of Major R.N.L. Hopkins as the first General Staff Officer, Grade 2 (Mechanisation and Armoured Fighting

Vehicles) at Army Headquarters following his own attachment to the British Army. The armies of the British Empire had pioneered the use of armoured vehicles in the Great War, and were well aware of the growing importance of mechanisation and motorisation and its implications for the conduct of war from at least the mid-1920s; government policies reflected in cutbacks to establishments followed by the financial problems of the Depression explain their relative lack of progress, rather than notions of hidebound conservatism or a refusal to understand the changing reality of warfare.

War broke out at the beginning of September 1939, and Captain Daly (as he now was, following promotion) and other Australians on courses and attachments were faced with trying to return to Australia at a time when commercial shipping was being taken up for war work. He got himself to Bombay (now Mumbai), and there spent a pleasant week at the Taj Mahal Hotel, which had been taken over as an officers' mess, while he waited for the *Strathaird* and a passage home. After some confusion in posting orders when he reached Melbourne, he found himself posted as adjutant to the new 2/10th Battalion, Second Australian Imperial Force (AIF), then in the process of being raised at Woodside, a former militia training camp outside Adelaide.

The raising of the early battalions of the Second AIF was a chaotic affair, often characterised by scrounging for equipment. Most of what the army had was Great War surplus, brought home in 1919 – some modern gear, such as Bren light machine-guns and 25-pounder artillery, would reach some units only when they actually arrived in the Middle East. Daly's previous service in South Australia, ties to local militia units, and the activities of the quartermaster, Captain Frank Allchin, MM (a Great War veteran of the original 10th Battalion and, along with the CO, Lieutenant-Colonel A.D. Verrier, one of the few veterans among the officers) helped the new battalion to make ends meet. Training began in earnest, however, only once the battalion moved to Ingleburn, outside Sydney, just before Christmas 1939. They were to spend four months there before departing for overseas service and the Middle East, as they then assumed.[29]

The 2/10th was part of the 18th Infantry Brigade, commanded by Brigadier L.J. Morshead, and Daly had got to know him a bit during the battalion's working-up period; Morshead visited his units regularly, and as adjutant Daly usually accompanied him and the CO during their rounds. On an early visit Morshead told Verrier to 'leave the thinking to Daly, and you do the barking'.[30] The original conception was that the

Photo 10 2/10th Battalion officers, 1939. (AWM P00828.001)

16th, 17th and 18th Brigades would form the 6th Australian Division, the first Australian formation committed to the war in the Middle East; the 2/10th had taken over lines at Ingleburn vacated by the 16th Brigade when it had shipped out. However, a reduction in the number of infantry battalions in a brigade from four to three meant that two of the battalions in Egypt were now surplus to establishment. The 2/11th, part of the original 18th Brigade, had embarked separately from the remainder and ended up in Egypt, where it formed part of a newly constituted 19th Brigade in the 6th Division. The rest of the 18th Brigade was diverted to England following the fall of France and the disastrous string of defeats in Western Europe in the spring and summer of 1940 and, instead of the sands and heat of Egypt, the 2/10th found itself in camp on Salisbury Plain.

The brigade spent the rest of the year in training, and defending the south and east coasts of England against a possible German invasion. The battalions had personal and crew-served weapons, although no transport, but were still relatively well equipped compared to British units evacuated from France and forced to leave their equipment behind on the beaches of Dunkirk. Daly was hospitalised with pneumonia, although he recovered fairly quickly, and he thus filled the role of ship's adjutant when the battalion embarked from Glasgow in November 1940 as part of his new

Photo 11 Captain T.J. Daly, England, 1940. (Daly family)

duties as brigade major of the 18th Brigade. He was not to serve in the 2/10th Battalion again until late in the war, when he returned as its commanding officer.

The 18th Brigade was part of the recently raised 7th Division, commanded by Lavarack; Morshead relinquished command of the 18th Brigade and was appointed to command of the newly raised 9th Division on 1 February 1941, soon after the convoy reached the Middle East. The brigade staff had turned over in the interval between leaving Australia and arriving in Egypt, and Daly worked up a mostly new staff during the voyage. The training they had undertaken in Britain was of limited relevance to conditions in the Middle East, and the experiences gained during the early operations of the 6th Division at Bardia against the Italians were fed into the training regime for the newly arrived units.[31] Despite some limited training on board ship, the brigade required a certain amount of refresher training before it worried about the technicalities of 'desert warfare', which, as it evolved over the course of the North African campaign, bore little resemblance to the early operations against the Italians in Libya in any case.[32]

Daly met his new brigadier, George Wootten, in slightly unusual circumstances. Wootten had graduated in the first class at RMC in August 1914 and served through the war, being mentioned in despatches four times. He was selected to attend the first postwar course at the Staff College, Camberley, while still only twenty-five, with many Empire officers senior to him in age and rank. He had left the army between the wars and worked as a lawyer but had returned to a militia command in 1937. A large man of large appetites – by 1941 he weighed 127kg – he was intensely able and charming but ruthless when required. He had extensive experience as an operational staff officer during the previous war, and Daly was somewhat apprehensive at the prospect of working for him. Accordingly, Daly and his staff captain took a night's leave in Alexandria before reporting to their new commander, only to be told that he was there in the hotel bar. 'So we went round the other side of the bar and here was this enormous man, this huge brigadier, glasses, big smile. And I said, "Sir, I am your new brigade major and this is Hayward, your staff captain." He said, "Right, well, let's have a party." So there it was. We got home to the battalion about three o'clock in the morning.'[33]

The previous brigade major had been Ragnar Garrett, and Daly now followed him into the post as he had done earlier at Mount Gambier. Garrett was helpful in the handover, while many of the tasks as a brigade major involved the mixture of tact, firmness and clear-eyed intelligence that had been noted regularly in Daly's confidential reports. Authority and responsibility were delegated within the brigade headquarters in broadly equal measure on a daily basis, and the brigade major was often charged with explaining the commander's intent and with getting a group of sometimes difficult and forceful unit commanders to see matters his way, which is to say in the manner that the brigade commander (and, beyond him, higher command) had decided. Wootten, like Morshead before him, 'expected the Brigade Major to know exactly what was in his mind at all times, because we lived very closely together, and we talked a lot together ... I was always very careful that what I asked them to do was what I knew beyond doubt was what the brigadier wanted done.'[34]

There was much to be done, especially since the brigade had received warning orders to prepare to move to the coastal city of Tobruk, newly captured by the 6th Division from the Italians in an operation that Daly observed personally.[35]

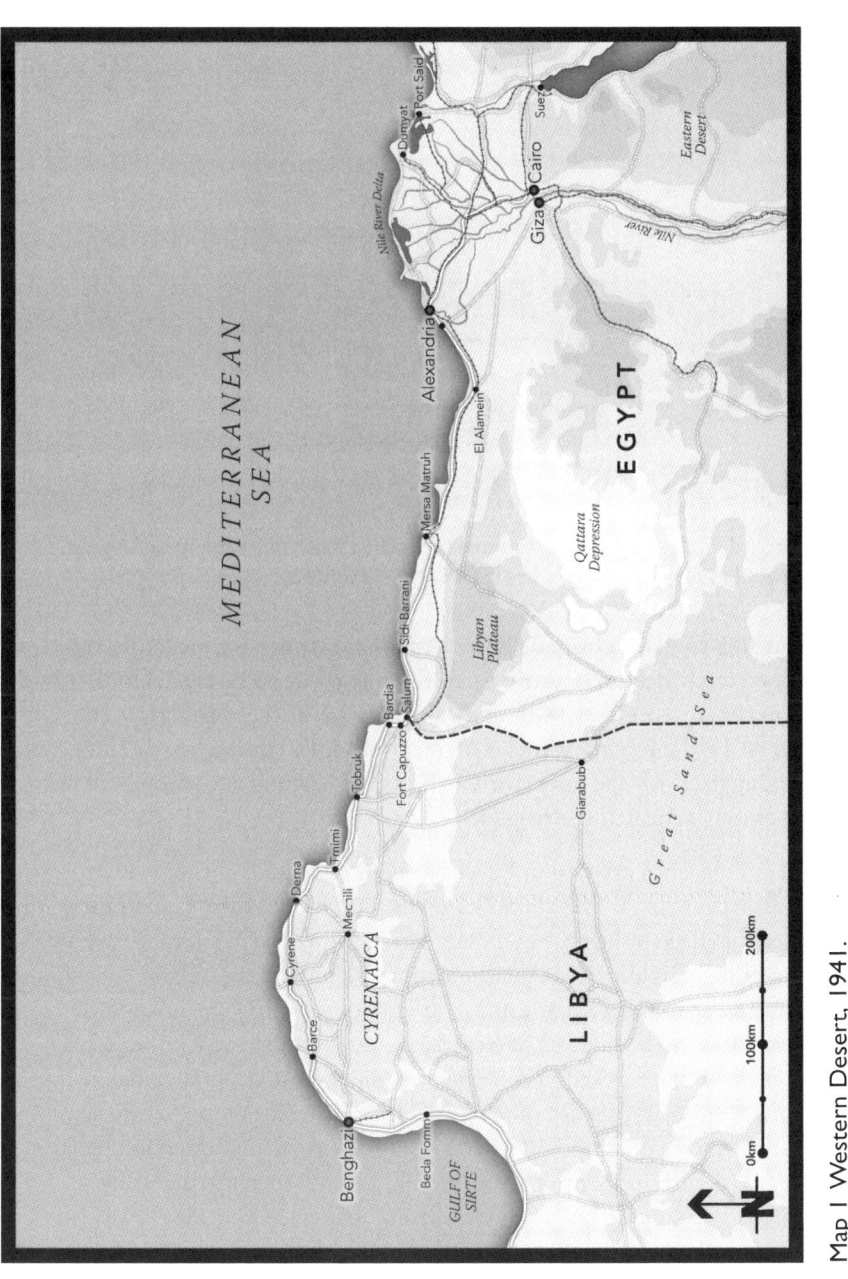

Map 1 Western Desert, 1941.

Photo 12 Officers' Mess, Headquarters, 18th Australian Infantry Brigade, Giarabub, Libya, 21 March 1941. (AWM 030385/16)

At this stage the brigade had virtually no transport, since the vehicles shipped from Britain had not arrived while those to be issued locally had not materialised either (although, in the way of these things, a consignment of load-carrying vehicles arrived ten days later as the brigade was readying itself for the move forward). As the brigade diary noted, in terms that closely reflected the brigade major,

> Training since arriving in Egypt has been restricted, in the first instance owing to the almost complete lack of transport, and in the second place to being on 6 hours notice. However, much time was spent in marching and other hardening training, designed to overcome the inevitable softness after a long sea voyage. In addition each unit carried out night exercises on at least three nights per week, resulting in a marked improvement in night work generally, and much valuable practice in the use of the prismatic compass. Dawn attacks were practised on several occasions, particular attention being paid to staff duties prior to the attack, i.e. movement to assembly areas, forming up places and laying of tapes etc. Altogether it was felt that, in spite of interference, and inevitable disadvantages resulting from the arrival in a new country, the month's training had by no means been wasted.[36]

Higher-level training dictated a shift in the style of operations as well:

> from operating in relatively enclosed country, or quite enclosed country in the south of England, to wide open desert... we did exercise after exercise insisting on being spread out and that sort of thing. When we went down to Giarabub, the convoy – if you could call it that – was operating on a front of about two to three miles. We were really spread out because at that time we had no air cover, and all that required a lot of control. Otherwise you'd lose half the people.[37]

Given the deficiencies in equipment and the short time available for training, it was perhaps as well that the brigade's first major operation was a defensive one, in Tobruk.[38]

Daly's first operational experience, with elements of the 18th Brigade, came before this, however, in an operation to take out the Italian garrison in the small town of Giarabub. With a strength of about 2000, well fortified and commanded by a capable and aggressive officer in Major Salvatore Castagna, Giarabub was the southernmost of the Italian positions along the border with Egypt but was vulnerable to concerted attack because of the parlous state of Italian logistics, notwithstanding the operational airfield that it possessed.[39] When the 18th Brigade arrived in Egypt in late December 1940 Morshead had been warned about the operation since at that stage his brigade was the only available reserve of trained units. Shortages of transport, the demands of the main offensive against Italian forces in Libya, then preparations for the expedition to Greece meant that the force tasked with the close investment and capture of Giarabub (dubbed 'Wootten Force') was to consist of a single battalion, the 2/9th, supported by a single company of the 2/10th, a composite machine-gun platoon drawn from the latter and the 2/12th Battalion, and the field guns of a battery of the 4th Regiment, Royal Horse Artillery.

The initial problem was the lack of a detailed intelligence picture of the Italians' dispositions, especially to the south of the town. Wootten conducted one such reconnaissance and sent his brigade major, Daly, forward on a second, which confirmed that the approach from the south had the best chance of a quick success. Time was a factor in the operation because Wootten had been given just ten days in total to move from Matruh, capture Giarabub and return in expectation of embarking for Greece. The supporting artillery also had only the ammunition they carried, and there was no possibility of replenishment.[40] The attack was made on the night of 19 March with an Italian outpost designated 'Daly House' as the

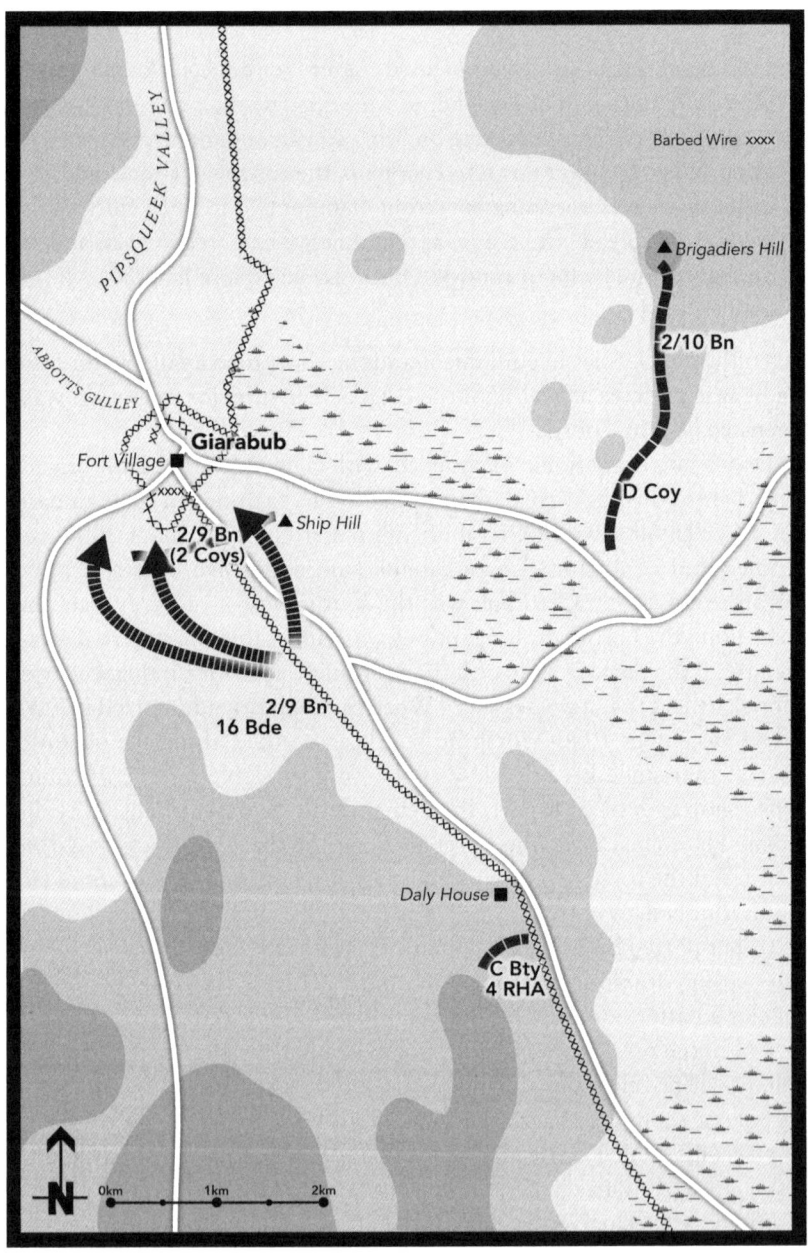

Map 2 Giarabub, March 1941.

Photo 13 The town of Giarabub, Libya, from Ship Hill, March 1941. (AWM 030385/06)

first objective; Daly went forward with the attacking companies because Wootten was unwell (and in any case should properly have been at the headquarters coordinating the various phases of the attack). The Italians laid down heavy but not very accurate artillery and machine-gun fire in response, and Daly now suggested to Lieutenant-Colonel J.E.G. Martin, CO of the 2/9th, that he mount a company in lorries and 'charge' down the road to the town itself. Although Daly enjoyed reasonable relations with all three battalion commanders and although he spoke with Wootten's authority in the latter's absence, Martin was inclined to be 'very strong headed and I had to handle him very delicately'.[41] The objective was secured – and indeed for a time one platoon was actually inside the main Italian defensive position before prudently withdrawing. The local success in the south now confirmed that this would be the main axis of the assault on the main defences, and while dense sandstorms during the morning and evening of 20 March clogged weapons with fine grit they served also to mask the Australians' preparations from the Italians, who were left guessing what would happen next.

The assault went in at 5.15 on the morning of 21 March, and the companies of the 2/9th were inside the Italian defences within ten minutes. As Wootten later wrote, however, 'in the initial stages strong resistance was encountered and it was not until 0800 hrs that it was definitely ascertained that the first phase of the battle had been completed and that the Southern objective was clear of the enemy'.[42] Progress was not helped by an unfortunate incident in which Australian soldiers were shelled by their own artillery, incurring casualties of 11 killed and 20 wounded (the infantry were out of position and visibility was appalling due to the ferocity of the dust storms). Another company from the 2/9th working forward on the left encountered further opposition for a time, but by 10.00am this, too, had ceased while the company advancing on the defences to the north-east likewise encountered crumbling resistance. By about 2.00pm all resistance had ceased, about 600 Italians had surrendered and the Australians were mopping up and salvaging equipment. The Australians lost 17 killed and 77 wounded while taking 50 officers and 1250 prisoners, together with 26 artillery pieces and numerous supplies. Perhaps 250 Italians were killed, but the winds whipped up again and bodies were quickly buried in sand, making an accurate count unlikely. Gavin Long noted the importance of the operation in gaining 'valuable experience of mobile warfare in a desert', while for the Australian soldiers the success had instilled 'increased confidence in their officers, in themselves and in their training'.[43] Daly recalled that soldiers in the other two battalions 'were very jealous of this early success of the 2/9th', but concurred that, while Giarabub was a 'little operation', it had nonetheless constituted 'virtually our blooding in proper war'.[44]

Having 'gallantly observed the battle all day' (a characteristic understatement on his part), Daly returned to Brigade Headquarters that afternoon 'to share with the Brigadier a bottle of Scotch which had been saved to celebrate victory, only to find that it had been consumed by a gang of war correspondents. He has never felt quite the same about them since.'[45] This wry observation offered years after the event belied the impact on him at the time, something conveyed to Gavin Long in conversation towards the war's end. In Long's words, 'It was a trying experience for him. His first show (apart from some time on 6 Div staff in the desert), and when it began Wootten was sick and on his back much of the time. And it nearly went wrong when our arty began falling among our own men. It was partly the arty's fault and partly the inf's. Both were out of position.'[46] We may be sure nonetheless that, standing in for the brigade commander, Daly felt some indirect responsibility for the casualties that eventuated, marring an otherwise outstanding small operation.

Consummation of the Allied victory in Libya was derailed by the need to send forces to Greece to take part in the quixotic campaign that

Photo 14 Major T.J. Daly (right), Giarabub, Libya, March 1941. (AWM 030385/17)

led to sizeable losses in April, and which stripped Egypt and Libya of experienced Allied formations and assets, especially in the air. The British high command did not count on a German–Italian riposte so quickly, and moved the 9th Division and the British 2nd Armoured Division, both only partly trained and equipped, forward to replace more experienced formations such as the Australian 6th Division, which was sent to Greece and Crete (and which suffered such heavy losses there that it took no further part in the fighting in the Mediterranean theatre). Rommel's forces cut communications with Cairo to the east and invested the town on three sides (all save the harbour, which was subjected to relentless aerial attack), utilising parts of two German and four Italian divisions, infantry and armour. Morshead deployed his brigades (three from the 9th and one from the 7th Australian Divisions) together with British and Indian infantry, gunners and some armour in an aggressive defensive strategy. Enemy attacks in March and April concentrated on the strongest parts of the town's mostly well-established defences, and were beaten back, sometimes inflicting heavy losses.

The siege of Tobruk and the role of the iconic 'Rats' of the 9th Division has acquired quasi-mythic status that tends both to trivialise the actual importance of the battle and to obscure the fact that forces other than

Australian – and other than the 9th Division units – were involved.[47] Tobruk's significance lay in the port facilities of the town – one of only two along the North African coast before Tripoli – together with Hitler's decision to send the *Deutsches Afrika Korps (DAK)* to retrieve the Italians' fortunes after their catastrophic defeat at British and Empire hands in the first Libyan campaign, recently concluded. Although the German contribution to the subsequent campaigns in North Africa has received the lion's share of attention, especially among film-makers and popular writers, the German effort could not have been sustained without the Italian logistic system in the Mediterranean or the efforts of the Italian navy and air force. Furthermore, Italian forces made up the majority of the Axis command in the theatre, and the Italians, in the end, held out a week longer than their much-vaunted German partners following the latter's surrender in Tunisia in early May 1943.

At the end of April the enemy launched a fresh and concerted attack against the Salient, and penetrated three kilometres before losing momentum and coordination. By 4 May the attack was called off, but a number of fortified positions were lost by the garrison and, despite Morshead's repeated attempts, were not recovered. Enemy losses were sufficiently heavy, however, for Rommel's subordinate commanders to argue against further assaults, and the German commander was content to maintain a close siege of the town through the summer months while he awaited further reinforcements and improved the training of his units for positional warfare. Pressure on the British high command led to the relief and withdrawal of Australian units, beginning with the 18th Brigade in August. The siege was broken successfully by a British advance in November.

As Daly later recalled, the 18th Brigade 'didn't prepare for Tobruk at all. We didn't know about Tobruk.'[48] Orders for the 18th Brigade to go to Greece were cancelled at short notice, and they went forward by sea to Tobruk, instead, to establish a defensive perimeter around the town while awaiting the return of the 9th Division, which was further forward to the west.[49] The decision was made to defend at the perimeter (the Red Line), utilising the Italian defensive works that were still extant and largely undamaged. Daly remembered that the 'Italians had very substantial wire all around the perimeter': 'We repaired that. They had these very sophisticated dug-outs, which were concrete and you could go underground, and there were circular concrete line pits running off the main position. There wasn't a great deal for the brigade headquarters to do [at this point], other than to allocate sectors to the battalions, and when they got there they had to sort it out themselves.' When the 9th

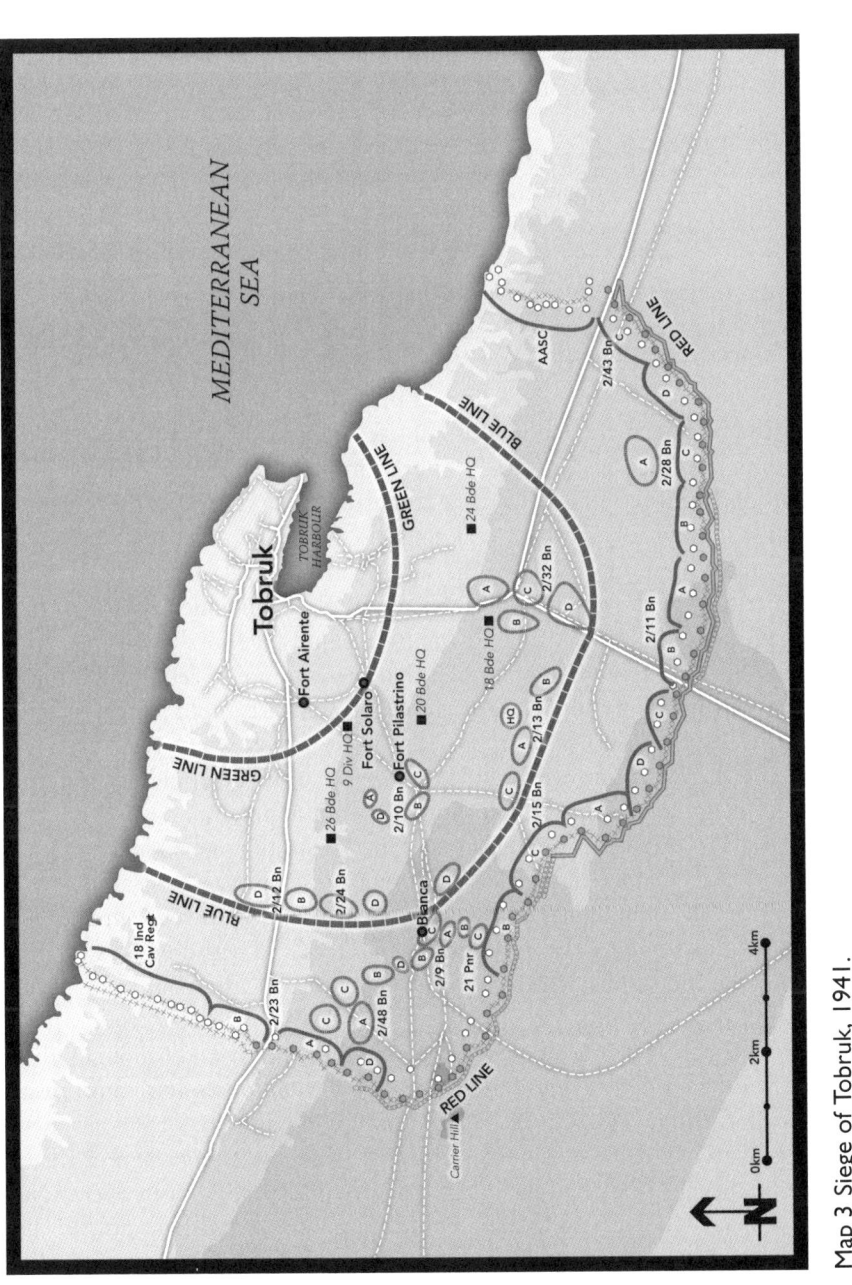

Map 3 Siege of Tobruk, 1941.

Division returned the defences were reorganised and regularised but, in Daly's view, 'it was all ad hockery, there was no preparation for it, no training for it. It was just something that had to be done on the spur of the moment because of the fact that Rommel had appeared outside Benghazi.'[50]

The 18th Brigade formed a central reserve for the defence of the town, but its battalions were scattered rather than concentrated in order that they might respond rapidly if called for. At the beginning of May the enemy switched the axis of their assaults and attacked towards 'the Salient', taking Hill 209 and driving back the defences to the Blue Line and thus gaining excellent observation as a result. The 18th Brigade was put into a deliberate counter-attack. Because of his size and a bout of dysentery, Wootten was not especially mobile, and when Morshead wished to tour the brigade's area he was usually accompanied by Daly as a result. The latter formed a fairly good appreciation of his senior's views and intent and believed that he became 'obsessed' with regaining the Salient. 'I think strategically it was a very sensible thing to do, because that was the highest piece of ground in the whole garrison,' Daly recalled.[51] But the attrition of the garrison and the seemingly open-ended nature of its commitment in defence of the town also meant that Morshead was loath to risk his only reserve in an attack that might more or less wipe it out. Success in pushing the Germans right out again required 'a really first class, well-organised, well-supported attack, which we weren't able to do', and merely confirmed Daly in the view that 'if you couldn't produce the goods to do it properly you shouldn't do it at all'.

The 18th Brigade's counter-attack failed in its aim of evicting the Germans. The 2/9th were late reaching the start line through over-ambitious planning and communications breakdown; they killed and captured some Germans, lost quite a few casualties themselves and withdrew, disorganised by the conditions. Much the same befell the 2/12th, while the 2/10th got one platoon onto the objective – Hill 209 – but they, too, withdrew through lack of support and communications. Daly thought the plan was at fault, but that underlying this was 'an obsession with those perimeter posts... the Germans were occupying a sector of the perimeter, a relatively narrow sector... and this [was] attacking them in their strength because they had the greatest degree of depth.'[52] As an operation it 'encapsulated everything that shouldn't be done on a night attack'. It was, nonetheless, an important and salutary lesson and one that Daly never forgot: 'In future we should never do a night attack unless we had information, plenty of reconnaissance, rehearsal, good communications and so on. Very thoroughly, well prepared operation.' He extrapolated more generally from his experiences in Tobruk, to conclude:

> If you're going to do one of those attacks against a prepared position, you have to have plenty of information, plenty of intelligence. You've got to know exactly what your targets are, what your objectives are... you can't take on one of these positions unless you know what you're going to be attacking and what the objective is, what its strengths are, what it looks like, how long it's going to take you to get there... And of course your troops have got to be well trained [with] good leaders.[53]

He was to follow these conclusions in his own exercise of battalion command against the Japanese in 1945. Equally, he took from his observation of Morshead the lesson that 'a tough aggressive defence with good soldiers and good leaders, lots of courage, lots of skill, can keep a vastly superior force on the back foot most of the time'. Foremost in his mind, however, remained 'those half-baked attacks and the casualties that were caused... deliberate attacks, unless they are very well planned, are very, very costly'.[54] Wootten was in agreement, noting in his after-action report that 'in view of the enemy's defensive strength and dispositions it appears that any further large scale inf operations will require the support of many more guns and [tanks]'.[55] It can have been of limited comfort to know that in Morshead's opinion the 18th was 'the best brigade here'.[56]

The 18th Brigade was relieved by a Polish brigade and withdrawn in mid-August for rest and refitting. Daly left on board the destroyer *Napier* at night, and reached Alexandria after most of the brigade had already departed for the camp at Kilo 89 in Palestine. The reunion with them was brief, and on 1 October he took up duties as GSO2 on the headquarters of the 6th Division, by then located at Baalbeck in Syria after a mauling in the Greece and Crete campaigns a few months previously. The divisional commander was now Major-General E.F. 'Ned' Herring; the brigade commanders – Allen, Savige and Vasey – had all been with the division since its departure from Australia; and the headquarters staff was tremendously experienced – Daly thought it 'magnificent'. The division was assigned occupation duties in the former Vichy French territory but was engaged as well in preparations for winter warfare against an apprehended move by the Germans south through Turkey, in the winter, as a means of outflanking the Allied position in the Middle East. Daly was tasked with producing a short manual on ski warfare to go with the ski school established in the north of the country at Cedars – one of the

Australian Army's few serious forays into the peculiar demands of winter warfare.[57]

Despite having held successive staff jobs in the acting rank of major, Daly had not attended Staff College. There was nothing unusual about this in the circumstances; the Australian Army possessed a handful of Staff College graduates in 1939 (the same situation, only worse, had existed in 1914), and with the rapid expansion of the army following the raising of the Second AIF many junior Staff Corps officers were posted to staff jobs well above their substantive rank. The army likewise met the shortage of technical staff officers (signals, engineers etc) through the simple expedient of commissioning senior warrant officers from the Australian Instructional Corps as captains.[58] As we have seen, Daly had been cleared for attendance at the Staff College in the normal manner before the war's outbreak. The Middle East Staff College was at Haifa, in Palestine, and Daly attended the course there between February and June 1942. The decision that Grade 2 staff officers would all complete formal staff qualifications appears to have originated with Blamey; as the Second World War went on there emerged a clear view and intention on the part of many older regular officers (those who had fought in the Great War as junior officers then seen their careers stagnate in the interwar years) that their younger counterparts should be given as wide a range of staff and field experiences as possible in order to prepare them for running the army after the war, whenever that might be.[59] Wartime necessity in its turn demanded that the course cram what would normally have taken two years in the pre-war course at Camberley or Quetta into a greatly truncated period, and course members worked very hard.

Some of the instruction had little to do with the problems of the desert, but then many of those who passed through the courses at Haifa would find themselves in other theatres facing other enemies sooner or later – very much sooner in the case of many of the Australians. Daly concluded that he became 'a far better Staff Officer than I was when I started. I certainly had a little more polish', and the course authorities agreed. He graduated with a 'B minus' grade and a recommendation for further employment on the staff; the commanding officer commented that he 'has done well', while the Directing Staff's notes remarked on 'a quiet, industrious officer with a good deal of experience... an excellent manner and a pleasant personality'.[60] The latter comment was not some pre-war affectation or reflection of more gentlemanly times; as Daly (and many others) had found already, an ability to persuade fractious and sometimes egotistical senior officers to see things from their commander's point of view was essential to success as a staff officer on a formation headquarters, and Daly would need those qualities again.

And with that his war in the Middle East, at least, came to an end. Even before the Japanese attack on Pearl Harbor widened the war and brought it measurably closer to Australia's shores, the army had begun returning drafts of officers and senior NCOs from the Middle East to improve the standards of training and fitness among the militia formations and impart awareness of the advances that had occurred in warfare since the end of the Great War – which, for many older militia officers, had been their last experience of combat. Shipping was at a premium (which remained true throughout the war and its immediate aftermath), and Daly returned to Australia with a handful of other officers aboard a Norwegian cargo vessel, the *John Bakke*. It was a lengthy and rather tedious trip, at least by comparison for those who nowadays take international air travel for granted; they embarked from Suez on 3 June and reached Melbourne only on 13 July. Promoted to temporary lieutenant-colonel, he was assigned as the GSO1 to the headquarters of the 5th Division, a militia formation located in north Queensland. Allowed time for a brief family reunion with his parents, he reached Townsville a week later.

The 5th Division was mobilised after the beginning of the Pacific War and charged initially with the defence of north Queensland during the uncertain early months when some believed that the Japanese might attempt an invasion of Australia.[61] The division was commanded by Major-General E.J. 'Teddy' Milford, an RMC graduate and artillery officer who had fought on the Western Front and attended Staff College, Camberley, in 1930–31. His service with the 7th Division in the Middle East was truncated by his appointment as Master-General of the Ordnance (MGO) at Army Headquarters in January 1941, and in this position he oversaw the rapid expansion of the army and its re-equipment. Command of the 5th Division in mid-1942 posed some significant challenges of a kind faced in all the militia formations charged with the defence of Australia and its territories while the Second AIF was being returned home.

When Daly reached them the division consisted of the 7th, 11th and 29th Infantry Brigades, each with three militia infantry battalions, and assorted divisional troops. The division spent most of its time preparing defences, undertaking reconnaissance of its potential area of operations; training ('lots of training', as Daly remembered it), including considerable initial emphasis on preparations for chemical warfare against an anticipated Japanese use of gas (probably a hangover this early in the Pacific

War from memories of 1914–18); and air cooperation exercises, which reflected more recent experience.⁶² Daly thought the division 'wasn't in terribly good shape' when he arrived, which was not really surprising given the short time since its mobilisation and the fact that most of the modern and serviceable equipment, together with experienced or simply willing manpower, available to the militia in 1939 had been sent to the Second AIF; most of this was still in the process of returning to Australia. This state of affairs was reflected especially in the officers on the divisional headquarters, none of whom 'had any experience except a very few of the chaps from the Middle East who were sprinkled about the division, and a lot of [the former] were pretty old' and, Daly thought, over-promoted.⁶³ Those, like Daly, with 'sand in our shoes',⁶⁴ were posted to the divisions and brigades in Australia ahead of the AIF's return precisely to compensate for these structural deficiencies, which the army's leadership fully recognised but about which, until then, they had been able to do little.

These new appointments undoubtedly improved the efficiency and degree of recent military experience found in formations in Australia, and not only within the 5th Division, and the area in which this had the greatest influence was training, a field in which Daly excelled. This was reflected in the divisional training instruction no. 4, issued under his signature and bearing all the hallmarks of his personal style. Allotments for individual, platoon, company and special training were laid down – many of the soldiers were deficient even in basic matters such as weapon proficiency and marksmanship – together with specifications for brigade exercises designed to provide practice for the troops in the defence of Townsville and utilising 'the principle of mobile defence and [calling] for initiative and determination on the part of leaders and troops'. The lessons and observations from Tobruk were clearly evident as well: 'exercises will cater for further experience in . . . letting [tanks] through "soft spots" and dealing with accompanying inf[antry] . . . Emphasis must be made on the importance of speedy and accurate communications. There is always room for improvement in this and particularly at present . . . The value of the detached [troop] of art[iller]y for mobility and rapid production of fire must be brought out by exercises and the problems attaching to a non-self-supporting sub-unit overcome.'⁶⁵

Above all, Daly emphasised the importance of strong battle drills, something that Australian soldiers quickly came to appreciate in both world wars and beyond: in his view, 'one of the greatest obstacles in most operations is the time factor. An efficient automatic drill will do much to overcome this but such a pitch can only be reached by constant [training] based on a sound and simple system.' This relentless emphasis on preparation, training and anticipation reflected the fact that, as he observed years later, 'I can't think of any operation in which I was involved in which there wasn't some degree of confusion.'[66] The elements of his own command style were being honed.

Daly regarded Milford as 'first rate, very easy to work with', which was not always the experience of Staff Corps officers working in senior staff positions in militia divisions; nor, indeed, was it his initial experience with Milford.[67] The tensions, antagonisms and outright antipathy felt between some members of the interwar Staff Corps and their militia counterparts has been well known for some time and forms the context of various biographies and other studies of the senior ranks of Australia's Second World War army.[68] Equally, and unsurprisingly, there were feuds between individual members of the Staff Corps while a substantial number of militia offers were critical of the behaviour of one of their own most senior officers, Major-General Gordon Bennett, following his decision to leave his command in Singapore before the surrender to the Japanese took effect; reactions were rarely and simply defined by the source of an officer's commission. Officers newly returned from service in the Middle East were not always greeted warmly by those they were sent to replace, a situation sometimes exacerbated by the failure of Army Headquarters in Melbourne to inform individuals that their replacements were on their way. There were many reasons why individuals did not volunteer for service overseas with the Second AIF – age, health, family circumstances, restricted occupations – and some older militia officers who had done their best in difficult circumstances were left unimpressed by the advent of younger, brasher officers who appeared intent on undoing and redoing things that they had already put in place. Initially the 5th Division headquarters struck Daly as divided and unhappy, but this soon passed with the replacement of several members of the A Mess 'and after that everything went swimmingly'.[69] This was just as well because, as we have seen, there was a great deal of work to be done, not least in reorganising the headquarters and placing it on an operational footing before, in January 1943, the 5th Division was ordered north to Papua.

The field army and that back in Australia defending against an increasingly improbable Japanese invasion underwent substantial reorganisation in the early months of 1943, following the defeat of the Japanese offensive across the Owen Stanleys that had ended in defeat and disaster for them in the tangled swamps of Buna and Gona. As a result, the 5th Division was sent to Milne Bay and the 11th, another militia division, was posted to Moresby and Buna. The 5th Division's task was to defend against the possibility of a further attempt by the Japanese to take Milne Bay, although, after the defeats of 1942 and the simultaneous reversals suffered in the Solomons, it seems unlikely that the enemy had the resources to do so, even if he had formed the intent. Characteristically, the emphasis was on hard training in jungle conditions, further emphasised by Milford's insistence on walking regularly around his command and observing their activities. Daly and his staff, too, 'did a colossal amount of walking... We planned defensive positions, counter-attack roles, put the troops through the rehearsals for them, that sort of thing.'[70] The truth, however, was that the war had moved north, and in time the 5th Division moved with it.

The rivalries that rent the higher command of the army during the war intruded into this process, to Daly's discomfort, although, fortunately, not to his disadvantage. Savige's 3rd Division had been involved in the heavy fighting in the Koniatum–Mount Tambu area as part of the Australian and American offensive to clear the Japanese and take Salamaua in the early stages of the drive north along the coast of New Guinea. The 3rd Division was to be relieved by the 5th and Savige replaced by Milford; ahead of this, Daly was posted to replace Colonel J.G.N. Wilton as the divisional GSO1.[71] The sticky part was that Savige was unaware that he was to be relieved – although Daly knew – and that the relief was to be effected by Major-General Frank Berryman, Blamey's chief of staff and one of the oldest and most inveterate of Savige's Staff Corps antagonists. In the interval between these two events, Daly was in an invidious position and felt 'very uncomfortable, embarrassed, because my loyalty was to General Savige as his GSO1, but I knew that the axe was about to fall but I couldn't say anything'.[72] As it happened, upon his return to Australia Savige was elevated to command of II Corps and lead it in operations on Bougainville in 1944–45. His promotion was probably owed to Blamey's long-standing personal patronage, and aroused further comment among those who believed him unfit for higher command in modern war (which, in fairness to the regulars, was an opinion voiced as well by the commander of New Guinea Force, Lieutenant-General Sir Edmund Herring, another senior militia officer). Daly was fortunate to have come no closer to the nastiness that characterised relations between too many of his seniors at this time.

The 5th Division now undertook operations aimed at the reduction and capture of Salamaua. Their role was a supporting one, since the main operation was mounted by the 9th Division with the landing at Lae; the 5th Division aimed to keep the Japanese further south occupied so that they could not reinforce their comrades opposing the landings. The terrain was rugged, maps were inadequate and conditions were generally tough, although the 5th Division reported very few malaria cases because of a ferocious emphasis on prophylactic measures, which proved highly successful. Daly was becoming increasingly frustrated by his role, however; after Salamaua fell, he felt that he really had very little useful work to do. While the Japanese continued to resist he was out visiting the brigades and forward positions regularly, accompanied by a native policeman as an escort because the latter was able to move quickly, and this activity was not without its dangers (chiefly from Japanese patrols). As he subsequently explained to official historian David Dexter, 'in that period I walked miles and miles':

> Due to the elongated front (in terms of time) and the difficulty of visualising the exact piece of country in which the various small operations were taking place, I spent three days a week at least visiting units so that I could give the GOC [i.e. Milford] a first-hand account of what was happening, and the difficulties being encountered... It will be clear to you that intelligent planning on a Divisional level was dependent on an intimate knowledge of the country and as visibility was very restricted, this took weeks of detailed reconnaissance.[73]

Once this phase of operations had ended, however, most of the work was being handled by other staff sections within the headquarters, such as the engineer staff, while the 5th Division increasingly was left behind to occupy and consolidate areas already taken by other divisions, which then continued to move forward against Japanese positions in the Markham Valley. For his work in this period Daly was to receive a mention in despatches 'for gallant and distinguished service', and would receive an OBE in 1945 for his service in New Guinea overall that highlighted his 'sound judgement, attention to detail and lively foresight', but he was clearly ready to move on.[74]

A visit to the operational areas by the CGS, Lieutenant-General John Northcott, provided a solution, and towards the end of the year Daly's request for more meaningful work resulted in his posting as an instructor in the senior wing of the Australian Staff School, at that time superimposed on the Royal Military College, which had relocated at Duntroon at the end of the 1930s. The staff school trained captains, majors and lieutenant-colonels in the duties and responsibilities of Grade 3, 2 and 1 staff officers; this was another example of the manner in which the

Australian Army came to meet its needs from its own resources during the second half of the war, rather than defaulting to its allies to provide all those functions and services that it could not (which had been the invariable practice in the small army of the interwar years).[75] The chief instructor was Colonel Reg Pollard, an RMC graduate of the Class of 1924 and subsequent CGS in the early 1960s whom Daly was to serve as Adjutant General.

While serving in India Daly had contracted malaria and his service in New Guinea brought a new and more serious bout together with a hookworm infestation, both of them relatively common occurrences derived from service in the islands. The principal drug used to safeguard Australian troops against malaria in the Pacific War was Atebrine, which did not necessarily cure malaria but was an excellent suppressant while used. In keeping with general practice, Daly had ceased taking the drug after a set period having returned to Australia, and the infection flared up. The medical officer at RMC had practised in Rabaul before the war and thus possessed first-hand understanding of the disease, and Daly was put to rights within weeks after first being treated with sheep dip (carbon tetrachloride) to clear up the hookworm. Of his instructional duties he later recalled that he 'worked very hard, but at the same time had a bit of time off to play golf and enjoy the social life of Canberra at night', such as it then was. Once again, a course that was taught pre-war across the span of a year was crammed into four months through wartime exigency, which made it a 'pressure course' both for those who undertook it and for those who taught it.[76]

The instructional billet was intended as a short-term appointment before further posting, and for Daly it had provided something of a respite while he regained full fitness. He was there less than a year before receiving orders to report to Kairi on the Atherton Tableland to take command of his old battalion, the 2/10th.

CHAPTER 2

BALIKPAPAN, 1945

Daly assumed command of the 2/10th battalion on 14 October 1944. The battalion was located at Kairi on the Atherton Tableland in Far North Queensland and was heavily engaged in training and refitting, having returned to Australia in May 1944 following the fighting in the Ramu Valley. The battalion had lost sixteen killed and thirty-one wounded during the campaign phases in the Finisterres, and underwent a period of rebuilding; as the battalion history noted, reinforcements 'were received and welcomed as the battalion was considerably under strength... brought about by large numbers being medically down-graded or discharged as medically unfit'.[1]

There can have been relatively few men in the battalion with direct experience of the new commanding officer from his days as the unit's adjutant at the war's beginning. Casualty rates among infantry battalions were nowhere near as severe in the Second World War as they had been in the Great War (unless one was unlucky enough to be in the 8th Division and suffered under the vicious bastardry of Japanese prisoner administration), but turnover within a battalion across five or six years of war was still considerable. Disease rates in New Guinea and the islands were high, even with strict enforcement of anti-malarial and other hygiene regimes. In the course of the war the 2/10th Battalion suffered 938 casualties of all kinds (killed in action, died of wounds or disease, injured or prisoners of war), which was roughly the whole of the battalion's strength at any given point in time. Admittedly imperfect records gave a total of 167 officers and 3274 other ranks as having served on the battalion's strength during the war.² On top of the obvious wastage through active service, officers and men were posted to training establishments, to other units on promotion, or had their medical status revised and were thus no longer fit or suitable for deployment in a combat unit.

The battalion had not had an entirely happy time during the fighting in New Guinea: successive commanding officers, Lieutenant-Colonels J.G. Dobbs and C.J. Geard, had both been 'relieved for cause', which is to say sacked. Dobbs had been widely liked and respected within the battalion (the unit history described him as 'one of the best COs in the AIF'); by the end of the fighting at Buna he was 'depressed, malaria-stricken and utterly exhausted', and his relief from command was as much for his own good as that of the men he commanded.³ As one of his junior officers who had served with him before the war observed, 'his two great qualities were...administration, and his ability to train troops. I don't think his tactical ability was equal to these two qualities.'⁴ Geard was brought in from the 2/12th to succeed him; he was 'well known to older members of the unit' and possessed a 'pleasant personality', but was sacked by his brigade commander, Chilton, after the battalion returned from New Guinea.⁵ This was not a trivial matter; nor were its consequences confined to the individual COs concerned. Chilton thought Geard 'a nice enough bloke' who should never have been placed in command of a battalion. Several of the respondents to Garth Pratten's thorough and wide-ranging study of Australian battalion command observed the difference that the change in command made after Geard's removal: 'I've never seen a greater transformation in a battalion, in morale, in everything, from bad to excellent'; 'Geard was quite hopeless, he couldn't make up his mind. 2/10 had difficulties with such a weak CO.'⁶ He clearly failed to 'grip' the battalion and place his own stamp upon them; in fairness to him, he had also contracted malaria in April 1943 and spent several months recuperating.⁷

An infantry battalion is the smallest self-contained force in the army, termed a 'unit' in the nomenclature of the organisation and, as 'Jo' Gullett has observed (writing of his own unit, the 2/6th, but his observations hold good for the AIF generally), possessed of its own spirit, character and characteristics.⁸ Another member of the 2/6th (and subsequently its historian), David Hay, wrote that a battalion 'depends heavily for its performance in action, indeed for its whole spirit and character, on how it is led and trained'.⁹ Garth Pratten has listed the challenges a CO faced: 'to train soldiers well; to employ supporting arms to the best effect; to improvise when plans went awry; to motivate soldiers to do things that self-preservation argued against; and to value the life of the individual, yet have the courage to risk it in pursuit of larger objectives'.[10] Pratten draws two important conclusions from his careful study of unit command: first, that there was 'no single distinctive manner in which command was exercised over Australian infantry battalions during the Second World War'; and second, that tactical and administrative competence were 'critical to effective command'.[11] The popular stereotypes that Australians sometimes attach to their image of their soldiers do not hold true in explaining the proficiency of Australian officers any more than they explain the capabilities of Australian troops more generally.

Appointment to command at various levels within the army was a somewhat vexed issue, especially early in the war, and has remained so in the literature since. The initial unit command appointments went to militia officers, and not a single Permanent Military Force (PMF) officer received an appointment as an infantry CO. This has generally been attributed to a Cabinet, or even prime ministerial, decision favouring militia officers for unit and formation commands, but the evidence for this is mixed. The official historian, Gavin Long, recorded a conversation with Menzies in his diary shortly after the war: 'As a matter of fact, in the Cabinet before the appointments were made I [i.e. Menzies] remember saying we did not want any funny business about regular soldiers in this war. I believe that a man who spends his life preparing for war is likely to be a more useful soldier than a man who hasn't done so.'[12] If there was a blanket directive to exclude regular officers in such a manner, it did not last long. Colonel H.C.H. Robertson (RMC Class of 1914) received command of the 19th Brigade on its formation in North Africa in 1940, and was succeeded by Colonel George Vasey (RMC Class of 1915). H.D. Wynter, commissioned into the A&I (Administrative and Instructional) Staff in 1911, was appointed to command the 9th Division in 1940, but his health failed before he could command in action. Vernon Sturdee (commissioned into the Royal Australian Engineers in 1911) briefly held command of the newly raised 8th Division in mid-1940, before being appointed as Chief of the General Staff (CGS) on the death of Brudenell White, while John Northcott (commissioned into the A&I Staff in 1912) was held back from this command in turn because his abilities and knowledge as a senior staff officer were considered vital to the war effort at that stage.

The maximum age for enlistment in the Second AIF as a lieutenant-colonel was set at 45, but some officers appointed were at or indeed over that limit. The factors involved in selection and appointment at the war's beginning – when units were being raised from scratch – were complex, and involved a mix of experience, reputation, local identification (since battalions were raised initially on a regional basis) and personal relationships. By the middle years of the war, much had changed. The average age of command appointments had declined dramatically, reflecting the acute physical and mental demands these made upon individuals and mirroring the pattern established in the previous war. Active service winnowed the elderly, unfit, out of touch and incompetent, often ruthlessly, and the cohort of young, energetic officers who had demonstrated their capacities in previous campaigns came to the fore. Brigade commanders in 1944–45, such as Chilton and Dougherty, had been battalion commanders in 1940–41, and so on it went down the chain of command.

As with their seniors, battalion commands were given to PMF officers – over the course of the war, fourteen PMF officers commanded battalions in either the Second AIF or the militia (and to this number might be added a further seven former PMF officers) – but the demand for experienced staff officers and, in some quarters, a lingering prejudice against the perceived command abilities of permanent officers meant that these generally enjoyed shorter periods of command than their non-permanent counterparts and generally received only a single command.[13] Although he was far from being the first permanent officer to be a CO, when he received his command in October 1944 Daly was the only Staff Corps officer in such a position.[14] He was the last to hold such an appointment in the Second AIF. Some senior regular officers, such as H.C.H. Robertson, attempted to spread the opportunities for command experience among their juniors, mindful of the potential needs of the postwar army. Another regular officer (and subsequent CGS), Brigadier Henry Wells, observed to Gavin Long: 'It was a great pity that so many of the younger Staff Corps officers had so little active experience. Not only because of the value of the experience to the men concerned but because it weeded out the weak ones.'[15]

Although he had left the battalion four years previously, Daly had kept in touch with many of its officers and soldiers while serving with the 18th Brigade headquarters in the desert, and by the time he returned some of these men were company commanders and senior NCOs. His second-in-command, Major G.R. Miethke, had been his assistant adjutant in 1939–40, two of the company OCs had been subalterns while two more of the four company commanders, together with the adjutant and the RSM (regimental sergeant major), had been NCOs. Daly described returning as CO as 'like going home'. On the other hand, he had been briefed by Chilton that the battalion was not 'in very good shape' and that he had to 'get a grip on it and do something'.[16] Fortunately, he retained 'a

Photo 15 Lieutenant-Colonel T.J. Daly addressing a parade of the 2/10th Battalion, Kairi, Queensland, October 1944. (AWM 082067)

certain amount of authority' from his time as adjutant and from being a known quantity, by reputation at least – Daly himself thought it stemmed in part from his pre-war status as a regular officer among a group of mainly pre-war militia NCOs.[17] What is quite clear is that Chilton asked for him specifically to take over, and that the GOC of the 7th Division, Major-General George Vasey, concurred in the request.[18]

The arrival of the new CO of the 2/10th brought with it an upswing in the training cycle. Ten new subalterns arrived at the end of October, and the regimental medical officer noted that the health of the battalion was good, training was now 'at its full height with plenty of marching to do', while the malaria rate had dropped to about two cases a week since Atebrin prophylactic measures were closely supervised.[19] Selected officers and men were sent on training courses while training within the battalion became 'more intense' following Daly's arrival. There was an increasing emphasis on amphibious operations, first at the theoretical level in staff exercises and using sand models, and subsequently involving all ranks at Trinity Beach in November. 'We trained and we trained and we trained and we trained. I reckoned that by the time we were finished I could have just got on the radio, given about half a dozen quick orders and the battalion would have gone into action. It was so very very highly mobile and ready to go.'[20]

This first exercise, which lasted the whole of the month, involved practice in an opposed beach landing and incorporated training with tanks in the assault as well as cooperation with naval bombardment. Considerable attention was also paid to taking out enemy pillboxes – the fruit of long and sometimes bitter experience going back to the fighting at Gona and Sanananda in early 1943. Daly had studied American reports on beach landings ('We had no experience of that sort of thing. The 9th Division had done it in New Guinea but we hadn't'), and insisted that the companies practice supporting fire in such circumstances on the 30-yard range in order to get used to the idea that fire needed to be maintained right up to the point where the enemy was taken out.[21]

Daly paid careful attention to all aspects of the battalion's training, and to the internal economy of the unit as well. Routine orders for 27 November noted that in order to build up 'a stock of beer for Christmas', the weekly beer allocation would be halved, to a bottle per week per man issued once a week.[22] He paid similarly close attention to dress and turn out, to the proper consumption of Atebrin, to correct conduct in dealing with the remains of enemy soldiers when encountered (this latter had a very practical side since, as routine orders explained, 'the Japanese propose to return the personal effects of deceased personnel, on the basis of the return of the effects of an equal number of deceased Japanese').[23] Battalion and brigade training continued intensively until Christmas; at a unit parade on 21 December the brigade commander, Brigadier Chilton, 'touched on the subject of future movement of [the battalion]' (he had already briefed Daly on the battalion's role in the forthcoming operation at Balikpapan), while a Christmas screening of the Chips Rafferty epic *Rats of Tobruk* brought 'disgusted' responses from those men who had actually fought there: 'Its screening overseas will bring discredit to the AIF.'[24]

Mindful of the likely deployment of the battalion, Daly took leave in Melbourne 'determined to enjoy myself for four or five days'.[25] His sister set him up on a blind date with a friend, Heather Fitzgerald. The CO was gone for most of January, but his time was clearly productively spent. Before the battalion left Kairi for predeployment preparations en route to Morotai he had proposed, by telegram, and was accepted. He was now in his early thirties, which some sensibilities might consider a little late for the purposes of matrimony. The war, of course, had interrupted

Photo 16 Daly and Brigadier Chilton inspecting a parade of the 2/10th Battalion. (AWM 082068)

normal arrangements (it is likely that for every hurried early marriage before a man departed for service overseas, another was delayed by the same consideration), but that was not the only factor. Junior officers needed permission to marry before the war, and in any case were not paid enough to maintain a married household (few quarters were provided), and married women from respectable backgrounds did not work. As in so many other respects, it was a different world.[26]

At the completion of an intensive, eight-month training period the battalion left for Redlynch (near Cairns) and embarkation on 28 May. Loaded onto overcrowded American LSTs (Landing Ships, Tank), the soldiers endured a mostly miserable voyage with bad weather and rough seas resulting in a high incidence of sea-sickness.[27] The passage to Morotai took fifteen days, with the voyage interrupted briefly at Biak, and the convoy dropped anchor in Morotai harbour on 12 June. Final training, acclimatisation, planning and preparations now commenced for the battalion's role in the amphibious assault on the port town of Balikpapan, designated Oboe 2. Although they would get little opportunity for final 'toughening up', Daly believed his battalion was nonetheless 'fairly well acclimatised' after the eight months on the Atherton Tableland: 'the period spent on the landing craft was used to good purpose and included two PT periods per day... we [2/10th Battalion] had no casualties [at Balikpapan] from exhaustion. C Coy, who had the hardest day, were in fine form in the evening [of the first day].'[28]

The landings in Borneo (the others were made by the 26th Brigade Group at Tarakan on 1 May and the 9th Division against Labuan and Brunei Bay on 10 June) were approved by the Combined Chiefs of Staff in February as part of the strategic planning governing the final phases of the war against Japan, and had several purposes (although these shifted in the course of the deliberations and some of the accompanying declarations of intent were not to be taken at face value). With the end of the war in Europe imminent and the British Government desperate to play a larger role in the war against Japan in order to safeguard its interests in South-East Asia in particular, London despatched the British Pacific Fleet as a first instalment on a renewed commitment to the final battles in the Pacific. The seizure of Labuan Bay was intended, at one stage, to provide a forward anchorage and operating base for the British Pacific Fleet. More importantly from the Australian point of view, the operations in Borneo (and also those on Bougainville and on the north coast of New Guinea towards Aitape), were a means of keeping Australian forces in the war and fighting. Despite claims and blandishments to the contrary, MacArthur clearly had no intention of using Australian (or other Commonwealth) formations on offer in the final offensives against the Japanese home islands, just as he had frozen them out of the operations to retake the Philippines (again, despite earlier undertakings to do so). The Australian Government was determined to assert a place in the postwar deliberations on the future of the region and the nature of the peace to be imposed on the Japanese, and had clear and proper interests in being seen to restore Australian and Allied authority in territories to Australia's immediate north and for which it had direct responsibility, such as New Guinea. The final campaigns (as the official historian, Gavin Long, designated them in his final volume) have aroused considerable controversy ever since, with some questioning their rationale and purpose given that they could, and did, contribute nothing of value to the final defeat of the Japanese and the end of the war.[29]

All of this was well above Daly's (and Chilton's) pay grade, and whatever other men may have decided about the worth or otherwise of these final operations then or subsequently, at the time soldiers were committed to their comrades and units and to seeing the business through to its end.

This general view needs to be qualified in one important respect, however, regarding partial demobilisation before the war's end. Australia's small population could not sustain the size of the forces fielded in the course of the war while maintaining the demands of industry and supplying foodstuffs both to the Australian population and armed forces and to the Americans in the South-West Pacific Area, together with continuing supply to Britain. In October 1943 the army had released 20 000 men to the civil economy as part of the reorganisation of the field army overseen by Blamey and reflecting organisational demands of fighting in the Pacific that were very different from fighting the Germans in the Mediterranean.[30]

Further reductions in the strength of the army and the RAAF were effected in August 1944. There was also concern in parliament that men who had served in multiple campaigns after enlisting at the war's outbreak (or soon after) were continuing to fight and run the risk of wounds and death in combat, which struck some observers as inequitable given the considerable risks many had run already in the course of their service. The argument was given added force by the fatal wounding in action of Lieutenant T.C. 'Diver' Derrick, VC, DCM in the operation against Tarakan on 24 May 1945.[31] Ultimately, the War Cabinet directed the introduction of what was known as the 'five and two' scheme, whereby men with five years service including two years overseas were immediately eligible for discharge 'subject to operational needs'. This decision was approved only on 28 June, although it led to the reduction in the strength of the army and air force of 50 000 men by the end of 1945. This might have had direct implications for the battalions of the 18th Brigade as they prepared for their last operation of the war. Gavin Long noted of the 2/10th that all Daly's company commanders and all the company second-in-commands but one 'were eligible to go out' under this scheme. Daly believed that he could replace both officers and men if necessary so long as he had the time to retrain specialists and select more junior officers for promotion – but he greatly feared having captains and majors from outside the battalion foisted upon him.[32] The implications of this for Daly's command are underpinned by a simple check of the photographic archive at the Australian War Memorial to see the group portraits of men of the 2/10th Battalion due for demobilisation under the scheme and taken by the unit photographer just *after* the conclusion of operations.

The final period on Morotai enabled the battalions to brief all ranks thoroughly and to assimilate the latest intelligence on the Japanese positions and defences. Daly had already worked out the battalion plan in consultation with Chilton; he now took his officers through the details with the aid of a sand table. 'Never in the whole war did we have such information about our objective', he recalled. 'We had maps, we had photographs, we had information about the ground.'[33] The model was of Parramatta Ridge, the battalion's major objective located above the town of Balikpapan itself, and Daly briefed his company commanders, who in turn briefed their platoon commanders and these, in their turn, took their men through the detail. 'Of course, it was never exactly the same [as on the ground], but it was a big help.' In line with Daly's study of American experiences in amphibious assaults – bearing in mind that Balikpapan was an opposed assault and the Japanese were expected to put up strenuous resistance even this late in the war – the plan emphasised getting off the beach and inland as quickly as possible. To assist in this, 'my one little battalion... had enormous support planned', including air and naval gunfire (from the American 6-inch cruiser USS *Cleveland* and the Australian cruisers *Shropshire* and *Hobart*), a squadron of tanks (once landed), 4.2-inch mortars, anti-tank guns and a field regiment.[34] As Long noted, this was to be 'the last large-scale Allied operation of the war'.[35]

The landings were to be accompanied by very heavy bombardment, the belts of sea mines had been cleared by US minesweepers and the log barriers that the Japanese had constructed about a hundred yards out from the landing beaches were demolished by underwater demolitions, giving the landing craft a clear and unimpeded run. The enemy had fortified his positions strongly to cover the likely landing areas, deploying coastal defence and anti-aircraft batteries and utilising nearly 4000 troops of various categories. These were all subject to the attention of Allied firepower: 'the place had been very badly battered by the time we landed', Chilton noted.[36]

The divisional plan had opted to land in the middle of the Japanese positions around Balikpapan itself, rather than the alternative site of open and more lightly defended beaches several kilometres to the north (an option favoured initially by the US Navy), on the grounds that the latter would then involve protracted heavy fighting through close country with attendant additional casualties – a tacit recognition, perhaps, of the strains being felt at this late stage of the war and of the essentially minor nature of the outcome of the operation. Major-General E.J. Milford, commanding the 7th Division, had argued for this with the observation, in blunt terms: 'why land up the coast and have to fight miles through jungle, which suits the enemy, when you can go straight in under heavy supporting fire, which the enemy can't stand, in comparatively open and favourable country?'[37]

Photo 17 Assault barges at the beachhead, Balikpapan, 1 July 1945. (AWM 132509)

The 18th Brigade was to land in the Klandasan area with the intention of destroying Japanese defenders encountered there and opening the harbour for use by the Allied flotilla, and the brigade plan called for the 2/10th to land on the left at Red Beach, the 2/12th on the right on Yellow Beach with the 2/9th in reserve, ready to move through the 2/10th and capture Parramatta if the latter's attack stalled. In keeping with the conclusions he had drawn from studying earlier US operations, Daly was determined that his lead companies 'were not going to get caught on the beach', and his plan for the 2/10th involved an early concentration on the dominating feature of Hill 87 (the key to the ridge designated Parramatta), which had the potential to command the landing beaches all the way along in the brigade area.[38]

It is a commonplace observation that opposed amphibious assaults are among the more difficult of conventional operations of war, and Balikpapan proved true to form despite the obvious disparities in weight of fire and numbers of troops that favoured the 7th Division's operation. Although Japanese return fire was mostly light and inaccurate,[39] the assault waves missed their designated landing zones in several cases and found themselves ashore at the wrong place.[40] The hydrology of landing beaches is a complex problem, imperfectly understood at the time and still able to complicate amphibious operations even when aided by the full range of modern technologies.[41] The first wave of the 2/10th Battalion landed where they were intended, but the second and subsequent waves were off the mark by 800 yards or more, and this necessitated a quick reorganisation in order to establish the battalion's position correctly.

The battalion's tactical headquarters was ashore a few minutes after 9.00am. Daly's plan was straightforward; successful plans often are, but that does not necessarily make their execution easy, and the enemy is always a factor to be reckoned with. As Daly later told Gavin Long, 'my plan was for B Coy (Bray) to seize the high ground north of Red Beach by 9.15...while D Coy (Brocksopp) sealed off the left flank. Bray was told to ignore all opposition on the way to his objective, which he did, covering the 800-odd yards in the planned time of 15 minutes. This great haste was in order to secure some sort of depth to the beachhead before the enemy recovered from the bombardment.'[42] With his command post established ashore, the plan then called for A Company (Sanderson) to advance to the apex of the line between the first two companies and seize the road junction there, with tanks in support; C Company (Cook) would then mount the attack on Hill 87.

For whatever reason, A Company's early objectives were bare of the enemy, although Sanderson's forward elements soon began to take fire from Japanese positions on Hill 87, which nonetheless appeared to be lightly held. Although the supporting fire plans made a considerable number of units and weight of fire available to the battalion in the initial phases of the attack, in fact at this point the squadron of tanks detailed to assist them was still on the beach and had not yet worked its way forward, the field artillery likewise was unavailable because of communications problems while the naval gunfire support was also off-line at this point. Stripped of the major assets on which his plan had been formulated, Daly could only call on his own light mortars, a platoon of medium machine-guns and a troop of 4.2-inch mortars from the 2/2nd Anti-Tank Regiment.

Conscious of the critical importance of taking and holding Parramatta, Daly made what the official history later described as a 'bold decision'.[43] He could either wait for the promised support to become available or he could fulfil the plan's intent and attack forward with what he had; he chose the latter, knowing that the alternative was to give the Japanese time to 'recover from the bombardment and get back into their positions, and then we'd have a tough battle on our hands'.[44] With the mortars laying

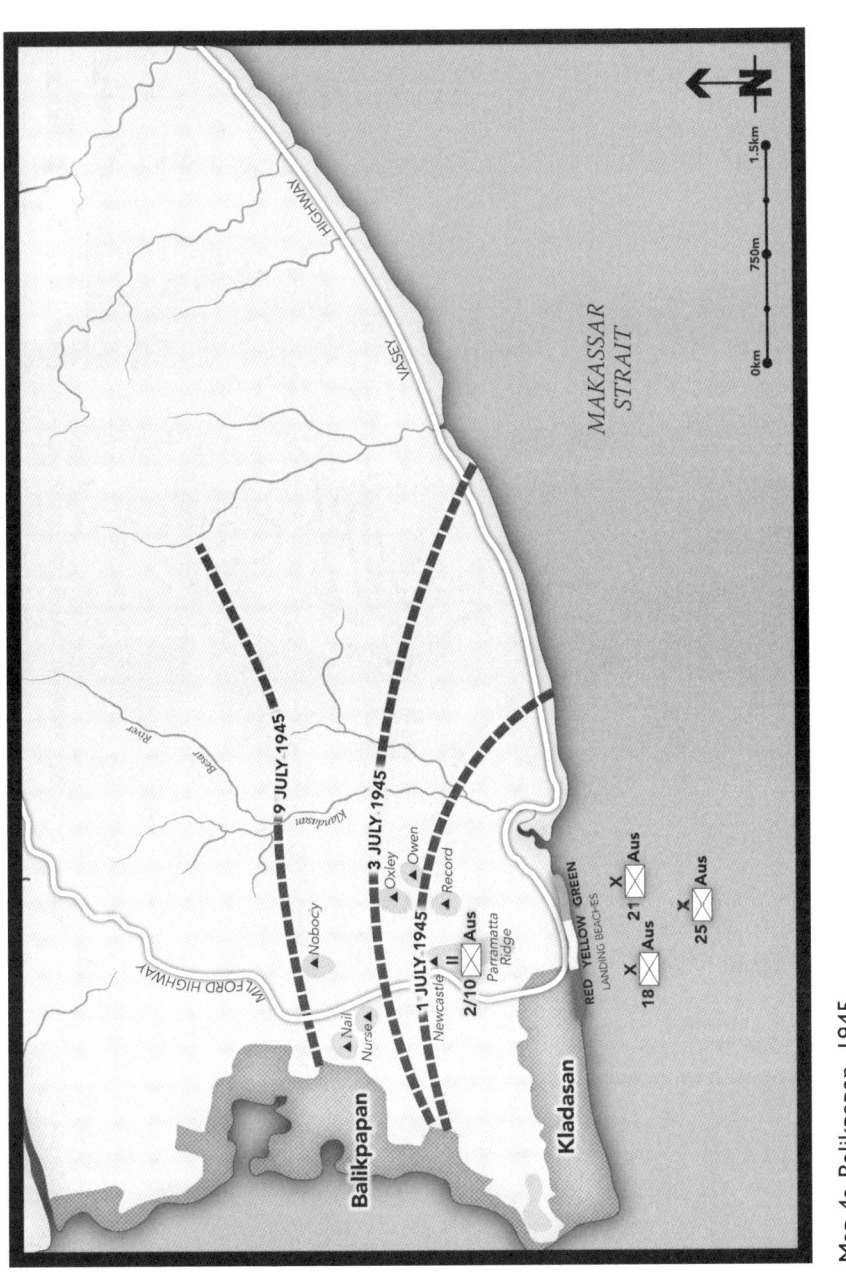

Map 4a Balikpapan, 1945.

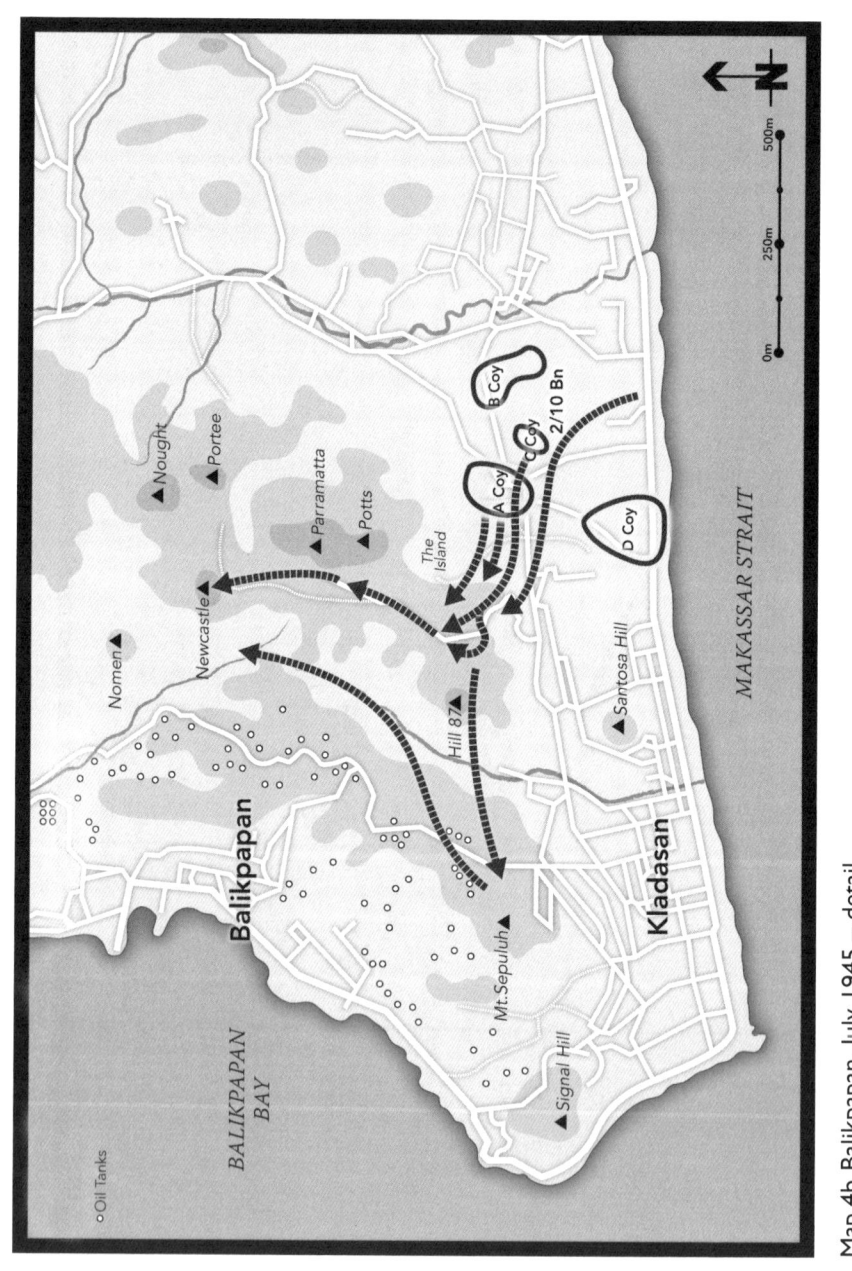

Map 4b Balikpapan, July 1945 – detail.

'a beautiful smoke screen between Hill 87 and Parramatta', Daly ordered C Company forward: 'Right, Frank [Cook], off you go.'[45] Despite taking fire from another enemy position, designated the Island, to the right of Parramatta, the platoons pressed forward and engaged Japanese defences on Green Spur, although they failed to clear it until the tanks started to arrive later in the morning. The Japanese began to recover from the early surprise and the effects of the bombardment, and the fighting intensified as the morning went on; the leading platoon had taken thirteen casualties so far, and there were several fierce encounters in the fighting for the hill.[46]

The arrival of the tanks just before midday ended Japanese resistance on Hill 87. Mortar and machine-gun support helped to suppress Japanese fire from Parramatta while the guns of the 2/4th Field Regiment were coming into play in support of the assault on the ridge as well; the guns 'rendered valuable service by engaging targets on Parramatta', while Daly was dependent for a time on the battery's radio net because his own communications had broken down.[47] Although enemy casualties were heavy, the rapid advance had been costly for the battalion as well; C Company had by now lost nine killed and ten wounded, and Daly moved A Company forward to relieve C Company in the next phase of the attack while requesting Brigade HQ to deploy the 2/9th to relieve his remaining two companies, then exploit and consolidate the positions through the afternoon.[48] A patrol pushed forward and cleared the enemy off the Newcastle feature as well, to complete the clearing of the ridge and offering good observation over the open ground to the north and towards the town itself. The overall advantage, as Daly noted later, was that 'it placed the enemy in a very poor position from which to launch a counter attack on the western end of the beachhead'.[49]

In keeping with his own command ethos, Daly had been well forward for much of the day, at times with limited communications to keep contact with his forward company ('I made a point of being well up...to see what was going on...sufficiently forward to see what was going on').[50] At one stage his command group was brought under fire by a Japanese anti-aircraft gun firing at only 2000 yards range, but Allied fire support could be equally lethal. A forward patrol from A Company was strafed by American aircraft during the afternoon after clearing a Japanese position, but far worse was the attack on the battalion headquarters, located just south-east of Hill 87. US carrier-borne aircraft bombed and rocketed the hill, probably responding to a request for air support made earlier in the day and subsequently cancelled when the advance outstripped the need.

Photo 18 Soldiers of the 2/10th Battalion moving along Vasey Highway towards Hill 87, Balikpapan, 1 July 1945. (AWM 128753/2)

Major Miethke, the second-in-command, the RSM and twelve others were wounded, and three men were killed, including one of the unit's early members, Lance-Sergeant Hackett, MM. Aircraft identification panels had been displayed, 'but they got bombed just the same'.[51] Although there were several hours of daylight left, Daly's request to Chilton at brigade headquarters to keep pushing forward across the valley was denied, and the battalion was ordered to consolidate and hold as far forward as the Newcastle feature with one platoon from each of B and C Companies and machine-guns from the 2/1st Machine Gun Battalion in place.

Desultory infiltration attempts by the Japanese that night were easily repulsed with heavy Japanese losses (the official history states 'about 40', on top of the 216 killed during the day), aided by star shells fired by the ships offshore that readily lit up the area.[52] The 2/10th's own losses had been thirteen killed and thirty wounded, but the day's action had been a considerable success. Summarising the battalion's assault years later, Long wrote in the official history that the main reasons for their success had been 'the swift advance of Cook's company up the sides of Hill 87 regardless of "mopping up", the speed and skill of the individual infantrymen and the way in which they went on despite heavy losses [and] Daly's action in ordering the company to press on when he had practically no reserves and little supporting fire'.[53]

The second day's objectives included final consolidation and clearing up of Hill 87 and Parramatta, and patrols forward of Newcastle towards the concentration of fuel storage tanks (the Tank Farm area) and the features dubbed the Reservoir, Nought and Nomen. Clearing up involved the sealing and destruction of Japanese positions in tunnels and shafts, usually accomplished through coordinated action between the engineers, infantry pioneers and 25-pound explosive charges. (Gavin Long records that 110 tunnels and pillboxes were destroyed in the Balikpapan area in this way, with more than 8000 mines and booby traps being defused as well.)[54] The Tank Farm contained sizeable quantities of fuel oil (Balikpapan had been the largest producer of petroleum products in South-East Asia before the war), and there was concern that fires might develop and threaten the Australians ashore as well as posing threats to the local people. The Japanese had not yet conceded their positions, and in the course of the day engaged the battalion's forward platoons and other positions on Parramatta with artillery and small arms fire, damaging several of the storage tanks and creating at least one large oil fire. They were eliminated through a combination of infantry action, artillery fires and air strikes. Daly used D Company to take the Tank Farm. The company was commanded by Captain W.A. Brocksopp, an Englishman (originally) who had given his occupation as 'gentleman' upon enlistment; Daly recalled pointing out to him later 'that it wasn't customary for Australian officers to lead their companies into battle with a swagger stick underarm', but when the company encountered enemy fire and initially went to ground it was Brocksopp's example that got them moving again.[55]

Isolated groups of Japanese continued to engage the companies' forward localities that night, and small-arms fire punctuated the darkness on several occasions. The tasks for the third day were to clear the main part of the town, the waterfront and the industrial area; pillboxes and tunnels were encountered again and neutralised, and a small number of enemy killed with no losses to the battalion. A handful of Japanese soldiers, possibly trying to break through and out of the now-occupied town, attacked the A Company position in the early hours and either were killed or managed to escape.[56]

The 7th Division had successfully established and expanded a bridgehead that was now five miles (eight kilometres) wide and a mile (1.6 kilometres) deep and had secured an operational airfield, which was now pressed into use.[57] After three days of fighting in which they had lost 16 killed and 40 wounded, and had inflicted 332 dead on the Japanese, the 2/10th's part in the operation effectively ended; 4 July was spent in 'consolidating and reorganising' in the official terms of the battalion war diary; 'a quiet day was had by all companies', as the unit history recalled. Now in brigade reserve, the men spent time clearing the great quantities of equipment left by the enemy ('many valuable souvenirs were collected'), processing the mainly Indian POWs freed from the camps in the area and the large numbers of Japanese captured in turn, and providing assistance to the local people as they emerged from wherever they had sought shelter. On 10 August the soldiers received their first beer ration on Borneo (three bottles per man, doubtless part of Daly's recollection that 'we didn't have much to do after [going into reserve] and I set about making the battalion comfortable'[58]), while news of the Japanese surrender came through the following evening. The war was over.

The priority now was to demobilise the army and return the tens of thousands of 'soldiers for the duration' to civilian life as quickly and effortlessly as possible. This was not an easy task; it would see soldiers awaiting repatriation into the early months of 1946 and would provoke disturbances among some disgruntled men who simply wanted to leave the army and go home. Daly, whose peacetime occupation *was* the army, found himself acting in command of the brigade as its members were repatriated and 'then in due course I became G1 and AQ of a disappearing division, and then finally the divisional commander when there was no division'.[59] As noted earlier, the government had given considerable thought to the way in which demobilisation would be handled, with an emphasis on fairness and efficiency and getting long-service men home first before those who had joined more recently. This posed some challenges, since many of the officers and senior NCOs were men with the longest service, and if they all went home first the machinery of demobilisation would likely fall apart.[60]

Ever meticulous in his arrangements and planning, Daly believed that the release of men under the 'five and two' scheme posed few problems. 'There were plenty of Lts who could become coy comds and the older NCOs could be replaced by good younger men.'[61] His concerns were practical: he didn't want numbers of surplus majors and captains posted into his battalion to prevent 'the promotion of his young and able men' as was happening in some other units. And he did not want to be posted to Japan as part of the occupation force then being put together, even though he was offered a battalion command in what would become the British Commonwealth Occupation Force (BCOF) and of a unit that would be a precursor of the Royal Australian Regiment (not that he could have known that). There was also talk of him being posted to Japan as senior staff officer on Lieutenant-General Northcott's headquarters.[62] Neither of these eventuated once he made his objections clear: he wanted to return to Australia and to marry Heather, the woman to whom he had become engaged before embarkation for the Oboe operation.

Refusing such appointments when offered in this manner might have proven a slightly risky option, given the usual drastic reductions in the military establishment that accompany the end of every major war and the shabby way in which Staff Corps veterans of the original AIF had been treated in the 1920s and 1930s – a process that Daly had observed as a staff cadet and freshly minted junior officer. Blamey attempted to persuade the government to treat older regular officers more fairly than their predecessors in the absence of an existing pension or superannuation scheme, and the senior Staff Corps officers in a position then to ensure that the mistakes made in the aftermath of the previous war would not be repeated after the latest one were generally successful in their efforts.[63] Daly's own immediate postwar appointments would prove professionally and personally rewarding, and conducive to early married life.

Daly was an outstanding success as a battalion commander, and made a critical contribution to the success of the Australian assault at Balikpapan, one recognised through the award of the Distinguished Service Order (DSO), the citation for which noted that the success of the first day was 'due in no small part to the courage, initiative and brilliant leadership of the commanding officer'. Gavin Long, who probably knew the Australian Army of 1939–45 better than anyone, described him as 'a quiet, shy chap, but has concealed beneath this outside great drive and sound military sense ... he comes out of this show with full marks – the outstanding CO of the campaign'.[64] The available evidence suggests that his soldiers concurred: writing years later, the unit history described his arriving to take command as a 'red letter day', which, given the uneven record of previous COs of the 2/10th, it must indeed have seemed to those who then entrusted their lives to his capacities and judgement. One NCO, an old soldier who had served with the battalion through Tobruk, Milne Bay and Balikpapan, and who had a clear basis for comparisons, might reasonably speak for all: while Daly might appear 'devoid of a sense of humour' and lacked the tendency to familiarity in behaviour of some officers, he struck them nonetheless as a first-class soldier and administrator: 'A soldier and a half... he looked the part... and had it all nutted out to the last round.'[65]

As Pratten has concluded in his meticulous study of Australian battalion-level command in the Second World War, professional competence came to be more highly prized by the ranks than the cliched mannerisms sometimes thought to be the attribute of a successful officer, not least because it kept them alive. Chilton, an outstanding officer in his own right, thoroughly concurred in these judgements: 'if the commanding officer's below par, the battalion won't perform terribly well, and its morale won't be terribly high and vice versa... it was just phenomenal, the change in that battalion after Tom Daly took over.'[66]

Command of an infantry battalion had been Daly's ambition 'for the whole war', and he had had plenty of opportunities to observe good and bad COs.[67] The keys to his undoubted success as a commanding officer were several. First, he virtually retrained the battalion: 'I didn't know what the state of training was and there was only one way to find out and that was to start from scratch and see how they performed.' The key to effective training, moreover, was realism. His men expected him to know his job, and he expected them to know theirs, and in most cases to have the capacity to perform 'one up', to take over the roles and functions of the next rank above their own in the event of casualties or other absences. They were encouraged to exercise their initiative in battle – hence the sand table model of Balikpapan and its availability to all ranks – but to obey the rules, respect the rank, and be fit for their tasks. In many respects he perfectly embodies the old saw about the command relationship between officers and men: 'firm, fair, friendly, but not familiar'.

Daly very clearly enjoyed the confidence of his superiors, especially Chilton. In his efficiency report written just after the war's end, Chilton summed up Daly in the following terms: 'A most outstanding officer in every respect – and the best all-round battalion commander I have known. I can think of no weaknesses. He is a strong personality but is tactful and universally respected and liked. Possesses in a high degree the ability to obtain the utmost from his officers and men both in training and in action.'[68]

Daly in turn enjoyed the trust and support of his own immediate subordinates and had a good understanding of the characteristics of his company commanders, 'what made them tick'. As noted earlier, he had known all his company commanders – in very different roles – when he had served as the battalion's adjutant at the war's beginning, and was in the fortunate position of knowing 'where their characteristics were best employed'. As a result he 'felt that my company commanders, whatever happened, knew what I wanted them to do and they would do it'. But a good commanding officer is not merely a manager of other men's capacities. As Gavin Long noted, citing Brigadier Ivan Dougherty, the Balipapan landing 'was a lesson on the use of firepower'.[69] At the critical moment, however, with the key terrain feature in reach and his men ready to move, all the major firepower assets failed and Daly opted to go forward regardless.

Soldiers are killed in operations of war – a melancholy fact increasingly unfamiliar to modern Western sensibilities. As noted previously, by the war's final operations there was a growing desire to preserve lives in contexts where their loss made no appreciable difference to the outcome, which was by now a clearly foregone conclusion. Excessive caution, however, could be equally, or more, dangerous, a dilemma for commanders at all levels and one with which they had to come to terms in their own way. Daly recalled later how 'you become very close to the men, very, very close because you know that some of them are going to die, and it may be your fault that they do. Not that you have much choice in the matter because you don't know what the enemy is going to do most of the time. But you do feel that.'

His style of command and as a commanding officer is encapsulated by an incident that occurred while the battalion was training on the Atherton Tableland before Balikpapan. A woman in town was badly assaulted by a soldier on a drunken spree, and in these circumstances Daly 'showed no mercy, none whatever'. 'I formed the battalion up, and I said this is what's happened. This chap's let the battalion down, and we've got to do something about it.' He instructed that a hat be passed around, and the assembled ranks contributed several hundred pounds in total to assist her, since she had few other means of support and was quite badly injured.[70] As Chilton observed years later, Daly understood his men, 'and they understood him'.

CHAPTER 3

'HE COULD FILL ANY APPOINTMENT WITH DISTINCTION'

Australia emerged from the Second World War on the winning side, and in far better physical and economic shape than most of the victorious combatant nations other than the United States. Like the other dominions of the British Empire, Australia had avoided invasion and occupation with their attendant destruction, division and trauma (although, unlike Canada, New Zealand or South Africa, Australian territory had been attacked sporadically by the Japanese in the course of 1942–43). As a major supplier of US forces in the South-West Pacific Area, moreover, Australia emerged from the war as one of the few net creditor nations under the US-inspired Lend-Lease scheme. The suspension of the scheme within weeks of the end of the war placed the battered British economy under still greater stress but had little effect on Australia's.

Australia had been on the victorious side in 1918 as well, but having won the war could arguably be said, in common with most of the world's democracies, to have lost the peace during the interwar years. The 'war to end wars' had done nothing of the sort, and the economic depressions of the early 1920s and throughout the 1930s had led some to question the value of the sacrifices of the Great War generation, and had contributed seemingly little to the creation of a 'land fit for heroes'. The political and strategic folly of the interwar years had been replicated in Australia as well: the general officers' conference of 1921 had identified the most likely direct threat to Australia as being posed by Japan and had made recommendations for force structure and capabilities with which to meet it. Not surprisingly, so soon after the end of the Great War their report was ignored and, equally predictably, the conclusions of the Washington Treaty on Naval Armaments Limitations in 1922 had seen the small Royal Australian Navy further reduced in size and effectiveness. In 1945, however, the wisdom of massive postwar reductions in the armed forces in a context of emerging Cold War tensions between east and west was less than strikingly apparent – at least to some – and within the senior ranks of the Australian Army there was a strong belief that the mistakes of the interwar period should not be repeated now, nor the costs of such reductions visited upon a new generation of Australians whether in or out of uniform.

The postwar reductions after 1919 had severely affected officers of the Permanent Military Forces, and the effects were still being felt during Daly's service as a young regular officer in the 1930s. He was now somewhat older and a great deal more senior in rank and experience, but this had been true of many of those who had survived the Great War and had done them little good in career terms. The difference this time was that the general officers at the head of the army were determined to maintain the army's capacities and talent in the face of the inevitable push to reduce the service, including the permanent force, in line with the obviously reduced requirements now that the Germans and Japanese were utterly defeated.

Although his professional future was a matter of very close interest, Daly had other and more immediately pressing matters to attend to: marriage. He used some of his accumulated leave to get 'to know my bride a little better and I think she was rather anxious to know me. And likewise my future in-laws who had seen even less of me than she had.'[1] Heather's father, James Patrick 'Jim' Fitzgerald,[2] was a prominent Melbourne businessman with Consolidated Zinc who had mixed feelings about an army officer as a prospective son-in-law: 'he had I think grave reservations about anybody who was silly enough to be a soldier'. Daly, on the other hand, both enjoyed the army and had his own reservations about his suitability for a civilian job. He and Heather, who was ten years his junior, were married on 19 February 1946 in the chapel at Xavier College and honeymooned at Portsea and on a road trip to Sydney, via Canberra. The wedding present from Heather's parents had been a Ford V8 motor car and, despite the extreme petrol rationing, they drove to Sydney and back, visiting friends, staying for a few days at the Australia Hotel, and easing into early married life. Now long gone, the Australia Hotel, located on the corner of Castlereagh Street and what was then Martin Place (now Plaza), was the most glamorous hotel of its day in Sydney. An Art

Photo 19 Wedding day. (Daly family)

Deco structure built in the 1930s, it was a modernist riot of glass, steel and marble and much favoured by the wealthy (in whose number one did not normally include army officers). Daly, however, was 'fairly flush with cash' and had plenty of leave in hand, since there had been few opportunities to expend either over the course of the last few years.

On his return to Australia he had been initially offered an instructor's position at the new Australian Staff College (later the Army Command and Staff College) soon to be located at Fort Queenscliff on Port Phillip Bay in Victoria, where it opened in time for the 1947 course intake. Not only had he done such a job already during the war, but also the college had moved around a lot and in the last year of the war was located in Cabarlah, near Toowoomba in Queensland (in order to free up space at Duntroon, where facilities were very cramped due to a range of wartime activities located there). He opted instead for a staff job in Army Headquarters, Melbourne (much more conducive to starting married life and with Heather's family nearby), and was appointed GSO1 (Training) from early February.

Domestic affairs were less easy to arrange. Australia was in the grip of an acute housing shortage after the war years during which construction resources had been diverted to supporting the services and the infrastructure needed to base the large US presence in the country, and accommodation was at an absolute premium – some estimates put the shortfall at between 250 000 and 300 000 houses. The government instituted a War Service Home Scheme under the auspices of the Commonwealth Housing Commission, but it had little utility or appeal to a regular soldier who could count on the numerous moves concomitant upon the posting cycle. They managed to find a house at Frankston, near Mornington on Port Phillip Bay, and Daly commuted to Army Headquarters at Victoria Barracks each day, which was 'quite a hike' by train and on foot.

It was not to last long. Army Headquarters was busy overseeing the return to peacetime affairs, the contribution to the occupation of Japan, finalisation of the repatriation and demobilisation of the wartime army, and formulating advice to government on the desirable shape of the post-war army and the influence of early developments in the emerging Cold War. Daly was put to work drafting the plan for the postwar army, but this job, too, clearly held him in a 'holding pattern' while his next appointment was finalised: a member of the Directing Staff (known in the parlance as a 'DS') at the Staff College, Camberley, in the United Kingdom. Such an appointment suggested strongly that Daly was being groomed for higher rank.

The Staff College was established in 1858 as part of the gradual process of educating and professionalising the officers of the British Army, later joined by a limited number of student officers from the newly established armies of the dominions and India.[3] In 1906–08 Brudenell White, later wartime chief of staff of the First AIF, became the first officer of the Australian Military Forces to attend, and a small number of Australians continued to attend Staff College courses there and at the Indian equivalent at Quetta with interruptions during the two world wars. The appointment of Directing Staff from the dominion armies was introduced only in 1945, and the first Australian officer posted was Lieutenant-Colonel N.A.M. Nicholls.[4] The course had been reformed just before the war, in 1938, and the old two-year course had then been replaced by an annual intake system.

Daly had to get there first, which was by no means a simple proposition at the end of the war. As with housing, there was an acute shortage of shipping in the war's aftermath: many passenger vessels had been taken up from trade and pressed into service as troopships, both during the war and now in order to return millions of men and women to their homes outside Europe and Asia; this was a more acute drain of available shipping than the wartime destruction wrought by the submarine campaigns, heavy though the toll had been, because many of the ships sunk through enemy action were cargo and freight ships. Distant points like Australia were particularly affected, as the Dalys now discovered, and the movements staff were unable to provide any details on their likely departure dates or even what ship they might join ('I didn't know when or how and nobody could tell me', he recalled).[5] In the curious way the army sometimes works, his wife found out the details of their voyage before he did, and they duly embarked on the *Empire Clarendon* on 19 July, bound for the United Kingdom.

The voyage was far from comfortable, much less luxurious. The ship was a refrigerated cargo liner of 8500 tons, built by Harland & Wolff for the Ministry of Water Transport in Belfast and launched in May 1945 as part of an effort to replace lost tonnage and get empire trade flowing again. She was operated at this stage by the P&O Line and had accommodation berths for thirty-five passengers, although on the early postwar voyages she was carrying many more in order to try to meet demand; Daly recalled '150 aboard... mainly expatriate Britishers who had been evacuated from England during the war and were returning'. He shared a berth with a naval officer while Heather shared with two other women, despite being pregnant with their first child, Betty-Ann, who was born in November. 'It wasn't the most comfortable of voyages.'

The housing shortage they had known in Australia was far worse in Britain, as were shortages of just about everything else. Rationing was still in full force. They eventually obtained a married quarter a little way from the college itself and, through connections that Heather's father deployed on their behalf, a small car, although they waited some time to acquire it, during which time Heather rode a bicycle. The quarter was entirely unfurnished, while Daly managed to supplement the petrol rationing allowance with extra coupons he was able to obtain through the local garage (excess coupons sold by local farmers, who enjoyed generous allocations that mostly they could not use), but rectifying all this took some time to arrange.[6] When his second daughter Susan was born in March 1948 in a local hospital near Aldershot, he had to visit wife and child by bus!

Daly was assigned at the end of August 1946 to the college's C Division, situated in an elegant former civilian residence, Minden Manor, which had been requisitioned for the Staff College's needs as a wartime exigency. The Commandant of the college was Major-General (later Field

Photo 20 Lieutenant-Colonel T.J. Daly, Camberley, 1948. (Daly family)

Marshal Sir Richard) R.A. Hull, a cavalryman who had commanded the 5th Infantry Division in north-west Europe in the last six months of the war. One of the youngest major generals in the British Army, he would become Chief of the Imperial General Staff (CIGS) in 1961 and Chief of the Defence Staff in 1965. Not only were the staff all experienced veterans of the recent campaigns but so, too, were the students. At this stage the curriculum was still organised according to wartime requirements with a foreshortened course lasting six months of the kind with which Daly was familiar from his previous instructional posting at Duntroon, and he fitted in easily. 'An outstanding young officer in every way', commented Hull on his annual confidential report.[7]

The 1947 course year reverted to the full twelve months and was marked by another change. Field Marshal Montgomery, appointed CIGS the previous year, had mandated that all officers of colonel rank who had not attended the Staff College were to do so. This meant that syndicates and course materials designed for majors were now hurriedly adapted to cater for a course whose make-up ranged from the majors for whom it was intended all the way through to officers with wartime rank as acting or temporary brigadiers. This made for an interesting situation given that the Directing Staff were lieutenant-colonels, in Daly's case a temporary one with a substantive peacetime rank of major. Reflecting older patterns and habits within the pre-war British Army, some of these officers had no desire to be staff officers or ever serve outside their regiments, and managing them must have demanded all the tact and charm for which Daly was often noted. He thoroughly enjoyed the work, especially the planning exercises, which drew on recent campaigns in which he had not participated such as Burma and the north-western Europe campaign of 1944–45 with its heavy emphasis on armoured and mobile operations on a grand scale. The course methodology included that invaluable tool for instruction in military history, the staff ride, and the 1947 course visited the sites of recent operations in north-western Europe. 'We had on the course chaps who had been involved in every aspect of every operation from Caen right through to Arnhem to the crossing of the Rhine and so on, and this was great stuff... having people like that to show and tell you what happened was almost as if you were there.'[8]

Daly's syndicate that year included Lieutenant-Colonel John Frost, who had commanded 2nd Battalion, the Parachute Regiment in the four-day defence of Arnhem Bridge in September 1944. Among the course members in the first year, 1946, was Wing Commander (later Air Marshal Sir) John Grandy, the only air force officer to command a squadron in the Battle of Britain and subsequently become head of the RAF.

There were opportunities for travel – around Britain and on a camping trip through southern France and northern Italy – sport (especially cricket, in which Daly captained one of the college teams), and the resumption of a normal social life after the abnormality and restrictions of the war years. Daly enjoyed his time at Camberley, and his superiors clearly appreciated him. Hull rated him as 'an outstanding young officer' in both his subsequent annual reports, recommending in his final remarks that his future appointments 'should be carefully planned and he should... be given command of a Brigade at an early date'. Successive assistant commandants echoed these sentiments: 'He has an alert and thoughtful mind and considerable skill in handling men. The latter attribute has been well tested in the past year [1947] when many students have been far senior to him.' Another noted 'a most engaging and cheerful personality and a good sense of humour' and thought, despite an acquaintanceship of only seven months, that Daly possessed 'the brains, determination, and personality to take him right to the top of his profession'.[9]

In an age when long-distance travel was by sea, any form of overseas travel or assignment was expensive and the Australian armed forces lacked the resources or facilities themselves to provide many areas of technical and higher military education, it was common for officers posted to the United Kingdom to undertake a further posting or assignment there before returning to Australia and so it proved with Daly. The Joint Services Staff College (JSSC) had been established in 1947 at Latimer House in Chesham, Buckinghamshire, and Daly was sent on the four-month course in the first half of 1949. The college was intended to provide a tri-service dimension to the professional education of officers of lieutenant-colonel rank (or equivalent), and it was assumed that successful graduates would attain at least three substantive ranks above their current one (i.e. reach at least the rank of major-general or other two-star equivalent). The new posting meant that the Dalys had to relinquish their married quarter at Camberley, no small matter with a young family and with no ready pool of other accommodation to be had. Heather somehow found a private rental near Camberley itself while Daly 'lived in' at JSSC and returned at weekends.[10]

The course completed, the Dalys returned to Australia on board SS *Orion*, an Orient Line passenger ship built in 1935 that could carry more than 1200 passengers and was loaded to the gunwales with 'ten pound Poms' on assisted passages to settle in Australia. The voyage home was more comfortable than the earlier one, but no less crowded. To the strong reports he had received at Camberley was an equally positive endorsement from JSSC: 'A most likeable officer with a charming personality... a hard worker with a determined outlook... has commonsense and is not afraid to speak his mind... He does not speak much but when he does it is expressed clearly and much to the point... an excellent all-round knowledge.'[11]

After a brief period of leave, Daly took up his new appointment as Director of Military Art at RMC Duntroon. Like most pre-existing service training and educational facilities, the college had undergone considerable changes occasioned by the war. As well as the Staff School, which Daly had instructed at in 1944, the site had also contained an officers' training wing for commissioning into the AIF while in January 1945 the Army School of Civil Affairs had opened in buildings vacated by the Staff School. The four-year curriculum that Daly had known as a cadet before the war was compressed, some classes were graduated early – especially in

1942 to meet the needs of the Pacific War – and the intakes had been increased in size. Younger members of the military staff went overseas on active service, female personnel (members of the Australian Women's Army Service) were employed on the administrative side, and the small number of civilian academics was supplemented by retired professors who returned to fill gaps. The war brought other changes as well. Reflecting a sense that the curriculum and training methods at RMC were obsolescent in the light of the challenges of modern war (riding had been dropped from the syllabus only in 1940 and was in fact restored temporarily in 1945), Blamey formed a committee of three senior RMC graduates (Generals Robertson and Vasey and Brigadier Combes) to recommend changes to the way in which RMC prepared officer-aspirants for service in a modern army. It was also tasked with reviewing the resources and facilities of the site and with assessing the subsequent utilisation of graduates once they entered the army proper.

The resultant report stressed a commitment to the educational mission of RMC and expressed the hope that the standards and qualifications of the college would mirror those of the nation's universities; it was to be several decades before this became a reality with the brokering of an agreement with the University of New South Wales for the delivery of degree-granting programs from the late 1960s. The Vasey Report also recommended that only 'tried and experienced officers be appointed to the military staff instead of officers appointed on the basis of availability and convenience'.[12] The new Commandant, Brigadier E.L. Vowles (Class of 1914), who was appointed in February 1945, possessed a clear-eyed understanding that regular officers would need not only 'a sound military education but also a high standard of technical and general knowledge'.[13] The recommendations of the Vasey committee were then endorsed by a further committee, chaired by Lieutenant-General S.F. Rowell, Vice-Chief of the General Staff, which convened and reported in 1946. The decision to create an Australian Regular Army (ARA) in 1947, partly to meet the force demands of Australian participation in the British Commonwealth Occupation Force in Japan, partly reflecting the recommendations of the Military Board for a new approach to postwar force structure and planning that avoided the perceived shortcomings of the interwar era, further underpinned the need for a revised approach to the preparation of Staff Corps officers. The four-year course was reintroduced for the intake in 1947 (the Class of 1950), which meant that as on occasions in the past there was no graduating class in a given year, in this case in 1949.

Changes to the curriculum would occur, and be debated within senior army circles, over the next several years, while in January 1952 the Officer Cadet School (OCS), Portsea began operations to supplement the flow of regular officers in light of the army's enhanced needs flowing from the war in Korea and the government's decision to adopt a National Service scheme. Much of this lay in the future, however, and would not concern Daly until he was leading the army as a whole in the second half of the 1960s. Other, more immediate matters would do so, however, including the seemingly perpetual problem of finding somewhere to live. An ambitious rebuilding program at RMC was scrapped on grounds of likely cost, but the expansion of the Corps of Staff Cadets and the generally dilapidated state of many of the existing facilities led to a more modest redevelopment program that would continue for most of the following decade.[14] The growth in the corps meant growth in the number of staff, and the provision of married quarters for army families posted to the college was a perennial source of difficulty for most of the 1950s.

The quarter traditionally assigned to the Director of Military Art was deemed excessive to his needs by the Commandant, Major-General Henry Wells (Class of 1919), and was in the process of being subdivided and renovated when Daly received his appointment. Daly lived in the Officers' Mess for a while and Heather and the children stayed in Melbourne with her family, but postwar soldiering in a family context must have been a strain; as Daly himself later characterised it, his wife came from a background which 'had everything and then suddenly [she had] been thrown into living in substandard accommodation, two little children and trying to cope with rationing in England... [and] with always having to pack and follow'.[15] In a manner familiar to all those who lived in army quarters in the postwar era, the modifications to the now subdivided house resulted in an interior wall being placed between the living areas and the kitchen so that there was no access to the dining room! The house had been empty for a while and the garden had run riot, and once he took possession Daly found himself spending 'a lot of time in that garden. I got it right eventually.' Canberra in the 1950s was still a small country town, the presence of the federal parliament and other national institutions such as RMC notwithstanding. Several officers on the staff took night courses at the fledgling Canberra Technical College; Daly did a year-long course in woodwork and gradually acquired a stock of woodworking tools, which was 'marvellous to have, bearing in mind the sort of houses you were going to live in'.[16]

The position of Director of Military Art had been held by some distinguished officers before the war, including C.W. Gwynn (a British officer on exchange, the first occupant of the position in 1911, subsequently Major-General Sir Charles Gwynn and author of the seminal military text *Imperial Policing*, first published in 1934); E.F. Harrison (1915–17, the first Australian to attend the staff course at Quetta, and a subsequent Commandant during the Second World War); H.J.F. Foster (1917–18, previously Chief of the General Staff and, between 1906 and 1916, Director of Military Science at the University of Sydney); J.D. Lavarack (1919–24, a divisional and corps commander in the Second World War); and H.C.H. Robertson (1934–39, the first RMC graduate to command a brigade in the Second AIF and Commander-in-Chief of the British Commonwealth Occupation Force in Japan between 1946 and 1951). The role of Director of Military Art had originally been 'to instruct in strategy, military geography and history and to supervise the instructors in technical subjects'.[17] By the late 1940s it was the senior military instruction position at the college and usually, as in Daly's case, tied as well to the position of Commanding Officer, Corps of Staff Cadets.

Although significant changes were on the horizon at RMC, especially in terms of the increased emphasis on more rigorous, university-standard academic work, many aspects of college life had changed little since Daly's time as a staff cadet. His passion and talent for sport was given free rein. He played cricket and managed the Australian Rules team because 'nobody else seemed to want to take [it] on', and he did so in addition to managing the rugby club. In fact AFL, to give it its later generic title, had only been introduced to RMC in 1942 over the Commandant's objections that rugby should be the only code played on the grounds that it was 'still considered the best suited for personnel in the Army'.[18] Coached by Roy Leaper, who had played sixteen games for St Kilda between 1926 and 1928, the RMC side won the local competition in 1943 undefeated, but its fortunes slumped after the war and it withdrew from the ACT competition in 1947. Under Daly's encouragement it re-entered in 1950 and won the flag again in 1951. In his confidential report for 1949–50 the Commandant noted 'the reorganisation of the extensive sporting activities of the Staff Cadets' on which Daly had embarked with 'equal ability, keenness [*sic*] and interest'.[19]

His time as Director of Military Art struck Daly as mostly 'the hum drum life of a senior instructor... trying to keep them in order'.[20] Part of the challenge here lay in restraining the urge to 'Fourth Class training' on the part of senior cadets, or 'bastardisation' to give the practice its modern, and more accurate, title. Harassment and physical punishment of junior cadets by their seniors was a long-running problem at RMC that went back to the college's foundation, and Daly himself had felt the Commandant's displeasure in his own senior year for having acted against it with what was deemed insufficient vigour on one occasion. It was a practice with which he 'certainly didn't agree... [and] in my day [as a cadet] I didn't agree with that at all'. Although he did not believe that there was 'very much of it', it was nonetheless the case that the junior class was 'still treated like outcasts'. If Daly was mistaken in his recollection of a comparative decline in the practice – and he probably was – he was at least in good company; Major-General R.N.L. Hopkins, Commandant between 1951 and 1954, believed erroneously that he himself had largely eradicated it.[21]

Daly's time at RMC was a happy and productive one, if undramatic. A third daughter, Edwina, was born, which further emphasised the cramped nature of the family's living arrangements. When the Korean War began in June 1950, and with an Australian commitment of troops in September, Daly was considered for command of the 3rd Battalion, Royal Australian Regiment (3RAR), the unit still based in Japan on residual occupation duties and being rapidly built up before deployment to the fighting. The reinforcement and retraining was conducted in a great hurry, and the Military Board thought it advisable to appoint a commanding officer who had commanded an infantry battalion in war; Daly was one such, and within the regular establishment there were scarcely any others. Problems ensued with his release and replacement at short notice, however, and in the end the appointment went to Lieutenant-Colonel C.H. Green, who had commanded the 2/11th Battalion in 1944–45, had left the army but returned in 1949 and who was attending the Staff College in 1950; he was killed in Korea in October 1951. Disappointed at missing out on the appointment, Daly was posted nonetheless in mid-1951 as Director of Infantry at Army Headquarters, an important posting because of the war and because the Australian Army now had regular infantry units for the first time in its history. He was also promoted to temporary colonel.

In any case, in his annual report Hopkins had recommended Daly as suited for brigade command and noted that his 'most outstanding characteristics are determination and tenacity coupled with a useful streak of toughness'.[22] The first two were tested once again through relocation to Melbourne and the seemingly perennial challenge of finding somewhere suitable to live. There were very few married quarters in Melbourne at this time, and the Dalys solved the accommodation issue by buying a house in Ashburton, one of Melbourne's south-eastern suburbs and an area characterised by then mostly recent, postwar development. Even with much more favourable house price-to-income ratios than pertain today, this was no small matter for army officers of the day, even those who might be able to call on family resources to assist in the purchase.[23] The biggest challenge he faced professionally as Director of Infantry was managing the flow and training of suitable reinforcements and replacements for 3RAR in Korea, made more challenging when a second battalion (initially 1RAR) was deployed alongside it in April 1952, although the 'work up' had been in hand for months; the battalion was brought up to strength with drafts from its remaining, uncommitted sister unit, 2RAR, and with drafts of special enlistees – dubbed 'K Force' – a proportion of whom were recruited in Britain. The manpower pressures within the army have been noted already, and one of Daly's tasks while in Melbourne was to assess the suitability of the former quarantine station at Portsea for acquisition as the site of the new Officer Cadet School.[24]

Developments in Korea became an increasingly large part of his job. The manpower pressures – accentuated by the Korean commitment although not caused by it – manifested themselves in the shortage of both officers and other ranks even though the initial Australian commitment was a single infantry battalion. Reinforcement drafts had to be found, trained and adequately prepared for the conditions they would encounter, and Daly ensured that he was 'closely in touch with what was going on'; he interviewed officers returning from Korea and read all the operational reports forwarded to Army Headquarters, and even penned a short article on Operation Commando for the *Australian Army Journal* based on the available evidence and testimony.[25] The staff of the Directorate consisted of just one major and a captain in addition to himself, so of necessity he was familiar with a lot of the detail himself. A considerable amount of information was also sent back through the Australian Army organisation based in Japan. As a result, when he was appointed to command of the 28th British Commonwealth Infantry Brigade in Korea he was, he recalled, 'pretty well up with everything that was happening there'.[26]

The Australian force contribution to Korea had increased to two infantry battalions in April 1952, the increase having been announced the previous year as a result of requests from Washington. In July 1951 the three separate infantry brigades fielded from the British Commonwealth – the 25th Canadian, 28th (formerly 27th) Commonwealth and 29th British – were combined into the 1st Commonwealth Division, under

Photo 21 Colonel T.J. Daly is farewelled before departure for Korea, 1952. Left to right: Lieutenant-Colonel E.G. McNamara, Lieutenant-General S.F. Rowell (CGS), Lieutenant-Colonel C.E. Long, Daly, Colonel R.G. Pollard. (Daly family)

British command but with a combined staff.[27] The 28th Brigade now disposed of four infantry battalions, two British and two Australian, with supporting arms from New Zealand (artillery) and India (medical). In addition, the Australian battalions were considerably larger than their British counterparts as a result of Australian policy to provide a 10 per cent 'boost' to establishment to cover wastage (sickness was a constant hazard in Korea), and the shortages of British manpower occasioned by multiple simultaneous commitments around the world.[28] The general principle that 'he who provides the greater proportion of the troops also exercises command' now came into play, and the Australian Army assumed command of the 28th Brigade. The CGS, Lieutenant-General S.F. Rowell, directed Daly to provide a list of suitable candidates, then ignored the list and appointed Daly himself to the job: 'I was slightly taken aback and very chuffed and very excited about it.'[29]

He took over from a British officer, Brigadier J.F.M. MacDonald, who had commanded the 1st Battalion, King's Own Scottish Borderers (KOSB or 'Kosbies' colloquially) in north-western Europe in 1944–45 and was in command of the same battalion again in Korea in 1951. He had stepped up to take over the brigade in October 1951 after the previous commander, Brigadier George Taylor, was relieved and sent home at the end of Operation Commando. In fact, British authorities in London had canvassed the issue of an Australian replacement informally with the Commander-in-Chief, British Commonwealth Forces, Korea, Lieutenant-General Bill Bridgeford, who was a senior Australian officer in command of all administrative and non-operational support for Commonwealth forces in Korea and Japan.[30] This discussion, in February and March 1952, was caused by the announcement of the imminent arrival of 1RAR and the hope, not subsequently realised, that the addition of an Australian unit might allow the removal and non-replacement of a British one. Bridgeford declined to be drawn on the command issue, suggesting properly that the matter be referred to Army Headquarters in Melbourne; Rowell's response was favourable, as we have seen. The British Army was hard-pressed by competing demands in Korea, Hong Kong, Malaya (where the Emergency was now in its fourth year) and in building commitments to NATO in Germany, and the manpower shortages were manifested in commanders and staffs as well as in formed units: 'I think it would be fair that Australia should provide the Brigade Commander if they provide two of the battalions,' noted the Vice-Chief of the Imperial General Staff. It would also be fortuitous.[31]

And so, at the beginning of July 1952, Daly arrived at Headquarters, 28th Brigade to take over command. He had made a brief visit to Japan and Korea in February to familiarise himself with the situation, while administrative changes to the brigade headquarters were already underway in any case 'with particular emphasis on the KOREAN Theatre of War'.[32] In military terms, a brigade is neither a unit (a battalion) nor a formation (a division or corps), but at that time was the smallest all-arms organisation in the army able to fight at the tactical level and sustain itself administratively from its own resources for a finite period without necessarily calling upon external sources of support. The 28th Brigade consisted of the headquarters with a staff of twenty, supported, defended and maintained by a defence and employment platoon, a light aid detachment, K Troop of the 1st Commonwealth Divisional Signals Regiment and a provost section from the divisional provost company. Daly made two more or less immediate changes. He inherited an 'entirely British' headquarters, and proceeded to internationalise it: the brigade major, intelligence officer, one of the three liaison officers and one

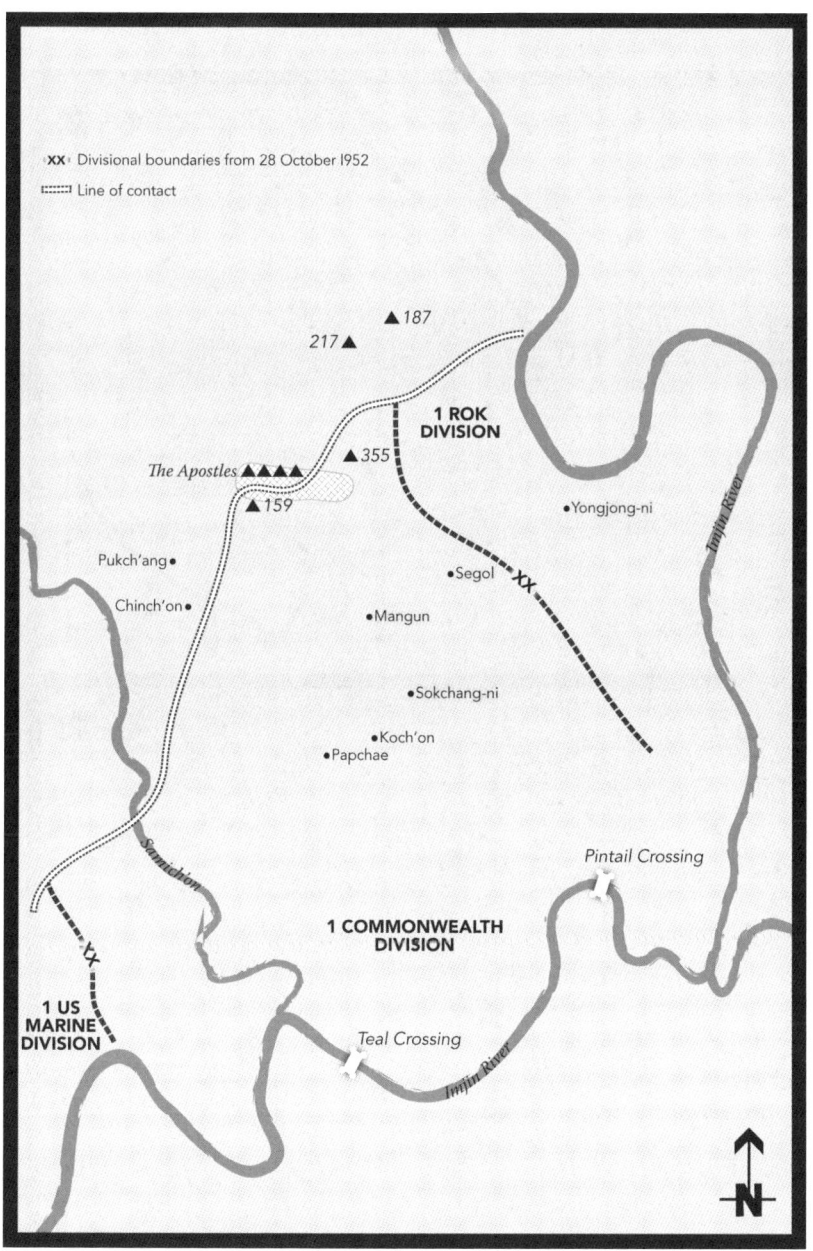

Map 5 Area of operations, 1st Commonwealth Division, Korea, 1952–53.

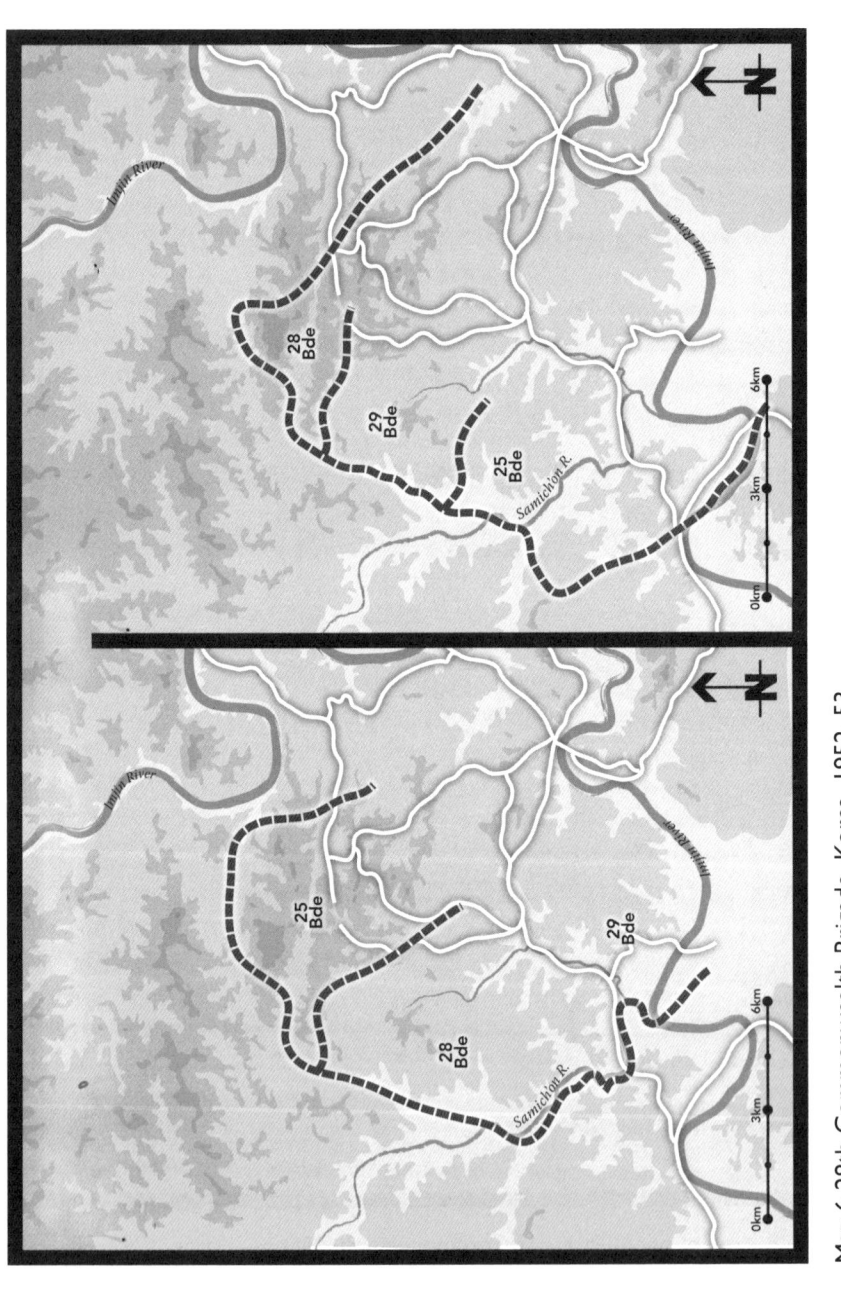

Map 6 28th Commonwealth Brigade, Korea, 1952–53.

of the two staff captains were now drawn from the Australian Army.[33] He also moved the headquarters forward ('it had been way, way back'), and instituted a tactical headquarters (Tac HQ) 'to enable him to ex[ercise] personal op[erational] control'.[34] Daly had demonstrated his penchant for commanding well forward at Balikpapan, and he did so again now in Korea: 'not necessarily to get yourself shot but to get the feeling of the battle... be able to visit your battalions quickly if need be or if something blew up and a commanding officer wanted to talk to you'. He later recalled being shelled by the Chinese 'once or twice', but it wasn't very effective. In any case, he thought that 'it's a good idea for the Brigade [headquarters] to get shot up every now and then... it brings you into the war a bit. You don't become detached.' On one occasion he was in a forward observation post on Hill 217, with his radio operator, when the position was mortared by the Chinese and suffered a direct hit. Both occupants emerged unscathed, although Daly later admitted to permanent deafness in one ear, a sign of how closely the round had impacted.[35] One of his staff recalls 'following him up almost vertical slopes as he headed for some remote OP. He had a habit of doing this as the sun was rising... we (quite affectionately) called him "Daly at Dawn".'[36]

The first year of the Korean War was replete with mobility and manoeuvre; the southern capital, Seoul, changed hands four times in less than a year, and the infantry on both sides covered considerable distances, much of it on foot. By the time Daly arrived, however, the character of the war had changed and become largely static and positional in nature. A series of offensives and counter-offensives between the American and South Korean-dominated United Nations Command (UNC) and the (mainly) Chinese and North Korean forces demonstrated that neither side had the means or the will to push the other out of the Korean peninsula entirely, and the fighting settled into a style of warfare dominated by trenches, artillery, barbed wire and minefields that reminded some Western observers of the Western Front during the Great War.[37] Protracted negotiations for a ceasefire (convened first at Kaesong, then moved to Panmunjom), accompanied a vicious and often bloody tactical stand-off between the two sides in a line that ran more or less along the length of the 38th parallel, the inner-Korean border. The Commonwealth Division occupied positions on the Jamestown Line as part of the US I Corps; apart from a period out of the line in February and March 1953, the division occupied these positions for the remainder of the war. Some personnel were relieved and rotated individually, many others by unit (especially in the infantry), and most experienced the climatic extremes (heat and dust

Photo 22 Brigadier Thomas Daly DSO OBE, who is taking over the 28th Commonwealth Brigade, on a tour of the front line, Korea, c. 27 June 1952. (AWM HOBJ3281)

in summer, deep snow and great cold in winter), punishing terrain, primitive conditions and prevalence of disease that are a determining feature of most veterans' recollections.

Commanding a brigade offered rather different challenges from the command of a battalion. While there is always some distance between the CO and his company commanders, that between the brigade commander and his headquarters staff – many of them captains and majors – is far greater still. 'One can be a bit lonely in command like that.'[38] The headquarters mess was a convivial one nonetheless, abetted by some genial characters such as the Australian staff captain, A.L. 'Alby' Morrison, who possessed a sunny personality, a good singing voice and a knack for relaxed social intercourse as well as being highly proficient and professional.[39] In any case, Daly and his staff were kept mostly very busy. With operational responsibility for four battalions and their activities 'you were up all night every night, virtually, there was something happening somewhere on the front [while] in the daytime along came the "visiting firemen" – bishops, film stars, politicians, American generals, Australian politicians, senior officers visiting the base'.[40] As a result, Daly usually slept after lunch.

As an Australian brigadier in a multinational Commonwealth division that operated within an essentially American environment, Daly had responsibilities and relationships both up and down the chain of command that far exceeded those normally entrusted to an officer at his level. The British had long resisted placing British units and formations under dominion command; they had been forced to accept this with the appointment of an Australian lieutenant-general in command of the British Commonwealth Occupation Force in Japan in 1946, unhappily, but as the composition of the brigade headquarters demonstrated, even after the Second World War they were still inclined to place the needs and aspirations of the dominion armies at a discount when it suited. The most senior levels of the British Army might view the prospect of an Australian commander for the 28th Brigade with equanimity, as we have seen, but this view was not necessarily shared elsewhere in the organisation. Daly enjoyed warm relations with the commanding officer of one of his British battalions, the Durham Light Infantry, but the officer in question had held temporary rank as a brigadier himself in the closing stages of the Second World War and could be expected perhaps to take a broader view. His relations with his other British CO were much less comfortable. Daly felt that he was viewed 'with a certain amount of suspicion' both because he was 'a colonial' and because he was therefore an unknown quantity to those he commanded.[41] Daly in his turn had mixed views on the battalions in his brigade. While appreciative of the quality and courage of the soldiers, especially the Durhams ('a first rate battalion'), he felt that the company commanders were, on the whole, too old for the demands of the campaign ('rather elderly'). Many of the British platoon commanders were freshly commissioned National Service officers who, while individually brave ('very young subalterns ... very good chaps. They knew their basic stuff'), lacked experience, which showed when they were caught in tight tactical situations where judgement mattered.[42]

Daly answered to two different divisional commanders in his time in Korea: Major-Generals A.J.H. ('Gentleman Jim') Cassels and M.M.A.R.

('Mike') West, both British officers. Cassels had commanded a brigade in the Normandy campaign and a division immediately after the war's end, and knew Australians from his time as head of the UK Services Liaison Staff in Melbourne where Daly had met him previously.[43] West had commanded a brigade in Burma in 1944–45 and was GOC-in-C, British Troops Austria during the Allied occupation. Cassels went on to become CGS (1965–68) while West was subsequently GOC Northern Command and Head of the British Defence Staff in Washington DC (where he was nicknamed the 'swinging general' because of his prowess on the dance floor).[44] They were very different characters, although both excellent divisional commanders, and Daly got on well personally with both. 'Every commander is different from every other commander, they all have different personalities. Cassels was a man's man... he'd talk to the digs [diggers], talk to the troops. Mike West again was a very pleasant personality, he wasn't the same type of temperament as Jim Cassels. Cassels was more of an outgoing fellow – Mike was a little less so... Jim was a great cricketer and played the guitar, and sang and what have you. Mike was a most entertaining, amusing man which Jim Cassels wasn't necessarily. Mike was amusing, he was a funny man in many ways.'[45]

The Commonwealth Division was part of the US I Corps and the divisional commanders were the filter through which the decisions and directives of higher (US) authority were conveyed to the brigades in the line. As one of West's senior staff subsequently observed, within the Commonwealth Division 'the chain of command [was] more a chain of suggestion'.[46]

This was more important than it might at first seem. The US Army operated under different organisational assumptions and observed different staff and tactical doctrines, and command style could be very different again. Over time the higher US formation commanders came to a tacit understanding with their senior Commonwealth subordinates, such that they outlined intent and objectives and left it to the Commonwealth units to achieve these; US commanders were allowed little such latitude.[47] During Daly's time in Korea there were two US commanders of I Corps – Lieutenant-Generals John W. 'Iron Mike' O'Daniel and Paul W. Kendall, both with distinguished records in the Second World War – whose command styles and insistence on aggressive and seemingly continuous action against Chinese positions caused considerable friction with Cassels and West. The static phase of the war featured a variety of patrol activities with differing or complementary purposes, often mounted at night and frequently involving severe conditions (especially in winter) and the constant danger of bumping into Chinese patrols since the enemy operated on many of the same assumptions regarding the domination of no man's land between the two trench systems.

Fighting patrols were designed to keep the enemy well back on his own positions to avoid a situation where they sat too close to the UN positions and could mount attacks with the element of surprise on their side ('stacked up almost on our wire at last light', as Daly put it), which happened frequently with battalions that maintained a lax patrolling regime.[48] Standing patrols were designed to give warning of Chinese movements in this manner. Patrols were intended as well to gain intelligence, either through observation and reconnaissance or through taking a prisoner – a 'snatch' patrol or, if mounted by a larger body, a raid. These latter were difficult to mount successfully and were dangerous for the troops involved. The Chinese were often experienced and well trained, toughened in many cases by fighting in the Chinese Civil War in the late 1940s. They were generally well supplied with automatic small arms – ideal for this sort of fighting – and their discipline and combat drills were of a high standard. Being 'bounced' by a Chinese patrol at night in no man's land in mid-winter was no joke.

The problem was that the US senior command elements pressed constantly for prisoners, at a rate of at least one every three days and usually for generalised or unspecified 'intelligence purposes'. Daly knew that 'they were very concerned about this capturing a prisoner in order to identify what was opposite and whether there was a changeover in divisions and that sort of thing or whether there was an attack being planned'.[49] This was an alliance war and the first one waged under a United Nations mantle; despite being given considerable leeway at the tactical level, it was not politic for the Commonwealth divisional commanders to simply ignore the directives of the chain of command, and Daly was 'pushed... quite a lot' on the matter of obtaining prisoners, at least initially. West subsequently took the view that the inevitable losses did not justify the meagre returns obtained and, further, that his intelligence staff had a very good idea of what was happening generally on the Chinese side opposite them and did not need to mount regular actions of this kind simply for the sake of doing so. As Daly later summarised the position:

> The Chinese were not easy to take as prisoners, they were prepared to fight it out to the finish or disappear into the darkness. Generals Cassels and West... strenuously opposed it. Still we were ordered to carry out some raids... during my time in command. I don't believe

that any of them achieved their aim of taking a prisoner. They were successful in other ways, in destroying enemy positions, in killing a lot of enemy, and preventing them from encroaching into the valley.[50]

The point was underpinned by a large, company-size raid conducted by B Company, 1RAR, under Major A.S. Mann (designated Operation Fauna), in December 1952. The results were twenty-two wounded, three missing (one of whom was recovered the next night) – and no prisoner. This was not a new conclusion; Daly had observed soon after taking up command that 'efforts in this direction have met with little success', while 'the system of employing fighting patrols for this purpose has been found costly and relatively unsuccessful'.[51] Nothing that occurred subsequently was to modify this judgement.[52]

The other major issue that arose, and which was prompted in part by Australian objections, concerned the redeployment of the brigades in the line at the end of 1952. Previous practice had involved relief on a brigade basis with the division's defences manned on a 'two up and one back' system; that is, two brigades in the forward positions with the third in reserve on a rotational basis. West altered these dispositions and placed all three brigades in the line, with one battalion in each brigade area held in reserve. The explanation for this differs. Some dissatisfaction was expressed by Australian officers in the 28th Brigade when relieving Canadian units because of the latter's relatively lax patrolling methods, which gave the Chinese the local advantage and which had then to be wrested back from them by the relieving unit, with attendant casualties.[53] In his careful and very thorough study of Canadian operations, William Johnston fully accepts the shortcomings in some Canadian units, as alleged, but suggests that the change was made by West in order to rationalise and simplify the command problem for the brigade commanders and was undertaken without regard to complaints from the Australians, which would, in the nature of things, have been communicated to divisional headquarters by Daly.[54] The new system certainly made it easier for the individual brigades to develop their defensive localities in keeping with their own tactical emphases and manpower limitations (the latter being a particular concern for the 29th British Brigade), and made internal reliefs in position easier, although it increased the wear on the brigade staff who, as a result, never really got a break.[55]

Daly was relieved by another Australian, Brigadier J.G.N. Wilton, at the end of March 1953, and flew back to Australia from Iwakuni, Japan, on the 30th of that month. The two were near contemporaries (Wilton

Photo 23 Brigadier T.J. Daly, Commander, 28th British Commonwealth Brigade (left), talks to unidentified soldiers at a camp in Korea, September 1952. (AWM LEEJ0619)

was slightly senior), but although their years as senior officers would see them working in close proximity, following each other as Chiefs of the General Staff, and although they are often judged to be the two most influential senior officers in the history of the postwar Regular Army, they do not appear to have been personally close. Daly's focus was always the army itself as an institution while Wilton spent most of his senior career, from late in the Second World War, concerned with strategic policy (his time in command in Korea being the major exception).[56] Wilton was sometimes thought of as a 'cold fish' with little personality or small talk; he did not suffer fools gladly (neither did Daly), but his social circle existed largely outside the army of his time (which was unusual in those days). Daly later wondered if he had been relieved prematurely, but in fact command tenure of the 28th Brigade was always of less than twelve months duration and his nine-month stint was in fact one of the longest.[57] Wilton, at least, couldn't wait for him to leave: 'In April the weather is still extremely cold in S[outh] Korea', he wrote. 'My first few nights there were miserable cold ones for me and I was very glad when my predecessor as Bde Comd departed and I could then move into the comparative warmth of his Command caravan.'[58]

For his service in Korea, Daly was awarded the CBE, together with the Legion of Merit by the Americans. The Australian citation lauded command traits that by now were a feature of his style and approach to his profession: 'personal example', 'constant visits to all forward positions', 'timely advice and confident support', 'cheerfulness, devotion to duty and care for every soldier in his Brigade'.[59] When the Commonwealth Division was relieved in the line by the 1st US Marine Division for two months in February–April 1953, Daly instituted a vigorous training program for the units in his brigade.[60] As with the officers and men of the 2/10th Battalion, he knew what he expected from those under his command and left them in no doubt on that score.[61] For himself, he thought that he returned 'a much wiser chap than I had been when I left'.[62]

Daly now returned to the army as Director of Military Operations and Plans, reporting direct to the CGS, Lieutenant-General Sir Sydney Rowell, the first RMC graduate (Class of 1911) to attain the post. His new posting was one of the key positions in Army Headquarters and an important one from which to gain an understanding of the army's place in wider strategic policy and Australia's emerging Cold War alliance structures and commitments. (Wilton held the position between 1947 and 1951, after which he went to Britain to attend the Imperial Defence College.) The post of Director of Military Operations had existed long before the war (C.B.B. White had been appointed to it in 1911 on his return from Staff College in the United Kingdom, with the rank of major), but the postwar reorganisation of the army and the creation of a permanent force with field units had led to an expansion in the size and functions of Army Headquarters, and the post of Director of Military Operations and Plans was created in April 1946. The position, along with Directorates of Military Intelligence, Survey and Public Relations, formed part of the higher operations or General Staff within the office of the CGS. Directorates of Military Training, Royal (Australian) Artillery, Signals, the Engineer-in-Chief and the Director of Staff Duties, which included sections for armour, infantry, organisation, equipment and air, worked to the CGS through the office of the Vice CGS.⁶³ Various staff branches and directorates elsewhere in Army Headquarters answered to the other principal positions on the Military Board, which was reformed in early 1946 after being suspended during the Pacific War. Although the range and complexity of roles and tasks within Army Headquarters had expanded greatly in recognition of the more complex strategic and technological contexts that Australia faced compared to the period before 1939, the army remained ludicrously small in size, especially when the demands of the occupation of Japan and the Korean War are considered.

Army Headquarters still operated on a relative shoestring basis. As Director of Military Operations and Plans, Daly's staff comprised 'a couple of G1s... and a couple of G2s down the line somewhere' for a total of five Regular Army personnel and two Citizen Military Force officers, the latter on part-time duty.⁶⁴ The directorate discharged a wide range of responsibilities, including daily briefing of the CGS ahead of various meetings and committees, the agendas for which could include almost any subject from the mundane to the strategic. One of his other principal tasks was membership of the Joint Planning Committee. There were a number of joint committees within the Defence Department in the postwar era at a time when the services all had separate ministers and ministries, the powers of the Minister for Defence and his department were very much less than they later became, and when the three services competed with each other in budgetary terms and provided advice to government through separate channels. Like many other aspects of policy and administration, pre-war structures (such as the Joint Planning Committee) had gone into abeyance during the emergency of 1942–43 and began to re-emerge only with the defence reorganisation undertaken in March 1945.⁶⁵ The higher machinery for defence policy-making evolved rather gradually in the decades after the end of the Second World War; this is sometimes ascribed to the dead hand of the long-serving Secretary of the Department, Sir Frederick Shedden, who stoutly resisted attempts at reform or reorganisation that might diminish his influence in any way, but other factors were involved as well. (The Morshead Committee's recommendations for structural reorganisation, made in 1957–58, were mostly shelved by the Menzies government, while Shedden had in fact retired at the end of 1956.) There was, clearly, some long-standing dissatisfaction with the way in which advice was formulated and transmitted to government; as an example, in November 1952 Menzies had requested the production of a paper dealing with strategic policy to be prepared by the Joint Planning Committee.⁶⁶

Daly thus joined the Joint Planning Committee at exactly the point where its activities took on a greater seriousness of purpose and on-going concern with issues of national strategy and defence and alliance policy. As the army representative he found himself increasingly involved in planning meetings concerned with the Five Power Staff Agency, ANZUS, ANZAM (with responsibility for the defence of Malaya and the prosecution of the Malayan Emergency), and the South-East Asian Treaty Organisation (SEATO), created by the Manila treaty in 1954. His closest involvement was with the establishment of SEATO; he attended the Manila conference and subsequent meetings in Bangkok (where the SEATO Secretariat was established),[67] and in Washington DC and Hawaii for joint talks with the Americans. Invariably accompanied by representatives of the RAN and RAAF, he usually led these delegations. There seemed to be 'quite a lot' of such meetings 'and one was constantly on the run... and I rather tended to forget about the down-to-earth business of the commanding of a brigade or the day-to-day running of the Army, because it didn't come into my purview to any great extent'.[68]

Australia's defence assumptions were in transition, largely as a result of the Second World War and its influence upon Britain's standing in the world. Shedden ('a law unto himself'), and perhaps at this stage the prime minister, Menzies, continued to emphasise a strong British connection reflected in the planning for an expeditionary force to the Middle East in the event of a general war with the Soviet Union – a sort of Third AIF. At the same time, the military planners ('and, I am sure', Daly averred, 'the Chiefs of Staff') believed that 'Australia's destiny was irretrievably bound up with that of South East Asia', and accordingly that Australia should abandon the assumptions around a deployment to the Mediterranean and instead 'concentrate on a South East Asian contingency'.[69] The strategic lessons of the Pacific War provided a powerful stimulant to thinking so soon after the war, while in any case Australia's slender military resources (which, in Daly's view, 'for the most part existed only on paper') precluded two simultaneous commitments to separate theatres. The underlying assumptions were based on some form of Chinese attack, either against the 'protocol states' of Indo-China or Thailand, or further south into archipelagic South-East Asia, and successive iterations of SEATO planning considered the possible scenarios and the likely or possible counters, including the possibility of the use of atomic or nuclear weapons on both sides. The period of transition between the two positions – an emphasis upon the Middle East as opposed to concentration on the security of South-East Asia – in which Australia's means were simply insufficient to meet both possible contingencies was a difficult one, although it lasted only a few years, but, as Daly observed, 'politics and logic are not always compatible bedfellows'.[70] Given the recent fighting in Korea, developments in South-East Asia and the fact that both the British and Americans recognised the growing Chinese threat, the army planners 'didn't take the M[iddle] E[ast] contingency very seriously'. Daly recommended that the army make a contribution to the forces in Malaya and request access at senior levels to the British Headquarters, Far East Land Forces (FARELF) in order to develop capacity 'for the types of operations in which we would be involved' in any regional conflict; to become familiar with the challenges of climate and terrain; and 'to exercise a continuing influence on the planning and conduct of operations'.

Although the government did not signal a formal end to a putative Middle East commitment until late 1954, the focus on the growing strategic importance of South-East Asia was clear, at least in military planning circles, from 1953. By the time Daly left the Planning Committee to attend the Imperial Defence College in London, the pattern of future commitment to Malaya (later Malaysia) was set, although it had not yet eventuated (it was to do so in the second half of 1955). Army units were to fight against the communists during the Malayan Emergency from then until 1960, against the Indonesians during Confrontation from 1962 to 1966, and to remain in Malaysia as part of the regional security guarantee until finally withdrawn in the mid-1970s.

The Imperial Defence College (now the Royal College of Defence Studies) was set up in 1927 as a result of a recommendation of Winston Churchill.[71] The ruthless financial cut-backs to the armed forces overseen by the Geddes Committee in 1922 had included a recommendation for the creation of a central Ministry of Defence as an economy measure. Churchill believed that such a centralised ministry was incapable of creation while it had no staff possessed of a joint or tri-service perspective and experience, and it was this identified need that led to the creation of 'a Joint Staff College for officers of medium rank in the three Services' and with the expressed intent that this should result 'in a decrease rather than an increase in expenditure'.[72] The original syllabus concentrated on imperial strategy 'in the broadest sense' while, in order to ensure that it did not become 'too academic', specific problems in imperial defence were to be referred to the student body by the Chiefs of Staff Committee. The Imperial Defence College opened its doors at Buckingham Gate, near the palace, with an initial intake of twenty-five students, who included Lieutenant-Colonels Brooke and Auchinleck while the first commandant was Vice-Admiral Sir Herbert Richmond. Richmond was a serious military intellectual. He had founded the *Naval Review*, was a highly regarded naval historian, wrote widely on matters of imperial defence policy and coordination, and had most recently been president of the Naval War College. The new college and its curriculum were to bear his stamp for some decades.

From the beginning the student body included representatives from the dominions. The 1927 course was attended by two students from Canada, Australia and India, one from New Zealand, and two civilian officials from the British Ministry of Defence. The Australians were Commander (later Commodore) C.J. Pope, RAN and Wing Commander (later Air Vice-Marshal) S.J. Goble, CBE, DSO, DSC. The Directing Staff (which numbered just four in 1927, including Richmond), included Brigadier (later Field Marshal Sir) John Dill, a future wartime Chief of the Imperial General Staff. Australia was allotted two vacancies each year, which on a rotational basis meant that the army filled a slot every other year. In 1928 the army student was (Brevet) Colonel John Lavarack, CMG, DSO while the Defence civilian nominated was Frederick Shedden.[73] Attendance at the Imperial Defence College and its successor has long been recognised as a sign that the selected officers from Australia, at least, were likely to reach the highest ranks in their respective services. The CGS, Rowell, noted in his memoirs that at the end of the war both Wilton and Daly were marked 'for advancement to senior posts',[74] and Daly's selection to attend the Imperial Defence College as a member of the 1956 course was part of the process of further developing officers like himself who had excelled during the war and who needed additional skills and knowledge to lead the army subsequently.

The college closed early in the Second World War and reopened in 1946 in new premises at Seaford House in Belgrave Square, where it remains to this day. The curriculum underwent some changes, as did the student body, which was expanded in size and now included officers from the United States. The postwar curriculum emphasised 'international affairs and the relationship of foreign, economic and defence policies'.[75] The program of outside lecturers greatly increased, both in terms of subject matter in keeping with the evolution of the curriculum and in terms of the speakers themselves. Senior service officers were joined by a regular procession of ministers and MPs from all sides of politics, scientists and industrialists, academics, even the Archbishop of Canterbury, Dr Geoffrey

Fisher, who lectured to Daly's course in 1956. The postwar development of the Imperial Defence College included a program of overseas tours; the course was divided into groups, which would visit various European capitals, the dominions and India, and the United States for short periods, together with a regular visit to British industry conducted around Easter each year.

By 1955 there were five overseas tours in the program, while from 1956 tour presentations were required of course members. That year the program was disrupted by the Suez Crisis, which saw all the trips cancelled save those to North America.[76] The other Australian on the course in Daly's year was Brigadier (subsequently Major-General) J.W. Harrison (RMC Class of 1932), together with four Canadians, three Indians, a New Zealander, a Rhodesian, three Pakistanis, a South African and four Americans, including a civilian official of the US Foreign Service. The course produced two full generals, five lieutenant-generals, two air marshals, two air chief marshals and one Marshal of the Royal Air Force. Such distinction was not unusual. Among Daly's British Army contemporaries that year, the most significant were probably General Sir Alan Jolly who became GOC Far East Land Forces in 1964 during Confrontation with Indonesia and subsequently Quartermaster General (QMG) on the Army Council; General Sir Desmond Fitzpatrick, who was subsequently Vice-Chief of the General Staff and the Deputy Supreme Commander Europe during Daly's period as Australian CGS; and General Sir Victor Fitzgeorge-Balfour, Vice-Chief of the General Staff between 1968 and 1971.[77] Others, such as General Mohammad Musa, General P.N. Tharpar, Lieutenant-General W.A.B. Anderson and Lieutenant-General R.F. Armstrong, went on to senior roles in the Pakistan, Indian, Canadian and South African armies respectively.

Daly's three daughters were now aged nine, seven and four, and had already known something of the separations of service life while their father had been in Korea. The family sailed for Britain from Melbourne aboard RMS *Iberia*, one of the new *Himalaya*-class passenger liners operated by P&O on the long-distance routes between Britain and Australia and built as recently as 1952. Air travel was very expensive, slow and still hazardous, as the series of crashes that attended, then aborted, the De Havilland DH-106 Comet jet airliner attested.[78] Army officers on accompanied postings travelled by sea, which now seems wonderfully luxurious, even self-indulgent, but in the 1950s and 1960s represented much the cheaper option for the Treasury, which is why it was persisted with. In fact, Daly paid his family's fares himself; because the posting

Photo 24 The 1956 course, Imperial Defence College, London. Daly is second back row, tenth from the left. (Royal College of Defence Studies)

was only for a year, the regulations stipulated an unaccompanied tour. Wilton had also paid for his family to spend the year in London with him. Daly's eldest daughter celebrated her ninth birthday on the voyage, an event celebrated with 'a cake with green icing', and took part in the diversions and amusements typical of shipboard life in that era, including children's fancy dress competitions, which they won dressed as the 'three little maids' from Gilbert and Sullivan's opera *The Mikado*.[79]

They returned in February 1957 on the *Orion*, a ship of the Orient Line that had sailed the Australia–UK route before the war.[80] The Australian general manager for the Orient Line had been Leslie Morshead, who had returned to his pre-war business life the day after transfer to the Reserve of Officers in January 1946, initially as general manager for New South Wales and with national responsibilities from 1948. Daly later recalled being given especially favourable treatment on the voyage, which he ascribed to Morshead's gentle influence.[81] In fact, Morshead had retired as managing director of the Orient Line in September 1954 and, while he remained highly active in various business and government circles,[82] and had always been a very hands-on manager, this seems unlikely. In any case, the voyages to and from the year at the Imperial

Defence College were clearly a great deal more comfortable than those Daly or his family had taken in previous years.

The family returned to Australia at the beginning of March 1957, and Daly returned to Army Headquarters as Brigadier General Staff, a job he had held for a few months before leaving for Britain. He again reported directly to the CGS, who was by now Lieutenant-General Sir Henry Wells, and with the directorates of intelligence, operations and plans working under him. This was really a holding pattern again, and in August 1957 he was promoted to temporary major-general (a rank confirmed in September 1959) and posted as General Officer Commanding Northern Command, based in the state of Queensland and with responsibilities for the defence arrangements of the Australian territories of Papua New Guinea. He was thus one of the most senior officers (if most junior generals) in the army, and in one of its senior commands.

CHAPTER 4

THE CHALLENGES OF SENIOR RANK

The remaining years of Daly's army career, from his promotion to major-general in August 1957 until his retirement as Chief of the General Staff in 1971, were turbulent ones for the institution of which he was a part and to which he had devoted his adult life. There were major reorganisations in 1957 and, more radically, in 1959. The commitment to the Far East Strategic Reserve in Malaya that began in 1955 was relatively modest but so, too, was the army that maintained it. The mid-1960s saw another reorganisation – more correctly, perhaps, a reversion to an earlier model, but disruptive for all that – and the beginning of the deployment of increasingly larger forces to the war in Vietnam, which would be the main item on his agenda for every one of his years as the professional head of the service.

Daly's new posting was as GOC of Northern Command, based in Queensland but with responsibility as well for the 8th Military District, which encompassed the Territory of Papua and New Guinea (TPNG). The regional command structure was as old as the Commonwealth itself, although it had undergone a variety of name changes and partial or wholesale restructuring at various points during the previous half-century. In common with other, long-standing features of the army as an institution the origins of the system lay in the colonial structures that the army and the Commonwealth had inherited in 1901. Originally named 'military districts' with a numerical designator (Northern Command was the 1st Military District or 1MD), they were given territorial labels as part of the reforms recommended by the Inspector-General, Lieutenant-General

E.K. Squires, just before the outbreak of the Second World War. The crisis of 1942 prompted a clean sweep of the army's higher organisation and command structures under the direction of the second wartime CGS, Lieutenant-General Vernon Sturdee, geared to the defence of Australia and the prosecution of the offensive against the Japanese in the islands to Australia's north. Sturdee, Blamey's immediate postwar successor as Commander-in-Chief of the Australian Military Forces (AMF) and subsequently the first postwar CGS, reverted essentially to the model that Squires had recommended in 1939, reconstituting the Military Board along established lines as well.[1]

Squires' pre-war organisation had been designed to increase efficiency, remove command anomalies and institute a system in peacetime that would reflect the likely needs of war. In solving some problems it created others in their stead, and these were largely resolved in the postwar arrangements: the regional commands were no longer responsible for recruitment, for example.[2] The biggest driver in this process after 1945, of course, was the creation of the Regular Army itself. Put briefly, the role of the regional commands was to provide general support to the units based within their jurisdiction, whether regular or part time, to manage army assets (which could be extensive) and to act as a conduit between Army Headquarters and the various state governments, which played a somewhat larger role in defence matters than is the case today, especially during the 1950s with the National Service scheme and the prominence of the Citizen Military Forces (CMF) as a majority component of the army as a whole. The GOCs of the immediate postwar era had been substantial figures from the senior regular ranks of the wartime army – Robertson and Berryman, for example – and as Daly himself would demonstrate, the senior generals of the army could alternate between postings as GOC and membership of the Military Board.

These general observations were reflected in the structures and functions of Northern Command, although, as we shall see, it also had some particular characteristics. In Daly's time in command there the majority of army units and formations were supplied by the CMF. Although the National Service scheme was wound back in 1957 and suspended in 1959, there were still significant numbers of soldiers in its ranks and units on the CMF order of battle: the havoc wreaked by the Pentropic system lay slightly in the future. The CMF in Northern Command comprised the 11th Field Regiment, 2nd/14th Queensland Mounted Infantry (a light armoured unit) and the 9th and 25th Battalions of the 7th Infantry Brigade, all elements of the 2nd Infantry Division, which was headquartered in Sydney. The 11th (Independent) Infantry Brigade had its headquarters in Townsville and disposed of the 31st, 42nd and 51st Battalions, which were scattered across northern and central Queensland. There was a variety of CMF support units, together with the Queensland University Regiment[3] and the 1st Cadet Brigade with its five cadet battalions likewise scattered all over the state. The regular units were all support ones: engineers, signals, survey, supply and transport, ordnance and so on, and Command headquarters was at Victoria Barracks in Brisbane.[4] The basing of Regular Army combat units in Queensland was mostly a development of the 1960s (although 1RAR was moved to Enoggera in 1956–57).

The distinguishing feature of Northern Command as a regional command was responsibility for Papua New Guinea, which by the mid- to late 1950s disposed of two significant units: the Papua New Guinea Volunteer Rifles, a CMF unit with old roots manned by members of the white community, and the Pacific Islands Regiment (PIR), which could claim a lineage to the wartime Papuan Infantry Battalions and New Guinea Infantry Battalions and which recruited among the indigenous population. The League of Nations mandate under which Australia had held New Guinea (but not Papua) between the wars had disallowed the raising of indigenous forces, but the Pacific War had demonstrated the critical part that the two territories could play strategically in Australian security.[5] Australia retained defence responsibility for Papua New Guinea when the United Nations trusteeship (which covered New Guinea but not Papua) came into force in 1946, but the neocolonial nature of the relationship posed problems. Native men had fought ably and well in the ranks of the Australian units raised during the war, but some whites in the territories doubted the efficacy of raising units from among the native population, the evidence of wartime service notwithstanding. In fairness to this view, there had been a number of instances of collective indiscipline during the war, but it is probably also fair to say that the peculiar mixture of paternalism and racism that characterised some aspects of Australian oversight of Papua New Guinea played a part in shaping this view. The Vounteer Rifles was quite inadequate for the land defence of the territories, numbering only about 150 all ranks in 1952. It was, in any case, intended to provide a cadre of officers and NCOs for an expanded force in wartime should such an eventuality arise.[6]

The decision was made to reraise the PIR in 1951, gradually on a company-by-company basis over the ensuing twelve months or so.[7] In addition to the scepticism expressed by some members of the civil administration and the white expatriate community, tensions existed between the army and the Ministry of External Territories, and these would be a major factor in civil–military relations in the Territory until independence.[8] The new battalion was raised by a Regular Army cadre, and by August 1952 consisted of four companies based at Taurama Barracks in Port Moresby. The rank and file were drawn from native men, and no native soldier could rise beyond the non-commissioned ranks at this stage, ostensibly for educational reasons. The intention was to move the companies to outposts around the country, and these were established gradually, first at Vanimo, then at Nutt Point on Manus Island, and with a further station at Rabaul. Efforts were made to improve the training and efficiency of the men by, for example, the introduction of English-language classes, the successful completion of which would open the path to attendance at army trade schools in Australia. In July 1956 the PIR was presented with Queen's and regimental colours, a clear sign of its incorporation into the Regular Army establishment.

The army intended raising three battalions for the PIR almost from the very start.[9] In fact, the intended expansion and consolidation of the regiment took very much longer to achieve than originally planned, and the second battalion was actually raised in March 1965 while the establishment of a training depot came about only in 1964. Northern Command had wanted to avoid 'the piecemeal creation of an ad hoc organisation',[10] but this was essentially what they got in the course of the 1950s, at least. The changes in the 1960s were a response to the deteriorating relationship with Indonesia, reflected in Australian involvement in operations in Borneo during Confrontation; in Robert O'Neill's words, 'during the 1950s and early 1960s the PIR was maintained largely for reasons of Australian security'.[11]

There were some curious features to the structure and management of the army presence in Papua New Guinea. Civil administration was re-established at the end of the war, on 30 October 1945, but the army (including the PIR) did not come under the Administration, which nonetheless raised and maintained the Royal Papua New Guinea Constabulary as a 'national' police force.[12] The trusteeship over Papua New Guinea was exercised by the Department of External Territories (from May 1951 simply the Department of Territories), and throughout the 1950s the minister responsible was P.M.C. Hasluck.[13]

Relations between the department and the army were often problematic; O'Neill characterised them as 'difficult to penetrate' at a time when they were, by his own account, 'fairly smooth and perhaps better than they used to be'.[14] Part of the problem, although perhaps more a symptom than a cause, was the fact that the direct link between the two was exercised in Canberra, not Port Moresby, through the respective ministers. There were also tensions between the Administration and the local RSL, which offered regular criticisms of the civil administration and which was a more vocal and more powerful entity in such a small community than elsewhere in Australia, even in the 1950s.[15] Some of this may have rubbed off on members of the civil administration and coloured their attitudes towards the army more generally.

There had been 'disturbances' among indigenous soldiers before, including during the Second World War.[16] Causes were generally over such matters as differential pay rates (which applied to indigenous Australian and Torres Strait people during the Pacific War as well) and conditions of service. Discipline in the PIR was strict, not least because there were many more applicants than vacancies within the units; a consequence of the disagreements between Army and Territories was a strict manpower ceiling on native recruitment for the regiment. A series of more or less violent incidents and disturbances that broke out in the first half of December 1957 provided a significant challenge for Daly as the new GOC of Northern Command and threatened the existence, or at least the ready acceptance, of the PIR within Papua New Guinea itself.

Inevitably, there were immediate and proximate causes and deeper, underlying issues behind the 'riots' of December 1957. There are several versions of what happened and why, but tribal sentiments and loyalties lay at the heart of things: 'tribal loyalty within PIR was still strong in this early stage of its life', while the violence allegedly also highlighted '"deep ill-feeling" between the civilian population and PIR'.[17] The first incident occurred on either 7 or 12 December when a soldier, allegedly drunk, manhandled a young woman from the Orokolo tribe who was waiting outside a shop.[18] A scuffle ensued that was ended when more soldiers intervened and beat the woman's male companion, who had also intervened, badly enough to require stitches. At the centre of this and subsequent incidents were members of the Kerema tribe who originate in the Gulf of Papua. Many of these men had served in the wartime Papuan Infantry Battalion but had developed a reputation for indiscipline and were not recruited into the new PIR; many were subsequently unemployed or under-employed.

The Koki market provided both a natural meeting place for the native inhabitants of Port Moresby and a site for friction between antagonistic tribal groups. On 14 December a group of thirty PIR soldiers were set upon by up to 150 Kerema men in the market area, and the brawl was broken up by Australian officers, PIR NCOs and members of the civil police. A further altercation later in the day saw two PIR soldiers badly beaten by a large group of Kerema men who also attempted to assault the regimental sergeant major while he was in the act of rescuing the two soldiers concerned. Feelings in Taurama barracks ran very high, and the next morning more than 200 soldiers decamped to Koki market intending to settle scores with any Kerema they encountered. Being a Sunday morning, only three Australian officers were on hand and were unable to deter the men, although, contrary to later reports, no violence was offered to either officers or NCOs by their soldiers.[19] Gradually order was restored, and by ten o'clock that morning the troops had been returned to barracks; the violence provided encouragement to others, apparently, and more than a hundred arrests were also made against civilians in a neighbouring village, fighting in which soldiers were not involved.

Daly's report to Army Headquarters was unequivocal in its condemnation of the soldiers' behaviour: 'no excuse'. He was equally clear in his praise for the civil police whose 'exemplary' conduct in breaking up the brawls and apprehending the soldiers had saved 'a very ugly incident' from turning into 'a tragic one'. The matter did not end there, however. More than a hundred Kerema men had been arrested and were to face charges of riotous behaviour, and the Commanding Officer of 1st Battalion, PIR, Lieutenant-Colonel L. McGuinn, MC (who had taken over command only in August), had agreed with the acting Administrator, Dr J.T. Gunther, that the civil court would convene at Taurama Barracks to proffer charges and conduct proceedings against all those soldiers who could be identified as having taken part as well. The assembled soldiers, from A and D Companies, invaded the premises in an attempt to disrupt or halt proceedings, and in the end 120 native police, armed with batons, had to be trucked in to restore and maintain order. In the end, the soldier who had sparked the whole episode through his behaviour with the young Orokolo woman was sentenced to two months imprisonment, another 153 other ranks were fined £2 each while twelve were acquitted of involvement. Fifteen members were subsequently discharged.

Daly had been at Canungra while all this transpired, but arrived in Port Moresby early on the morning of 17 December. He was received by a ceremonial parade of the battalion, during which he addressed the soldiers and made it plain that their offence was a serious one and that the punishments would stand. He also made a number of calls on civilian officials, including the acting Administrator and the Chief of Police, both of whom had provided their full support during the disturbances. There was considerable unease among some sections of the white population, bordering on panic, reflected both in what Daly and others thought a 'scurrilous' coverage in the *South Pacific Post* and in the passage of a slightly hysterical motion in the Legislative Council calling for either the provision of Australian (i.e. white) troops to protect the civilian population from the PIR or the removal of the PIR from Port Moresby.[20]

The riots had revealed some serious weaknesses in the way in which the PIR was run, although Daly went out of his way to absolve McGuinn from responsibility given the short time that had elapsed since he had assumed command – he was also the fourth commanding officer in two years. There were clearly tensions between the army and some sections of the civil administration and hostility and suspicion towards the very idea of 'native' soldiers in other parts of the white expatriate population, while the army in Australia had clearly taken its eyes off the running of the PIR with potentially disastrous consequences. When he arrived at Headquarters, Northern Command as Colonel-in-Charge of Administration near the end of 1956, Brigadier I.M. Hunter was surprised to learn that the staff there had little knowledge of conditions in Papua New Guinea while, as a cost-cutting measure, none had visited the territory in some time.[21] Daly's conclusion was succinct: 'the breakdown in discipline was due principally to the officers not knowing their men sufficiently well and in consequence being unable to command their complete confidence and unquestioning obedience in an emergency.' He now faced two tasks: to reassert control of the battalion through immediate and wide-ranging changes to the practices that had grown up, and to re-establish relations between the army and the civilian community and administration to the extent that he could do so.

As an experienced battalion and brigade commander, Daly moved swiftly to restore a healthy and functional command environment within the 1st Battalion, PIR. 'The calibre of some of the officers leaves much to be desired', he noted, and ordered that henceforth vacancies were to be filled speedily, that junior officers were to become proficient in pidgin (a more complex language to *master* than is perhaps appreciated) and to spend more time with their men, that the 'nine-to-five' mentality was to end and that Army Headquarters should cease posting officers out of PIR before their full term had been served. The three officers who had been on duty at Taurama on the morning of the riot had, between them, just fifteen months service with PIR; of the eighteen officers on the posted strength of the battalion, only three had been there more than a year and only one, the second-in-command, spoke fluent pidgin. In short, in exonerating McGuinn from responsibility for the incidents Daly concluded that he had 'not sufficient officers, and of those he has, some are of indifferent quality'. As he further noted, 'far from requiring fewer officers than a normal Australian unit [PIR] requires at least an equal proportion, and of a definite type... there are many Australian officers who meet this requirement, but there are many who do not. These, if posted to PIR should be weeded out very early in their posting and replaced by more suitable types.' In addition to internal reforms, henceforth the PIR was to exercise jointly with the Vounteer Rifles at Goldie River rather than separately, as had been the case beforehand.

Relations with the civil community were a more intractable problem. Despite his support during the riot and the generally positive attitude he had displayed to Daly directly, the acting Administrator subsequently made disparaging and critical remarks about the army and PIR in a radio broadcast.[22] This attitude was not shared by the Administrator himself, Don (later Sir Donald) Cleland. With the wartime rank of brigadier he had been responsible for the civil administration of Papua and New Guinea under army control between March 1943 and the war's end. One of the great Australian servants of Papua New Guinea, he was to hold the position of Administrator from 1953 to 1967 and, in September 1958, became Honorary Colonel of the PIR.[23] In his subsequent discussion with Daly he offered 'the first bit of objective sense that I have been able to get out of Moresby since the affair', and shortly after made a formal statement in the Legislative Council 'giving the lie to a lot of the nonsense which has been talked'.[24] Daly felt that the Administration did not do enough to restrain the Kerema in Port Moresby and that the Constabulary often favoured them over soldiers when the two came into conflict, which was fairly often. Daly believed that the changes to the PIR that he had recommended would rectify the problems within the battalion, but recognised as well that good relations between the regiment, the army and the civilian population would take time.[25] Sufficient doubt about the attitudes of some in the Administration led the Secretary of the Department of the Army, A.D. McKnight, to suggest to the Minister, J.O. Cramer, that he show Daly's report to Hasluck, unofficially, in order to convey 'what the Army's understanding and views are on this unfortunate incident'.[26]

Daly later recalled that his recommendations for the PIR were based on his experiences and observations of the British Indian Army before the war.[27] The importance he placed on language policy certainly reflected this. Thereafter while he remained at Northern Command he would visit Port Moresby regularly to monitor progress.[28] He developed close relations with Cleland and became a member of the Papua Club in a bid to further relations between the army – or, at least, its most senior representative with direct responsibility for Papua New Guinea – and the leaders of the commercial and administrative elite in the Territory. Daly continued to take a strong interest in the PIR, later becoming its Honorary Colonel and stepping down from the role at Independence. In the remainder of his time in Northern Command, the main aim within PIR 'was to foster a feeling of national spirit and pride from soldiers who came from a very fragmented society and who often had difficulty in communicating with each other'.[29] There was a further and more limited riot within the unit in January 1961, this time over the tardiness with which the Australian authorities were considering pay increases for native soldiers and from which the majority of soldiers in the PIR held aloof. As we will see, his strong interest in, and support for, the PIR would remain with Daly beyond his period at Northern Command while the issues of pay, conditions, opportunities and fair treatment in the period before the grant of independence in 1975 would feature regularly on the army's agenda.

Daly had been involved in the army's contribution to the keystone strategic document, 'The Strategic Basis of Australian Defence Policy', produced in 1956 while he had been at Army Headquarters.[30] The implications of government policy, together with a requirement by the Menzies Government that the armed services should contract their budgets, led to a reorganisation of the army with which Daly had to deal in one of the senior regional commands. The idea was to prepare a regular field force (this had been the implication ever since the creation of the Regular Army in 1947), while the CMF was reduced in size (inevitable with the phasing out of the 1950s National Service scheme) and lost some support functions.[31] In fact, the army created the intended brigade-size force within the regular establishment but this reorganisation was, in any case, overtaken by a much more radical and wide-ranging reorganisation, associated with the creation of the Pentropic division, which began at the end of 1959.[32] The difficulties involved would impress themselves upon Daly much more forcibly when he became Adjutant-General with responsibility for manpower planning and policy: in that respect Pentropic was 'a pain in the neck'.[33] Equally difficult was the implication for the CMF that the new organisation meant the end of the citizen force as a viable military organisation and, more melodramatically (but not necessarily inaccurately) that the CMF had been handed its 'death warrant'.[34] The greatest blow, in opinions widely held at the time and subsequently, fell upon the CMF infantry units, many of which enjoyed lineages back into the colonial past and all of which had been organised on a regional basis with concomitant strong links into local, and often rural, communities. Within Northern Command, specifically, this meant the collapsing and consolidation of seven long-established infantry battalions into the two new, state-based battalions of the Royal Queensland Regiment: 1RQR and 2RQR. The PIR was not affected by the reorganisation at all, but the 9th (Moreton Regiment), 25th (Darling Downs Regiment), 47th (Wide Bay Regiment) and 41st (Byron Scottish Regiment) were reconstituted as companies of the 1st Battalion, while the 51st (Far North Queensland Regiment), 31st (Kennedy Regiment) and 42nd (Capricornia Regiment) suffered a similar fate as part of the 2nd Battalion. It was a very unhappy time in parts of the army and one with ramifications that extended well beyond Daly's own period as CGS; its echoes resonate still.[35]

On the whole, however, Daly greatly enjoyed his three and a half years in the position in Brisbane. The GOC's residence was the stately heritage property 'Tighnabruaich' (pronounced 'Teen-a-brew-ick') in the Brisbane suburb of Indooroopilly, a splendid example of the 'mature domestic style' of its architect, F.D.G. Stanley. Built in 1892 for his brother, the colonial engineer and prominent citizen soldier H.C. Stanley, the house enjoyed mixed fortunes as, alternately, a private residence and a boarding house while, during the Pacific War, it was requisitioned as an interrogation centre for captured Japanese officers by the Allied Translator and Interpreter Section (ATIS) and, towards the end of the war, as a personnel depot and records storage facility. In 1951 it was designated as the residence for the GOC Northern Command; Daly and his family were the third such occupants. The girls went to local Catholic schools, the older two attending Stuartholme Convent at Mount Coot-tha while Edwina went to the Brigidine Convent in Indooroopilly.[36] In the words of one recent guide to the property, the house 'evokes the affluent lifestyle of the wealthy professional elite in Brisbane' in the late nineteenth century.[37]

The job as GOC was busy and, with its frequent visits to Papua New Guinea, moderately demanding but essentially a peacetime regime. As GOC, Daly and his staff oversaw an annual exercise, sometimes in combination with RAAF elements based at Amberley. In 1957–58 the GSO1 on the headquarters was Lieutenant-Colonel Derek Sharp, a bright and imaginative officer responsible for writing more demanding exercise scenarios for the 1st Infantry Brigade, commanded by Brigadier J.S. ('Hans') Andersen. The army was still thinking its way through to a body of doctrine and the exercises reflected a mix of recent experiences in New Guinea against the Japanese, in Korea and of then current operations in Malaya as part of the Emergency. In 1958 the exercise was fashioned around 'an advance against a withdrawing enemy', and Daly found himself negotiating with local landowners for access since the exercises were to be conducted over private property. No doubt drawing on his experiences many years before in South Australia in the 1930s, Daly found that he could normally gain the cooperation of these 'rough, tough chaps' to facilitate ongoing movement for his troops. The exercise in 1959, dubbed Grand Slam, involved the concentration of the whole of the 1st Infantry Brigade Group (with the battalions based at Enoggera, Singleton and Puckapunyal) for an extensive field exercise over a ten-day period in the Colston's Gap area of central coastal Queensland, north of Mackay. The CGS, now Lieutenant-General Sir Ragnar Garrett, had requested the exercise on this scale in order to put the brigade headquarters through its paces, and it served this purpose at both brigade and battalion levels. The exercise also attracted attention in the newspapers, but was conducted in the characteristic 'bare-bones' manner of the day – the 1st Field regiment was involved, but no armour was available, although Daly had expressly requested it.

> One day, when Tom was due to arrive at Exercise HQ a few days before the action started, I got hold of a twelve-year-old boy from a nearby farm and between us we dressed his billy cart up to look like a tank. At an appropriate moment this 'tank' rattled past Tom, who was standing with a group of us beside the road looking at maps and air photographs, with the young driver waving and shouting: 'I'm a tank.' Those of us who knew Tom well knew that the angrier he became the quieter his voice became. On this occasion he turned to me and in nothing more than whisper said, 'Get rid of that thing, Sharp.'[38]

As noted earlier, Northern Command was a complex and diverse entity, and not only because of the responsibilities for Papua New Guinea and the PIR. Wide-ranging changes to the army's structure, roles and functions necessitated revisions to the ways in which higher headquarters in the regional commands were run since, in those days, these headquarters had much greater responsibility for the day-to-day activities of the army, both regular and CMF, than became the case later with the Hassett reforms of 1973 in which a functional command system was grafted onto the existing regional commands, which, in turn again, retained only local or regional responsibilities.[39] There was no Training Command, for example, in the 1950s (nor, for that matter, in the 1960s), and many of the functions and responsibilities that are centralised today through the functional commands structure were devolved to the regional command headquarters. On top of all this, Northern Command was a much more geographically dispersed command than others, such as Eastern (New South Wales) or Southern (Victoria) Commands in which many of the units were more concentrated and responsibilities could be devolved to higher formation headquarters, such as the CMF divisions. Daly's headquarters also suffered from understaffing in key areas, which tended to mean that the GOC (i.e. Daly) spent a lot of time attending to minor staff work and that policy formulation tended to go by the board because of the need among his senior staff to deal with lower-level responsibilities: the important being driven out by the immediate. Daly was an enthusiastic respondent to the proposal, floated by Army Headquarters in July 1958, for the introduction of a 'chief of staff' system in the major regional commands, but nothing seems to have come of this because of the, by then, impending shake-out that was the Pentropic experiment.[40]

This was not to say that the CGS, Garrett, did not appreciate the problems that confronted Daly and his counterparts. The Military Board members, senior regional commanders and commanders of the CMF met on a roughly quarterly basis at Army Headquarters to discuss the issues and problems facing the army; sometimes, the Minister and the Secretary of the Department of the Army were also in attendance. The army's senior leadership from around the country had few opportunities otherwise 'to leave their headquarters'.[41] Garrett well understood that the biggest problem facing the army at the end of the 1950s was money, which 'purchased less and less with each year. It was no use having an army which used up all its finances just to exist.'[42] The Pentropic reorganisation had greatly increased the workload on the regional commands, and to streamline communications with Army Headquarters the CGS authorised commands to make representations direct to specific officers rather than through the senior echelons, as protocol normally dictated.[43] The army ended the 1950s as it began them, stretched for resources and attempting to do much with too little.[44]

Daly left Queensland for Canberra and appointment as the Adjutant-General and Second Member of the Military Board in January 1961; indeed, he swapped positions with the previous incumbent, Major-General R.E. Wade, with whom he had pursued changes to the appointment of officers for the PIR. He now embarked on a period in the second most important general officer job in the army of the day and would spend the next several years at the heart of the army's day-to-day administration and decision-making.

The higher command and administrative structures of the army in the 1950s and 1960s had far more in common with those created at Federation than with those that apply in the early decades of the twenty-first century. The Military Board of Administration (to give it its full and formal title) was created on 12 January 1905 as a result of two factors. The first of these was the creation in Britain of the Army Council on 6 February 1904 as a result of the recommendations of the Esher Committee; this brought about an extensive reorganisation of the British Army prompted in large part by the shortcomings revealed in the South African War, recently ended. The commander-in-chief system, of venerable lineage dating back to the eighteenth century, was for much of the second half of the nineteenth century (1856–95) a position held by the Queen's cousin, George, Duke of Cambridge. Esher's reforms abolished it and replaced it with the post of Chief of the General Staff, reflecting another major thrust of the reform process in the British Army, the introduction of a general staff system.[45] The second factor working in Australia, with significant parallels in Britain, was dissatisfaction with the tenure of Major-General E.T.H. Hutton as General Officer Commanding of the nascent Australian Military Forces from 1901 to 1904.[46]

The first Military Board comprised five members, three military and two civil. The Minister for Defence chaired the board, and its general membership included a Finance Member, the Deputy Adjutant-General (the senior military member at that point), the Chief of Intelligence and the Chief of Ordnance. Beneath (or perhaps alongside) them were a number of directors: the Director of Works, the Secretary to the board, the Director of Departmental Services, the Deputy Assistant Adjutant-General and the Director of Stores. The position titles and, of course, the occupants, would change over time, but the range of functions exercised by the board in the higher administration of the army would remain remarkably consistent until its abolition in February 1976 as part of another great process of structural reform in the Department of Defence. It is also worth noting the relatively junior rank structure pertaining then (all were either colonels or lieutenant-colonels), and reflecting the small size of the pre-1914 army.

Further adjustments to the board's structure occurred in 1909 with the creation of the post of Chief of the General Staff and First Military Member, a role assumed by Bridges and reflecting developments in the British Army and other dominion forces.[47] Under the long-serving Labor minister George Foster Pearce, in 1911 the board acquired the final shape that it would maintain into Daly's time: Minister (chair), Chief of the General Staff, Adjutant-General, Quartermaster-General, Chief of Ordnance (subsequently the Master-General of the Ordnance), a Civil Member (usually the secretary of the department), and a secretary to the board. In the face of the crisis of early 1942, the government reverted to the model in Hutton's time and between July 1942 and March 1946 the board's functions were subsumed in the person of the Commander-in-Chief, General Sir Thomas Blamey. Thereafter, it reverted to the interwar model and, as the army grew in size and its roles and functions increased in number and complexity, the business of the board became accordingly very much busier. The only subsequent substantive change was the introduction of the post of CMF Member with the establishment of the Australian Regular Army in 1947.

The Adjutant-General (AG) bore responsibility for personnel administration from induction or recruitment through to discharge or separation from the service. Among the various responsibilities exercised by the AG were command of the Women's Royal Australian Army Corps (WRAAC), then a separate service within the army (and with naval and air equivalents in similar relationships to their service), education, career training and the army 'schools' system, and officer career development through the office of the Military Secretary. Many notable senior officers had held the office: Victor Sellheim, Victor Stantke, H.D. Wynter, T.H. Dodds, J.H. Bruche and Carl Jess among them. After the CGS himself, the AG ranked second in the board's precedence and his responsibilities were wide-ranging.

Daly's period as AG encompassed in full the attempted restructuring of the army along Pentropic lines. On his watch the army also maintained a commitment in Malaya (and later in Malaysia) that, by 1964, implied an active operational role in the developing war between Malaysia and Indonesia known as Confrontation, and into which Australian units would be introduced in Sarawak in early 1965. The National Service scheme of the 1950s had ended while that of the 1960s had yet to be introduced, and the army was forced to rely upon volunteers and to do its best to attract them; this was a problem that fully occupied the army's chief manpower officer, as Daly now was. There were ongoing issues with attracting enough young men for commissioning, long-running and seemingly intractable problems with accommodation both for single personnel and families, the management of female service, and a range of more esoteric issues that were his responsibility from honours and awards to colours, music and ceremonial. Very senior staff positions in peacetime lack all of the glamour of their equivalents on active service, but are no less exacting, time-consuming or important.

Many of the matters that crossed the AG's desk were short-term ones, or ones relatively easily resolved; issues that ran like a constant thread through Daly's tenure of office (and, indeed, before and long afterwards) were manpower and conditions of service. Getting people in – recruitment – and getting them to stay – retention – have been the two greatest issues facing the armed services through most of the last hundred years in both the regular and citizen forces. Just as the problems are recurrent ones so, too, the solutions tend to be as well. Making service in the armed forces attractive has always been a challenge in peacetime, especially in periods of economic good health. With one brief exception in 1961–62, the long period of Menzies' second prime ministership (1949–66) was characterised by 'a continually expanding world trade and a stable international monetary system... Between 1952 and 1965 Australian gross domestic product rose annually at a little less than five per cent, a rate greater than that of the United States or Britain.'[48] In 1950 the national unemployment rate stood at 1.2 per cent; in August 1965 it was the same, and at its height from late 1961 to early 1962 (during the so-called credit squeeze) it peaked at only 3.2 per cent. This was not a propitious context in which to entice young men into the army.

The strength of the Regular Army built slowly in the period 1961–64, matched by an equally steady but more dramatic decline in the strength of the CMF. Table 4.1 makes the point clearly.

Manpower issues are more complex than raw figures measuring increases and decreases, however. For one thing, strengths fluctuated across the course of a year, especially reflecting the expiry date of individual enlistments; it was much harder to manage personnel 'churn' in a voluntary system than in a conscript one with clearly identified intakes at specific times each year. The internal mix was also important in terms of age, qualifications and corps or branch of service. In what might seem a counter-intuitive process at a time when the army was seeking to boost enlistments, this meant that retrenchments had to be managed alongside

Table 4.1 Strength of the Australian Regular Army and Citizen Military Force, 1960–64

Year	Regular Army	Citizen Military Force	Total
1960	21 433	37 921	59 354
1961	20 459	26 958	41 417
1962	21 623	30 041	51 664
1963	22 639	27 341	49 980
1964	23 493	27 505	50 998

Source: Vamplew, *Australians: Historical Statistics*, p. 413.

the recruitment campaigns and balanced against possible parliamentary criticisms of the process.[49] Alongside all of this, the emerging crisis in the CMF in reaction to the imposition of the Pentropic structures had to be managed to the extent possible.

Daly neatly summarised the problem, and the frustrations, of the recruiting process in his last briefing as AG:

> The need for recruits was as great as it had ever been. The recruiting organization and methods had improved constantly, but in spite of this the Army was clearly unable to attract the numbers required, despite the fact that the annual requirement was only two per thousand of the appropriate male age group. The current increase in the demand for labour in commerce and industry would add to the problems and it was difficult at this stage to see a way out other than by a substantial improvement in pay and conditions.[50]

Neither the baby boom nor the large-scale programs of postwar immigration offered much assistance. Considerable resources were invested in paid advertising, including in the relatively new medium of television whose 'efficient exploitation', it was hoped, might produce results.[51] But, as Australian official historian Ian McNeill concluded, shortage of manpower 'had bedevilled the permanent army since the decision to form an infantry brigade in 1947. No significant danger to Australia existed to stir national sentiment, nor was the government, for reasons of economic policy, prepared to offer sufficient financial inducement to attract the numbers.'[52]

The army tried pretty well everything within its power. At the Military Board briefing in March 1963 Daly reminded his audience that 'the time had come to adopt a professional approach to recruiting', which was probably a tad unfair to both his own and others' previous efforts. The regional commands formed recruiting units ('a small body, trying to do a man-sized task' and with 'only a limited capacity to organise mobile recruiting tours, displays and the like'); produced more and better-focused literature aimed at the target demographic grouping; recognised, as Daly did, that young army wives were often the critical factor in a soldier's decision to re-engage and accordingly produced 'a booklet... which would inform wives of the virtues and advantages of the Army as a career for their husbands'; and regularly reminded unit commanders that 'the task was one of man-management... [and] a means of improving the standards of their units – keeping in the unit a man with previous service and who was known personally'.[53] Such efforts held the line and enjoyed occasional local successes, but could not hope to really boost recruitment in a sustained way in the absence of pay and conditions that were truly competitive with those on offer simultaneously in the civil economy. That was a task beyond the army's authority or resources.

Maintaining or enhancing numbers in the CMF presented an equally stark dilemma. The CMF had always been locally and regionally based and recruited, and, despite the sweeping changes brought in through the Pentropic structure, the Military Board recognised that this remained the basis of raising and retaining; the obvious contradiction inherent in the 'state regiment' structure seems to have been avoided, at least in formal discussions. Many citizen soldiers and especially many CMF officers resigned from the force and never returned, even when Pentropic was subsequently abandoned. This was the first problem. A second was implicit in Daly's remarks to the regional commands in late 1962, and which could stand as a critique of the basis on which CMF units were treated in recruitment campaigns for some decades thereafter. Conceding that 'there was not a great deal that could be done in a centralised way' and that the Director of Recruiting would continue to mount regular advertising campaigns, Daly undertook nonetheless that 'he would do all possible to ensure that no extravagant promises were made in recruiting advertisements, and that pictorial representations of new equipments were related to actual availability, not to expected issues'.

Wastage was then running at 'around 10 000 a year'.[54] Hollowness in the CMF was not the only issue; a significant proportion of the force had very little actual service to their credit, meaning that a very high 'churn' on an annual basis further undercut the capabilities that the CMF was intended to provide. In March 1962 CMF strength was 29 725. Of this, 42 per cent had less than one year's service, 77 per cent had less than two years while the average length of service was just one and a half years, with little variation between units or commands.[55] The CMF's capacity to contribute effectively in the event of war was suspect at best.

Amid a plethora of administrative issues that crossed Daly's desk on a regular basis three others stood out: training and education, the WRAAC and the needs of army aviation. All of these matters serve to emphasise once again how very different the army of the 1960s was from its descendant today.

As noted earlier, as AG Daly was responsible for education and career training throughout the army, but this bald statement disguises a number of significant realities. The army's training system was 'very haphazard', with twenty-eight separate schools scattered across the country answering, in the first instance, to the Director of Military Training, who was also charged with the provision of doctrine.[56] For administrative purposes, moreover, the regional commands exercised authority over those schools located geographically within their areas.[57] There were two functions involved: education, which the army traditionally does not really understand and often undertakes rather poorly, and training, which the army understands extremely well and at which traditionally it has often excelled. In Daly's view the problem with the training system was the relatively poor educational levels of many senior NCOs and warrant officers, which left them insufficiently qualified for instructional jobs (the army had once regarded instruction as a sufficiently specialised task to justify its own distinct organisational identity, the Australian Instructional Corps (AIC), which gave way subsequently to the A&I Staff). In those days it was common for Australians to complete their secondary education at the modern Year 9 level; indeed, as late as 1971, 51.3 per cent of adult Australians had completed Years 6–9, but only 18 per cent had attended Year 10 or higher. Those not attempting matriculation and a pathway to university and the professions commonly left formal education at the age of 15; put another way, in 1964, 70 per cent of boys aged 15 were in secondary education but only 8 per cent of those aged 18.[58]

In an effort to improve the general educational levels of soldiers, Daly ordered the introduction of a 'Services General Certificate of Education', accredited through the Schools Board of the University of Melbourne and to be equivalent in standing to the Victorian Leaving Certificate; he then made this a requirement for qualification as an instructor.[59] The other main point was that it should be recognised by Commonwealth and state authorities, an early step in the rush to accreditation and 'credentialism' that came to characterise the army by the 1990s. Reflecting his strong support for the PIR, Daly sought successfully to extend education for native soldiers beyond instruction in English to encompass the third-class certificate of education with subjects in English, arithmetic and social studies. The Army Apprentices School also benefited from attention, with Daly's decision to have army apprenticeships recognised by both unions and employers; this was not only good man-management, in terms of ensuring that soldiers had recognised skills for the civilian economy when they left the army, but also helped to ensure that a steady stream of qualified and motivated applicants presented themselves for each intake. Entry to RMC Duntroon was revised from 1964 with matriculation a requirement for acceptance in advance of the plans to introduce degree-level studies at the college; attracting sufficient candidates for officer entry was a problem in the early 1960s and, although the intake in 1963 of 77 officer cadets was 'the best ever', it remained well below the annual requirement. The impact of higher entry standards could only be guessed at, although initially it may have had a positive effect on applications for the Officer Cadet School, Portsea, which did not have the same requirements. Although Portsea received 365 applications in 1963 ('a record'), from which 54 were selected, in June 1963 there remained 38 fewer officers in the Regular Army than had been the case in June 1960 while there were 2200 more soldiers.[60]

The women's services had been re-established in 1951 after their wartime predecessors were hurriedly disbanded at the war's end, and their reinvention was very much a response to manpower pressures within all three services.[61] Members of the WRAAC had been granted permanency in the army in 1959, but the maintenance of a separate female service conveyed volumes about the perceived role and requirement for women soldiers. As Bomford has noted, 'The training of WRAAC members for employment in a discrete women's corps, which promoted ladylike behaviour and the notion that the members were feminine and very marriageable, encouraged the belief that women were separate and different. It also had the regrettable side-effect of making it more difficult to argue convincingly for better working conditions for women in the armed forces.'[62]

The *Army* newspaper noted in 1961 (as part of the WRAAC's tenth anniversary) that the presence of women in the army was 'becoming a more accepted fact as time goes by', which is scarcely a ringing endorsement of their role or contribution.[63] Daly had responsibility for the WRAAC as AG (again suggesting their marginality to the army's 'core businesses'), and later commented that he inherited the role 'for my sins'.

There was a tension within the WRAAC between those members (mostly younger) who saw themselves as soldiers who were women, and those (including the Director WRAAC between 1957 and 1972, Colonel D.V.V. Jackson), who declared that the 'aim of this Corps is that members perform normal efficient tasks for young women and that the wearing of a uniform does not point to a career of "playing at being soldiers"'.[64] Daly wanted to improve the status of women serving in the army (rates of pay between male and female members, for example, were even more discriminatory than in civilian life), recognising that 'there was an undercurrent of feeling about women being superficial [sic] to Army business' at the time.[65] The logical and inevitable end point of this was the abolition of the WRAAC in 1984 and the absorption of women into the mainstream army, but this was well after Daly's time.

The origins of military aviation and army aviation in Australia are synonymous. The Australian Flying Corps in the Great War was a component part of the AIF and of the Australian Army, and the fortunes of army aviation diverged from the mainstream only with the creation of the RAAF in 1921. The army began thinking seriously about utilising rotary aviation (i.e. helicopters) in the mid-1950s after their efficacy had been demonstrated in the Korean War and as the capabilities of newer platforms were demonstrated by the British in Malaya and the French in Algeria. The early postwar uses of army aviation were for reconnaissance and artillery observation, but the range of army applications grew with the capacities of the aircraft.[66] This led, inevitably, to clashes with the RAAF over ownership and tasking of aircraft. The RAAF believed that the 'unity' of airpower doctrine was to be equated with unity of control of air assets. The army increasingly came to understand that in this, as in so many other areas of capability, 'if you don't own it, you don't control it' and sought to acquire aviation capabilities of its own to support its tactical missions. The CGS, Lieutenant-General Sir Henry Wells, had made the army's case succinctly in 1956; while it was natural, he suggested, for the air force to pay little attention to light aircraft when its principal responsibilities were for bombers, fighters and transports, 'the Army should not be dictated to by another service in regard to these light aircraft, which were a prime need for the Army'.[67]

A compromise was reached in December 1960 with the formation of No 16 Army Light Aircraft Squadron, a composite unit with army and RAAF personnel under the command of an RAAF officer and based at Amberley, near Brisbane. In an effort to head off the acquisition of an army air corps the RAAF had offered positions in pilot training for army officers on RAAF courses, and in 1962 resisted the request to provide technical training to army tradesmen in aircraft maintenance. The story is a long and complicated one involving much bureaucratic in-fighting and organisational politics.[68] Daly would become involved again during the Vietnam War, in which heated disagreements over the performance of RAAF helicopters in support of the Australian units in Phuoc Tuy province would strain interservice relations severely. In the early 1960s in his role as AG, however, his involvement concerned attracting enough army officers to undertake pilot training as part of the development of the fledgling capability.

In the early 1960s the army decided to draw pilots from existing corps and services (the Royal Flying Corps and the German aerial service had done exactly this in 1914–15) rather than to create a separate aviation branch with a career stream as a pilot; Stephens suggests a desire to 'thumb their nose' at the RAAF by implying that pilots were nothing special.[69] If so (and there is no evidence either way), the subsequent establishment of the Army Aviation Corps in July 1968 suggested a fundamental rethink of the initial position. So too, perhaps, did Daly's difficulties in attracting officers with sufficient aptitude for pilot training. In June 1961 he reported that the previous shortfall the army had experienced in attracting suitable candidates had been ameliorated, to some extent, by a 'vigorous' recruiting drive in the regional commands that yielded 200 applications; only eighteen of these proved suitable for initial training, however, with a further ten being held back for possible further consideration. Two years later, as his tenure as AG neared its end, only fifteen applications had been received from regular officers for the 1964 intake of the army pilots course, forcing a further call for applications among Regular Army other ranks (something that would have been anathema to the RAAF at the time), the CMF and recruits straight from civilian life 'in an effort to obtain twenty-seven suitable members to undergo basic flying training' in light aircraft.[70]

In November 1963 Daly handed over as AG to Major-General J.W. Harrison and took over as GOC Eastern Command in Sydney from Lieutenant-General H.G. Edgar, the last three-star officer to hold the position. The duties of a GOC were, of course, familiar to him; the workload in 1964–65, however, was considerable, for several reasons. The end of Pentropic, while welcomed in most quarters, led to a wholesale restructuring of the army, again. Operations in Borneo as part of Confrontation with

Indonesia were hotting up in the course of the year, while the government decided belatedly in November 1964 to reintroduce a National Service scheme, something that had been under consideration for some time and which the army had resisted. The first infantry battalion and supporting units would be deployed to South Vietnam in mid-1965, but the deployment of the Australian Army Training Team, Vietnam (AATTV) from 1962, and its expansion thereafter, drained experienced NCOs and warrant officers from instructional positions before this and made gearing the army for a major war in South-East Asia that much more difficult. Eastern Command was home to the Headquarters, 1st Division and Headquarters, Logistic Support Force as well as the usual range of engineering, artillery, ordnance, medical and transport units, the 1st Task Force with its three battalions of the Royal Australian Regiment (by 1965), three university regiments and four battalions of the Royal New South Wales Regiment together with the 12th/16th Hunter River Lancers, all CMF units.

The Dalys moved into the Bungalow, the GOC's residence at Victoria Barracks in Sydney (originally the officers' mess in the nineteenth century). The family had lived in Deakin when Daly had come down to Canberra from Brisbane in early 1961, and in October 1962 built a house at 116 Empire Circuit, Yarralumla, which was to remain the family home through his years as CGS and into retirement. Betty-Ann was sent to board at Loreto Normanhurst in 1961 because her parents recognised that the posting cycle would disrupt her final exams if she continued to live at home, and her sisters both followed her there in succession.[71] The position in Sydney was a busy one socially as well as professionally; as the new GOC in December 1964, Daly noted, 'E Comd was very central. There was an international air terminal in Sydney, the Command had a relatively large Order of Battle and as a result of all this had a large number of visitors. Recently there had been an average of about 50 visitors per fortnight.'[72]

There were the usual problems that confronted the regional commands: pressure on resources, especially training areas and the supply of quarters, which became sharper after the introduction of National Service. There were long-term problems with existing training areas as Sydney expanded and with greatly increased air traffic and subsequent restrictions on air space, which held particular problems for field artillery ranges, for example (but these had a history extending before and after Daly's time as GOC). Pressure on housing was a seeming constant in the postwar army, one that Daly himself had experienced several times as a young lieutenant-colonel back from war service and with the needs of a young and growing family to accommodate. The flavour of the time may be savoured in Daly's description of the standard of housing with which some officers and their families were still expected to deal:

> In Eastern Command, the difference between the standards of Commonwealth owned quarters and Housing Commission quarters was great. In the former, such essentials as blinds, built in cupboards, reticulated hot water, fly screens and linoleum in bathrooms and kitchens was provided. In the Housing Commission houses the scale was much more austere – cupboards were reduced to an inadequate level, blinds must be provided by the tenant, the hot water was available at the bath only, and there were no floor coverings in kitchens or bathrooms. This was bad for morale... particularly aggravated when the rent for the austere Housing Commission quarter was greater than that charged for the Commonwealth owned house.[73]

Improving the accommodation and living standards of soldiers and their families had been an issue with him in successive posts, and he routinely found that he had a tough fight with the public service to secure funds for building and improving amenities.[74] Later he found that as CGS he needed 'a log of claims to improve the soldier's lot', but then, politicians didn't live in service housing.

Eastern Command ran a major annual logistics exercise, Exercise Longshot, to test the 1st Logistic Support Force, while the movement of 7 Field Squadron RAE and 111 Light Anti-aircraft Artillery Battery to Malaysia in May 1964 had revealed short-comings in HMAS *Sydney* in its operational role as a converted troop transport. A British-designed and -built ship, it lacked air-conditioning, while in tropical conditions the mess decks and laundry facilities were inadequate for the number of troops embarked. Sustained independent logistic support of Australian forces from Australian resources was still something of a novelty in the early 1960s, and Vietnam was to test the army's ability to lodge, maintain and sustain a task force in Phuoc Tuy for a period of some five years.

An early indication of the challenge involved the shipment of 1RAR and its support elements on board *Sydney* to South Vietnam, Operation Trimdon, in April 1965. The battalion was concentrated at Holsworthy and departed from Sydney, but the logistics organisation was based in Melbourne. The shift from the Pentropic to the Tropic establishment meant that tables of organisation were confused, equipment tables were incomplete, and stores and vehicles were still in the process of allotment even as equipment was being loaded. Daly later recalled the deployment as a 'shemozzle' with the battalion 'poorly loaded' when it left Sydney.[75]

In time the loading and back-loading of troops, vehicles and stores would become a smoothly run operation, but the dispatch of 1RAR was made possible only by almost round-the-clock staff work by the command and staff elements of the battalion, the RAN and Eastern Command. It had been a long time since the army had needed to do this for real. The impression sometimes given that the Australian Government made the decision to commit the battalion in haste is further supported by Daly's recollection that no prior consideration had been given to mounting a substantial combat force to Vietnam; 'when I was Adjutant General it was never considered'.[76]

Daly would succeed to the professional head of the army in May 1966 after three senior postings that had exposed to him to a range of the army's problems, capabilities and assets. None had been without their challenges, but these were as nothing compared to those he would face in leading the army in a war that was Australia's longest to that time, and among its bitterest and most divisive.

CHAPTER 5

CHIEF OF THE GENERAL STAFF

Daly's first meeting of the Military Board as CGS and First Military Member took place on 27 May 1966, barely a week after he had assumed the office. As was customary the Minister, Malcolm Fraser, extended a welcome from the chair, noting that 'recent years had seen big changes in the tasks facing the Army and the Army's preparedness to meet those tasks'. Fraser had been sworn in to this, his first ministry, on 26 January; Daly had been prepared for the top job for at least a decade. Both were acutely aware that much was still to be done; as Fraser observed, Daly would undoubtedly find his time as CGS 'at once stimulating and challenging'.[1]

Career management within the army receives considerable attention and resources, both for officers and enlisted personnel. It always has done. Within the Directorate of Officer Career Management (DOCM) today there is a section devoted to career management for senior officers; this, too, is a function with a long history, albeit perhaps a less bureaucratic one in earlier times. In Daly's day the management of promotions and selections came before the Military Board, while the day-to-day function was the responsibility of the Military Secretary's office. One thing that has not changed is that the most senior appointments in the service require the final approval of the minister.

Daly was groomed for senior rank through the 1950s; his attendance at the Imperial Defence College course in London was a clear sign of this. By the end of that decade as 'a young major-general of outstanding

Photo 25 Chief of the General Staff. (Daly family)

ability' his development was rounded out by appointment as Adjutant-General (AG), a senior administrative appointment to add to his 'wide and varied experience in Command and on the General Staff'.[2] From there he had gone to Eastern Command, which by the early 1960s was regarded as the most important regional command in the army.[3] While there he was awarded the CB in the Queen's Birthday honours list for 1965 in recognition of his 'most notable contribution to the efficiency and development of the Australian Army. To all his appointments he has brought great depth of vision and outstanding ability . . . [maintaining] the highest ideals and traditions of the Australian Army.'[4] His elevation to professional head of the army had been decided some time before this; in July 1961 the 'plot' laid out the succession as CGS for the next seventeen years with Daly to succeed Wilton in 1966, and to be followed in turn by Brogan, Hassett and MacAdie.[5] With the exception of MacAdie, highly regarded but whose health broke down leading to an early death, this was exactly how it transpired.

In the mid-1960s the CGS very much ran the army, in a way that current occupants of the position of Chief of Army can only imagine (or perhaps dream about). The Menzies Government had declined to act on the recommendations of the Morshead Committee inquiry into defence organisation in 1957, predicated on greater centralisation and heightened authority for the Minister for Defence.[6] The defence function was much more 'stove-piped', with separate departments for the three services, Defence itself and Supply, and the services each had their own minister, a junior figure in the outer ministry, as well as their own permanent head drawn from the public service. When he became chairman of the Chiefs of Staff in 1966 Wilton attempted to reform the Defence machinery aiming at greater centralisation of authority around the Minister for Defence (and away from the Secretary who, in the tradition of Shedden – and subsequently Arthur Tange – enjoyed considerable power to frustrate initiatives originating within the armed forces' senior leadership), but these would not be fully realised until the mid-1970s.[7]

The service ministers were a mixed bag; some were clearly rewarded for faithful service with a role that would not tax their abilities while others were being groomed for higher things, assuming that they did not make a mess of their first ministerial portfolio. Some of the service ministers were very good: John Gorton is remembered as a highly active and effective Minister for the Navy from 1959 to 1963, presiding over the service's modernisation and some very difficult political events after the *Voyager* disaster.[8] John Cramer, Minister for the Army from 1956 to 1963, owed ministerial office to his role as a founding member and long-standing New South Wales powerbroker within the Liberal Party. He was regarded as a partisan of the CMF, and his attempt to replace the Regular Army CGS with a CMF officer on the retirement of Lieutenant-General Sir Ragnar Garrett in 1960 came to nothing, foundering on complete lack of support in Cabinet. His successor, Jim Forbes, Minister from 1963 to 1966 after a short period as Navy minister (1963–64), had graduated from a wartime course at RMC Duntroon in 1942 and was presumed (by some) to have some special insight into the army. He held rather jaundiced views of the senior leadership of both the service and the department and had enjoyed a poor press while minister (although this did not stop his elevation to Health and then Immigration successively thereafter).

There were just five secretaries of the Department of the Army during its existence from 1939 to 1973. Two of these, Frank Sinclair (1941–55) and Bruce White (1958–73), left a strong mark on the department. Allan McKnight, secretary from 1955 to 1958, fell out with the Military

Photo 26 Military Board, 1966. (Army History Unit)

Board over matters of trust and confidence and was regarded as too dependent on his minister, Cramer; his attempt to centralise control of the army's financial affairs within the secretary's responsibilities led to his departure.[9] Bruce White, on the other hand, enjoyed the confidence of both successive ministers and members of the Military Board during one of the army's most difficult decades. His somewhat ingenuous foray into public commentary on the conduct of the war in Vietnam in October 1966 caused the government some embarrassment in the lead-up to the federal election that year, but he survived the fracas most probably because his views reflected those of senior army and civilian officials and because his minister, Malcolm Fraser, supported him unequivocally.[10]

The senior leadership of the Military Board had turned over completely since Daly's last stint in its membership. In addition to a new minister, the composition of the board with their dates of appointment was:

Adjutant-General	Major-General J.S. Andersen	11 May 1966
Quartermaster-General	Major-General M.F. Brogan	24 March 1966
Master-General of the Ordnance	Major-General C.E. Long	11 May 1966
Deputy Chief of the General Staff	Temporary Major-General A.L. MacDonald	18 April 1966
CMF Member	Major-General P.A. Cullen	1 December 1964

As a result, as it happened the CMF Member was the longest-serving current member of the board, ironically, because CMF Member was *not* classed as a 'Military Member' of the board, which implied a more advisory role than an executive or deliberative one. Cullen later reflected that 'the people on the Military Board with me – Tom Daly, Frank Hassett – we were great personal friends'. Indeed the common thread of service in the Second World War probably helped to smooth any clashes or acrimony that might have emerged,[11] although it would not save the CMF from further diminutions of its historic roles in the course of the 1960s.

The situation on the Chiefs of Staff Committee (COSC) was somewhat different. Daly's predecessor, Wilton, had been made chairman of the Chiefs of Staff Committee despite a lobbying process on behalf of the Chief of Naval Staff (CNS), Vice-Admiral Alan McNicoll, to succeed Air Marshal Sir Frederick Scherger in the post; this failed, not least because of resentment in some quarters at Lady McNicoll's blatant campaigning on her husband's behalf.[12] McNicoll had become CNS in February 1965 while the Chief of the Air Staff (CAS), Air Marshal Alister Murdoch, had joined COSC in June the same year. Murdoch had been a cadet at RMC Duntroon in 1929–30 before transferring to the RAAF and commencing flying training when the college moved to Sydney. Daly thought him 'a pain in the neck' on the Chiefs of Staff Committee, and clashed with him on a number of occasions over aviation matters in Vietnam, but others thought him intellectually very able if inclined to laziness.[13] McNicoll came from a distinguished military family: his father had commanded the 6th Battalion at Gallipoli and the 10th Infantry Brigade in France, one brother was a major-general and former Master-General of the Ordnance, while another was a noted conservative journalist and newspaper editor. This McNicoll was himself intensely able, if inclined to pomposity, and he wished to be left alone to manage the RAN as he saw fit.[14] He published poetry throughout his life, reflecting literary inclinations that ran through the family.[15]

The delay in the decision over who would succeed Scherger had the inevitable knock-on effect and meant that Wilton's successor as CGS could not be confirmed until his own future had been determined, notwithstanding the fact that everyone expected Daly to succeed as CGS and that Wilton had made that recommendation to his minister. In the manner all too familiar to service families, Daly had to uproot Heather and the girls at short notice once the decision finally was announced, and move from Sydney to Canberra even as he took over the job, while his successor at Eastern Command, Major-General J.W. Harrison, did the same in reverse.[16]

On the whole, and with the significant exception of the argument over rotary-wing aviation and a lesser fight over command positions within the Australian Force Vietnam, Daly thought in retrospect that 'the relationship was very good between the services. There was the usual battle in the Chiefs of Staff Committee and in the Defence Committee about carving up the cake of the Defence vote, who was to get what.'[17] He was much less sanguine about the state of the army, which was 'in something of a state of turmoil' with the reversion from the Pentropic structure, the need to supply forces to Vietnam and Malaysia, and the absorption of National Service: 'we weren't really properly manned to meet all these sudden requirements'. The expansion of the army was geared to the demands of the war in Vietnam, which would ultimately see a three-battalion task force deployed to Phuoc Tuy, but while the National Service intakes provided large numbers of good-quality young soldiers for units, it exacerbated the stress on the pool of officers and NCOs. The expansion of the Royal Australian Regiment from four battalions to nine added to the pressure; 'you take out the regimental commitment for Vietnam and Malaya, the training commitment, the absorption of National Service, the Reserve [i.e. CMF], normal staff duties and so on, and everyone was stretched, and every time that somebody moved [i.e. was posted], there seemed to be a chain reaction and somebody else had to be moved, and somebody else had to be moved, and this created a tremendous amount of upset with families.'[18]

Conditions of service had been an issue for Daly for many years, and the expansion of the army put renewed pressure on accommodation, which 'was just quite ghastly'. In Daly's view the attitude of governments 'of all persuasions' to the issue of service housing 'was quite deplorable', undermined morale – especially for soldiers serving overseas in the war zone – and led to family breakdown.

There is a tendency in retrospect to see the commitment to the Vietnam War as all-consuming for the army, the political process and for Australian society more generally. This is tempting, but it distorts the period and the issues: not every issue in politics or society was refracted through the lens of the war, and this was true for the services as well. For many Australians it was a distant event, an occasional distraction, notwithstanding the fact that the involvement of national servicemen in combat operations expanded the pool of Australian families with a direct stake in the 'Australian War'. Those directly affected by the twice-yearly call-up were affected very directly indeed, but it is worth remembering that the annual intake from 1966 was just 8400 young men (in two rounds of 4200 each), and that, although 63 735 men served in the army, most of these did not serve in Vietnam while the total pool of 'eligibles' numbered 804 286.[19] For every young man called into the army, therefore, a *dozen* others were not. Equally obviously, the war was the army's main business for the entire period in which Daly was its professional head; it began before he became CGS, and its last echoes would resound after his retirement.

There were three Ministers for the Army in Daly's time, Malcolm Fraser (January 1966–February 1968), Phillip Lynch (February 1968–November 1969) and Andrew Peacock (November 1969–February 1972). All three were in their first ministerial appointment (Lynch, in addition, had been elected to parliament only the year before), and all three were ambitious; Fraser was easily the most consequential and the most able, and had the greatest influence on Daly and the army. As Daly saw it, the minister was 'more concerned with the political side of things, such as personnel problems, the press, attacks in Parliament which he had to answer, which he had to fight off on behalf of the Army'. The relationship contained inherent structural difficulties since, as a member of the Defence Committee, the CGS was privy to intelligence and other information that was not disclosed to his minister. This position was 'extraordinarily invidious', the service ministers had a tough task, and on the whole Daly thought that his three ministers 'were good stuff... intelligent, hardworking and they had a lot of courage [politically]'.[20]

Fraser had entered parliament in 1956 and had been active on the back bench in defence matters. He was a prodigious worker who combined ambition with the desire to be noticed and a natural inclination to be involved and responsible for his portfolio. This led him to demand to see files before signing documents (such as letters from soldiers' families conveying a variety of complaints), and to seek advice outside the accepted channels that ran between the minister and his department (in this he was very much like Gorton had been as Navy minister – not a comparison that either would welcome).[21] Wilton worked with him for only a few months but thought him 'young, inexperienced and, rightly, unsure of himself but obviously ambitious and keen to make his mark – and at the same time avoid making errors... On the whole, we got on well together.'[22]

Daly and Fraser also enjoyed good personal relations. 'We had our problems, occasionally, because my views didn't always correspond with his on certain aspects of the Army's activities', Daly recalled. In an honest self-appraisal he added that as CGS he tended to neglect 'the political aspect of things... I had... a much too black and white view of things at the time. I couldn't really take into consideration political aspects as well as perhaps I should have.'[23] Fraser, in turn, thought that Daly had a 'passion for the Army and could get very tense and wound up about issues'.[24] Fraser's insistence on being fully informed made a great deal of work for himself, his department and the army: 'he wanted a copy of every signal that came in from Vietnam. It was into the hundreds, certainly nothing of importance to a Minister... guards and administrative things.'[25] Bruce White, by no means antagonistic towards his young minister, reportedly advised him at one point to 'stop trying to be a general. Your job is to administer your Department. Leave running the Army to the professionals.'[26] In retrospect, Fraser largely took the advice; he claimed to have 'enjoyed working in the Army and with the Department' and certainly never took the difficulties the portfolio presented lightly.[27]

What then did 'running the army' (as opposed to running the war) entail? It should come as no surprise that certain issues and themes run with unbroken continuity through the management of the army in the 1950s and 1960s (and, indeed, in some cases continue to do so to the present). The perennial challenges of the army's organisation and structure, its manning (recruitment and retention, for National Service did not provide the answer to all problems or in all circumstances), equipment acquisition and capabilities, the health (or otherwise) of the CMF, the development of the PIR, future developments in officer education, all required management and careful attention, war or no war. Some of these issues, of course, were connected, such as the structure and role of the army and the relationship of the CMF within it. Others were informed by the war, but had an existence outside it as well – the fight with the RAAF over army aviation preceded the Vietnam commitment and would continue to be fought into the 1980s and beyond. The war in Vietnam was the 'main game', but the army was more than the war.

The point is well made by a short paper updated in the CGS's files in January 1967 and providing an overview of the army's organisation in peace and its likely roles and missions in various levels of war.[28] Assorted contingencies were allowed for in army and defence planning and, depending on which variables came into play,

> it may be necessary to provide any grouping of field units ranging from (say) a battalion group, such as currently deployed to Malaya, to a Regular Army Task Force or to a large-scale effort of one or

more divisions. Australian Army field forces... may be integrated with Allied forces, in which case they may share some common logistic facilities. Alternatively they may be required to operate independently. Initial contributions to limited war would be provided by the Regular Field Force which would be capable of a rapid build up by the CMF as the situation may require.

It is now generally forgotten that National Service was not introduced specifically for service in Vietnam (since no such commitment had been made in November 1964) and that, while the first battalion group departed for service with the Americans in Bien Hoa, another battalion group was deployed to Sarawak fighting the Indonesians while the planned expansion of the PIR was proceeding with a possible expansion of Confrontation over the border from Irian Jaya firmly in mind.

The government had imposed a ceiling of 40 000 on the army, accounting for the National Service intakes once these had begun to flow regularly into the training system and including the WRAAC but not the PIR. Numbers were not simply an end in themselves, of course, and, as Daly observed, the strength of the Regular Army 'had to be related to the provision of a balanced tri-service force needed to meet Australia's assessed military commitments'.[29] The focus of the training system, naturally enough, was on the National Service intakes, and the needs of the Regular Army in 1966–67 meant that the regular cadres within CMF units were regularly plundered, or simply not renewed when positions became vacant. Rapid expansion and the stresses imposed by a protracted war pulled the army in different directions. On the one hand, by mid-1967 it was noticeable that increasing numbers of senior NCOs were applying for discharge as they qualified for a pension after twenty years service, and on the other hand there was a similar surge in the numbers of three- and six-year enlistments among the other ranks who were failing to re-engage. The result was an acute shortage in the rank of corporal – the section leaders in an infantry battalion, for example – and once again there were implications for the provision of instructors. By the end of 1968, Daly was forced to conclude that the shortfall in manpower 'was still a problem and would continue to be so for many years... the large number of recruits who joined on a three-year engagement... together with the high proportion of National Servicemen in the Army, produced so high a turnover' that the Military Board was forced to consider increasing the minimum regular engagement to six years.[30]

Daly was right in his assessment that the manpower problem was largely impervious to correction: in March 1970 the 'impending high wastage' of three-year men continued to cause concern.[31] Nor was the manning level for officers a cause for complacency either. Officer production in 1969 was 545 (334 Regular Army and 211 National Service officers), against a wastage of 388 of whom 68 resigned their commissions. This might have been adequate for the army's needs had not the establishment increased by 249, thus leaving a shortfall of 92. The resignation rate since 1966 had increased from 15 to 63 per annum across the four-year period, an increase of more than 43 per cent, with resignations justified in terms of pay and conditions, incompatibility and 'family reasons'.[32]

Opportunities for active service could bring both benefits and difficulties. Between March 1967 and October 1969, young men had volunteered for the army at levels 20 to 30 per cent higher than in the previous five-year period; the war provided opportunities that appealed to some and also greatly lifted the profile and 'newsworthiness' of the army. At the same time, large numbers of these men were three-year enlistments. On the other hand, Regular Army NCOs, in particular, faced family pressures over their continuing service since they had a strong likelihood of serving repeat tours in Vietnam. This may also have been a factor with some officers.[33] Daly himself certainly recognised the burden carried by the Regular Army in this regard, 'a burden quite disproportionate to its numbers' and involving second tours of duty in Vietnam and for some 'a third and [for] a few even a fourth'.[34] The combination of 'low input and high wastage' would create a reduction in army numbers as the Australian commitment to Vietnam wound down. Several solutions were attempted in the interim: a restructuring of the officer corps, the raising of the compulsory retirement age for lieutenant-colonels and below to 55 and, beginning in 1967, the recruitment of ex-British Army officers and single other ranks, subsequently extended to include married soldiers with specialist skills or trades. These men, and their families, were sponsored to Australia under terms consistent with the Assisted Migrant scheme.

The scheme proved attractive over and above the desirability for many of migrating to Australia, not least following reductions in the establishment of the British Army in 1967–68 and with the disbanding or amalgamation of regiments. Similar reductions in the Brigade of Gurkhas with attendant redundancies among (British) Gurkha officers prompted similar attempts to recruit from that source as well (although later suggestions that the Australian Army incorporate a battalion of Gurkhas into its order of battle went nowhere). The reductions in the British Army were highly controversial and the subject of concerted political and public discussion and disagreement in Britain, and many within the British Army opposed them, albeit quietly.[35] As CGS, Daly was only too well aware of all this, of the opportunities that the redundancies in the British service offered, and of the support for the 'Australian option' that was on offer. Major-General A.G. Patterson, GOC of the 17th Division in Malaysia, had attended the annual CGS exercise in August 1967 at which time he was briefed on the proposals; he wrote to Daly upon his return to Seremban that the proposal 'will be widely welcomed' and that he would personally encourage Gurkha officers affected by the cuts to consider applying.[36] In addition, Daly had visited Singapore officially earlier in the year and been told by the Commander-in-Chief, Far East Land Forces that 'an appreciable number of British Army officers were interested in accepting commissioned service in the ARA'.[37] The CGS also decided that selection should be based on the quality of the applicants rather than attempting to recruit a fixed number of captains and majors against specific corps requirements and thus risk denying the army the services of an applicant otherwise admirably suited to its broader needs.

The army had hoped that experience within its ranks might prompt numbers of national servicemen to re-engage upon completion of their period of compulsory service. Some did, including national servicemen who were commissioned through the Officer Training Unit at Scheyville in New South Wales and who later transferred to the Regular Army (on one estimate, 270 OTU graduates were still serving in 1983).[38] The Scheyville experiment was a highly successful one in the terms in which it was conceived: to graduate second lieutenants capable of meeting the pressing need for junior regimental officers and with few, if any, expectations that they would serve beyond the rank of major. The OTU graduated 1871 such subalterns between 1965 and 1972 of whom 328 served in Vietnam and eight were killed in action. Of the ninety pilots who served with 161 Reconnaissance Flight in Vietnam, forty-seven were OTU graduates.[39] Daly thought Scheyville produced 'excellent leadership material' and that OTU provided an opportunity for its members to realise their latent potential.[40] He was a strong proponent of National Service, publicly advocating its retention after his retirement as 'an essential component of the kind of army this country needs' but not, perhaps, entirely realistic in his assessment or expectation of its attractiveness to those actually called up.[41] The response of the first intake of national servicemen upon discharge in early 1967 had been 'disappointing' and the response low.[42] It remained so thereafter.

The other major manpower issue in Daly's time concerned the CMF, which, during the 1960s and early 1970s, appeared to some observers to have entered a near-terminal decline. The reversion from the Pentropic division structure contained some tacit recognition that the changes inflicted on the CMF had done serious, lasting structural damage. The CMF Member of the Military Board, Major-General Paul Cullen, was a staunch and combative advocate of CMF interests both within the army and, more particularly, outside it, including in his ability and willingness to lobby directly at the political level – an option certainly not available to regular officers of whatever rank. Beginning in mid-1965, the number of CMF infantry battalions increased from eight to fifteen and, while the detested state regimental system was maintained, a number of the new battalions in Queensland, New South Wales and Victoria were allotted traditional unit numbers, such as 51 RQR and 17 RNSWR.[43] An additional complication arose directly from the National Service scheme, under which young men who would become liable for National Service could exercise an option to join the CMF for six years in lieu of a possible call-up for two years. In order to permit young men in rural and remote areas to exercise this option the army raised a series of 'Bushmen's Rifles' battalions, 'special conditions battalions' that drew from all over the state concerned. The opportunity was taken again to associate these units with traditional CMF unit numbers, such as 28 RWAR and 49 RQR.

The potential pitfall in this system was realised, and many CMF units were undermined by members who joined in order to take themselves out of the call-up but who were essentially ineffective otherwise. The university regiments in particular enjoyed a surge in numbers in the first half of 1966, and Cullen pushed for the recruitment ceiling to be waived in such circumstances since the minister had declared that 'no volunteers for the CMF were to be refused'.[44] The shortages of regular officer and NCO cadres exacerbated the problem, as did shortages of new equipment for CMF units, since this was earmarked first and foremost for regular units destined for service overseas (a case in point being the US M-16 Armalite rifle, which Cullen argued should be made available in limited numbers to CMF battalions 'from a morale and public relations point of view').[45] The Military Board hoped that the new units would attract 'a number of ex-CMF officers and soldiers who would be able to assist in providing the unit command and administrative framework' since regular resources were stretched so thin, but this essentially did not happen.[46]

The CMF was basically broken, and events in the 1960s further reinforced that fact. With the various changes related to the National Service scheme the army allowed direct recruitment efforts to slacken since, as Daly observed, 'it was not clear what the effects of National Service would be on CMF ceilings'.[47] Efforts were made, and continued to be made, to improve recruitment and retention in the part-time force, but most analysts of the subject agree that by this stage the cause was largely hopeless. As the Adjutant-General reported in March 1970, 'the strength of the CMF continues to decline', the results from advertising campaigns were 'poor' despite substantial amounts being spent on them, and efforts to 'stimulate and sustain interest in the CMF' were largely abortive.[48] Fraser made it clear in Parliament as early as 1966 that the CMF's role now was to 'provide back-up forces in a situation of defence emergency in the time that would be required for the support of the Regular Army and National Servicemen', to provide 'for the expansion in the Army in the case of general war', and that the war in Vietnam 'does not require the employment of the CMF'.[49]

Cullen attempted to push the Military Board to raise a composite CMF battalion for service in Vietnam, with signal lack of success.[50] In Daly's view, the CMF was 'floundering in the doldrums with no purpose, no aim', and the idea of calling up CMF units for service overseas was unnecessary and impractical. It was unnecessary for the simple reason that the government had decided on a National Service scheme, and it supplied more soldiers than the army could use. Calling up CMF units was also impractical because so many CMF infantry battalions were under-strength ('two or three hundred whereas we wanted eight hundred') and would need an extensive period of full-time service for the effort to be worthwhile: 'They had to train for at least six months before you could send them off. And to make it economical and worthwhile they had to be away for twelve months after that... It wasn't realistic to think in terms of raising two or three CMF battalions for the kind of time they might be required... [and] there would have been problems if we had had battalions alongside each other in Vietnam with different conditions of service.' In Daly's view, 'it wasn't really a "runner" right from the beginning'.[51]

Cullen was replaced as CMF Member in December 1966 by Major-General His Honour Judge N.A. Vickery. Vickery had recently commanded the CMF 3rd Division, had served in the Second AIF for the whole of the Second World War and been awarded the Military Cross, and was also a judge in the Victorian County Court. In truth Cullen was probably happier outside the chain of command (although he had rarely, if ever, allowed it to restrict his freedom of action as he saw it). Although he professed to find the meetings of the Military Board 'fascinating', his creation of the CMF Association in 1969 as a lobbying organisation gave further expression to his reputation as 'a thorn in the side of the Regular Army'.[52] From his new position he urged Daly not to 'restrict' himself to 'seeking advice regarding the CMF from serving officers only', presumably a reference to himself.[53] Daly would have none of it. The CGS Exercise each year was concerned to a considerable extent with training, and advice on the training and employment of the CMF was best provided by the CMF Member and other senior CMF officers; it would be 'inappropriate' for the CMF Association to be represented, and that was that.

None of this should be taken to mean that Daly was hostile to the CMF or antagonistic to senior CMF officers in general (his views of Cullen, specifically, have not survived). He had served with CMF units as a freshly commissioned junior officer and thoroughly enjoyed it, and his links to the duration-only citizen soldiers of the 2/10th Battalion were maintained into his old age.[54] He gave very careful consideration to the appointment of successive CMF Members during his period as CGS and regarded their standing in the community as a matter of great importance and a factor in their suitability for selection (which was very much an issue close to Cullen's own heart). Vickery was extended for an additional year, in part because a suitable successor was not clearly evident, and Daly gave some consideration to appointing a successor from outside the ranks of serving CMF general officers, as had occurred with Cullen's own predecessor, although he did advise his minister, Phillip Lynch, that such a move 'will inevitably cause a reaction from the CMF "establishment" in Eastern Command' (a clear reference to Cullen). Of the two most likely choices, one had been Mayor of Woollahra on two occasions and was currently president of the Imperial Service Club in Sydney as well as being active in the Liberal Party, while the other was 'a well known and respected figure in Brisbane' and president of the United Service Club.[55] The point of all this was that both candidates had strong roots in the civil and ex-service communities as well as holding senior rank in the CMF.

The CGS often found himself acting as a court of appeal when other avenues seemed closed in personnel matters. In early 1967 one of Daly's predecessors as CGS from 1960 to 1963, Lieutenant-General Sir Reginald Pollard, wrote in his current role as honorary colonel of the Royal Australian Regiment to plead a case for one of the army's more controversial senior officers, F.P. 'Ted' Serong. Serong had worked for Pollard at the 6th Division headquarters in New Guinea during the war, and was well connected in other areas of the army. He had worked for R.N.L. Hopkins in the 1st Australian Armoured Division in Australia in 1941; his RMC classmates included C.A.E. Fraser; Stuart Graham had been two years behind him at RMC; and he had worked as well for M.F. Brogan when the latter was Director of Military Training in the mid-1950s. Brogan and Pollard were subsequently Chiefs of the General Staff, Graham commanded 1ATF, Fraser was Commander, Australian Forces Vietnam (COMAFV) while Hopkins held senior posts in the ten years after 1945. Serong was an inveterate networker and used his networks well.

In some quarters there grew, and remains, the view that Serong was Australia's home-grown counterinsurgency genius (at least until David Kilcullen!), a view regularly propagated by Serong himself and often underpinned by the claim that he had 'founded' the Jungle Training Centre at Canungra through which, in the second half of the 1960s, all battalions were cycled to assess their fitness for deployment to Vietnam. In fact the Land Headquarters Training Centre (Jungle Warfare) was founded in 1942 at Canungra under the command of Colonel A.B. MacDonald, a pre-war regular, and was re-established in 1954 on the site and structure of the former centre with Serong as its first commandant.[56] (Some would argue that the real author of the training at JTC in the mid-1950s in any case was the first senior instructor, Lieutenant-Colonel George Warfe, who had done all this before with the battle school at Haramura, Japan, during the Korean War and had extensive experience in New Guinea and, more recently, Malaya.)[57]

Pollard was out of line in seeking promotion for Serong to brigadier. The latter had effectively left army service in 1957 to work with the Burmese military then, subsequently, after commanding the initial deployment of the Army Training Team in 1962, was working in a civilian capacity for the Americans in South Vietnam. Even Pollard conceded that Serong was 'highly unlikely' to return to the army in the future, while Daly pointed out that he had been offered the position of Director of Infantry, which he declined, after the command of the AATTV. Serong 'could not have it both ways – enjoy the financial benefits of working for the Americans and, at the same time, be preferred in our own Service over a number of officers who have turned in sterling, if not outstanding performances over many years'.[58] In any case, Serong had attempted earlier to persuade the Adjutant-General of the merits of his promotion when Daly was in Saigon on official business. When he retired from the army in

August 1968 to further pursue his links with the Americans Serong was accorded the rank of brigadier in an honorary capacity, as was commonly the practice in those days.

In any case, Daly had more important things to do than pander to the ego of a self-promoting former subordinate. Over the course of his period as CGS he brought a younger group of generals with recent senior experience in Vietnam onto the Military Board, representing the present and future of the army. In his final year as CGS, in 1970, the board included Major-Generals A.L. McDonald and D. Vincent as successive adjutants-general, K. Mackay as QMG and S.C. Graham as Deputy Chief of the General Staff (DCGS); only T.F. Cape as MGO represented a (very slightly) older cohort within the army and one without Vietnam service. He pursued a similar policy in his immediate 'military family', the small personal staff comprising his aide-de-camp (ADC) and military assistant (MA); as a matter of policy he required the occupants of both positions to have had recent active service as a way of keeping in touch with what younger and more junior officers were thinking and experiencing. He inherited his first MA, Lieutenant-Colonel Ray Burnard, from his predecessor, Wilton (and in any case Burnard went to the command of the AATTV after leaving the post). Thereafter all satisfied the requirement: Lieutenant-Colonel J.M. Murphy had served with the AATTV then with 3SAS and was awarded a Military Cross; Lieutenant-Colonel C.N. Kahn had commanded 5RAR while Lieutenant-Colonel A.L. Morrison had been CO of 9RAR; Kahn had been at Duntroon (Class of 1951) when Daly was Director of Military Art while Morrison was known to him from his time as a staff captain on the 28th Brigade headquarters in Korea. Recognising that there were several different paths to a commission in the army of the 1960s, Daly also alternated the appointment of his ADCs between RMC and Portsea graduates.[59]

The job overall was relentless, even without the war in Vietnam. Pollard wrote to him in mid-1968 that he and Lieutenant-General Sir Sydney Rowell (CGS 1950–54 and the first Duntroon graduate in the position) 'agreed that we were jolly glad not to be holding the appointment today'.[60] Around the same time in a letter to an old friend, the Catholic Bishop of Cairns, the Most Reverend John Torpie (with whom he had served when the latter was an army chaplain in New Guinea during the war),[61] Daly gave an insight into the demands of the job: 'Being CGS is not a job I would recommend to my friends. It is the old business of robbing Peter to pay Paul, adding two and two, hoping against hope to make six, and the inevitable frustrations. I have been at it now for two years and rather hope to be relieved in another year (if my shortcomings do not become too evident beforehand).'[62]

Elsewhere he referred to the 'recurrent Canberra crises' that took so much of his time and attention while on another occasion still, after returning from army-to-army talks in New Zealand, he noted that he was 'now well and truly back at work, facing mountains of paper and not caring much for it'.[63] On top of the stresses and demands provided by the army, his father, Colonel T.J. Daly, now aged eighty-three, had his TPI (totally and permanently incapacitated) status downgraded in early 1967 and was forced to leave the Heidelberg repatriation facility, where he had been living happily, while his status was appealed. Daly was anxious to get him admitted to Anzac Hostel in Melbourne where he would 'be well looked after and that medical assistance was at hand should he be in need of it'.[64] He died the following year after a gradual further decline in health.[65]

The remainder of this chapter looks at a number of issues and crises that demanded the CGS's time and attention, and imparts something of the relentless nature of the top job. It was a time when the army grew but the size of Army Headquarters did not keep pace; an age of paper files, typewriters and strict delineations in responsibilities between civilian and military authorities and between the service departments and the Defence Department. Some were perennials with which Daly had wrestled in previous postings, others came seemingly from nowhere or were particular to their time and place.

One of the perennial issues that Daly had made a particular point of pursuing in successive senior positions was pay and conditions. We have already noted his condemnation of government attitudes to the standards of service housing, and to the 'churn' in the posting cycle that regularly disrupted families (a subject of which he, too, had extensive experience). This dissatisfaction was increasingly widely shared and voiced, and by 1970 the Minister for Defence, Malcolm Fraser, acted on these and a range of other concerns by appointing a committee of inquiry into pay and conditions in the armed forces chaired by Mr Justice John Kerr, a judge of the Industrial Court. The multivolume report would be delivered in 1971. The issues were different, or of differing severity, in each of the services but especially acute in the army and the RAN, and were reflected in the resignation rates among officers and the failures to re-enlist among the other ranks. As Major-General C.M.I. Pearson,

RMC Commandant, noted, this unrest over conditions 'and the publicity given them' even affected staff cadets at RMC who had yet to enter the army proper.[66]

The cumbersome nature of the organisation of the defence group of departments was well illustrated by the process of consultation between Fraser and the junior service ministers.[67] Issues such as the group pay rates that regulated pay and allowances for tradesmen in the armed forces in line with civilian awards were a *Defence* issue, but had to be dealt with by – and became rapidly bogged down within – interdepartmental committee structures. The seriousness of the delays this occasioned was underlined once again by disturbances over pay and conditions in the PIR – on this occasion, a strike that resulted in charges being laid against 274 indigenous soldiers. In this particular case the difficulties were further exacerbated by the long-running tensions between the army and the Department of External Territories, a fact of which Daly was only too well aware from his experiences in 1957. Other silliness abounded, such as the fact that army pilots received a lower rate of flying pay than their RAAF equivalents, a matter that had been referred to the Treasury in July 1968! The simple fact was that there was no mechanism by which service pay and allowance questions, or other conditions of service, could be dealt with in an expeditious manner.

Another problem was the lack of hard data available on such matters as service postings and the resultant family movements. At a meeting convened by the minister and including Wilton, the service chiefs and the Adjutant-General and his navy and air force equivalents, Wilton expressed satisfaction 'that the services give this matter the most careful attention and that postings are not made unless they are absolutely necessary'. He conceded, however, that statistics to support this belief were 'difficult to obtain at present but as statistical evidence is built up, this may lead to other thoughts'. Fraser in his turn wanted 'statistics of people posted outside the guidelines in the Minister's letters, i.e. how many people are posted for other reasons'. The major causes of discontent were the requirement to move house regularly, the fact that housing was often unavailable or unsuitable in a new posting, and the concomitant disruption to children's education. The commitment to Vietnam was not, of itself, the major cause of posting turbulence, with Fraser noting that it was far higher in the RAAF than the army.

With three children of his own, Daly was in a position to observe that the psychological aspects of continual changes in schooling arrangements were often as important as the reality, with service parents putting their children into boarding schools and finding 'that they cope much better' but with the corollary of greatly increased expenditure, which the system of educational allowances available to them simply did not cover. Drawing on a decade's involvement in these issues, as he stated explicitly, Daly commented that while 'the situation is better now than previously', the concept of the two-year posting 'is really a myth based on earlier Treasury rulings and qualifications regarding certain allowances'. There was also a problem with Treasury's view 'that an empty house [i.e. a service quarter] must be reoccupied quickly. This can cause turbulence which would otherwise be avoided.' Fraser requested that the services work to produce statistics 'in concentrated form on family movements, and the reasons for the move, for all ranks'.

Ultimately, the Kerr Committee would resolve some of these issues. The wider problem for the army was that it had not faced some of these problems in the past, or had done so on a much smaller and hence more manageable scale. Such *ad hoc* and localised arrangements were no longer sufficient in matters of family welfare, in particular, and the requirement clearly existed for a family liaison organisation, especially for families of men who were overseas or simply posted to other areas of Australia where there was no or insufficient married quarters (such as Townsville at this time). This was in large part a function in the growth of the Regular Army rather than of the war in Vietnam; national servicemen, almost by definition, were unmarried and so, too, were many young soldiers and junior officers.[68] Informal arrangements within units and commands, a reliance upon chaplains (not always the most appropriate resource, depending on the issues), and local arrangements in Eastern Command with the Australian Red Cross Society began to give way to a formal system of family welfare within the army on something other than a philanthropic or charitable basis. (It is worth noting that while the RAAF had no family welfare structure, the RAN had established a naval welfare service, employing trained social workers, in 1957, which reflected the protracted and repeated separation of families inherent in naval service.) The modern Defence Community Organisation with its emphasis on helping service families across the range of family welfare issues, from relocation and education for children to partner education and employment assistance programs, has its origins in the recognition of the army's increasing responsibilities towards soldiers and their families in the late 1960s.[69]

Daly was a rather formal man by nature, at least in public life, and throughout his career he made a point of insisting on a high standard of dress and turnout by all those under his command. In July 1962 while Adjutant-General he had drawn the attention of commands to an increasing tendency towards 'carelessness in matters of dress', especially on the part of officers.[70] He returned to the issue of 'professional standards' again when CGS in 1967, manifested in his view by poor standards of dress and bearing, the amalgamation of officers' and sergeants' messes and other infractions of discipline and good conduct.[71] He had been similarly strict as a battalion adjutant and when commanding the 2/10th Battalion or the 28th Brigade in Korea. There is an interesting military 'urban myth' that notwithstanding this, Daly was responsible for ordering personnel at Army Headquarters to wear civilian clothes in order to avoid unpleasant interactions with anti–Vietnam War demonstrators.[72] In fact, the move to have officers in Army Headquarters in Canberra (and at St Kilda Barracks in Melbourne) wear suits to work rather than uniform seems to have been a pragmatic one since officers were not to wear uniform in social or commercial settings, and this was clearly an inconvenience in a place like Canberra out of hours (on the way home from the working day, for example). The RAN already encouraged the wearing of civilian clothes. In any case the initiative came from the Adjutant-General, Major-General A.L. MacDonald.[73]

His concern for professional standards in the army cannot have been reassured by the publicity that attended the 'bastardisation' scandal at RMC Duntroon in 1969. The long and sorry history of physical and psychological harassment of junior classes by some of their seniors at RMC has been extensively documented and does not need to be retold here.[74] Daly had undoubtedly experienced hazing as a junior cadet not least, as Moore has noted, because the absence of an intake in 1931 meant that his year was the junior class for two years rather than one. In his final year he received a temporary demotion from the Commandant for insufficient vigour in curbing such excesses, although again, as Moore and Clark both note, historically the senior class generally did not engage much in harassment practices because they were too busy in their final year completing the requirements of the course.

The 1969 scandal needs to be seen in the context of the move towards university status and the award of degrees as part of the RMC course. Daly was a strong supporter of this process, reiterating frequently the importance he placed on academic training 'in producing a professional officer of the highest quality'.[75] He had been a member of the committee that had explored the 'ANU option' in 1961–62 whereby degree-level education would be provided through ANU. This never eventuated, for a number of reasons, and was an arrangement whose merits 'were geographic rather than scholastic'.[76] Ultimately the 1968 affiliation made with the University of New South Wales was a triumph of mutual enlightened self-interest leading to the establishment of the Faculty of Military Studies and the expansion of the teaching staff (previously small and not necessarily qualified to hold university appointments) along the lines expected of a tertiary institution. Like almost any graduate of the place, Daly was proud of his association with RMC and slightly defensive of the institution on those occasions when it attracted criticism and external opprobrium. This likely informed the observation made to him by Professor Ridley Bryan (head of the English Department at RMC) on the news that he had been extended in the office of CGS: 'apart from all the other merits in the appointment, a number of us at RMC will find comfort in the thought that you are in the chair during the early years of our link with UNSW'.[77]

The scandal's impact was exacerbated by the fact that the government, which in the eyes of many commentators had seemingly lost its way, was facing an election on 25 October 1969. The general 'tenor of the times' in the late 1960s also helps to explain some of the reactions to the revelation of 'Fourth Class training' abuses. The Minister for the Army, Lynch, bore much of the political brunt of the scandal and was generally held to have acquitted himself well. In Dennis's words, 'what could have been a disaster, coming as [it] ... did on the eve of a general election, was turned into a minor triumph of positive action for a Government not especially noted for its decisiveness'.[78] Lynch's performance in parliament was excellent; labelling the practices 'in varying degrees ... humiliating, stupid or simply a waste of time', he laid out before the House of Representatives in some detail the findings of the internal board of inquiry and the actions he proposed in response to it.[79] The Committee of Inquiry, chaired by Mr Justice R.W. Fox of the ACT Supreme Court and agreed to in discussions with the Military Board, was the principal result.

As CGS, Daly was obviously closely involved in the deliberative processes concerned, although the detail of them is now lost if, in fact, they were ever recorded. He clearly appreciated Lynch's efforts as minister in such difficult circumstances and was grateful for his political courage. As he observed in a letter shortly after the minister was returned in his seat following the election, 'There can be few more difficult portfolios than the

Army. Its affairs are conducted in the full public view; to the Opposition its shortcomings, real or manufactured, are a useful stick with which to beat the Government; to the news media the only news worth publishing is bad news, and the views of a relatively small number of articulate ill-wishers are given far more prominence than is fair or equitable.'[80]

Lynch in fact was promoted to Immigration in the new ministry, and the Army portfolio given to Andrew Peacock. The latter had to deal with the fall-out from a further instalment of the bastardisation affair in May 1970 with the broadcast of the ABC's program *Four Corners*, which claimed to 'expose' bastardisation practices at RMC (quite how one exposed something that had already been the subject of a judicial inquiry was not explained). The Fox Committee had tendered its interim report just before Christmas 1969, and these recommendations were incorporated more or less in full into RMC policy and procedures. The full report was submitted on 24 April 1970.

As with similar exposés in more recent times, the blend of fact and fiction and the line between truth and 'dramatic recreation' was fairly blurred. Peacock noted in the House that the ABC had asked permission to film at RMC, Duntroon. 'The timing was related to the presentation of Colours by the Queen. A week was spent filming most aspects of a cadet's life, including academic studies, military training, range practice, a class room sequence, lectures and discussion groups, as well as a ceremonial and drill segment... although three-quarters of a cadet's life is taken up with academic studies at degree level this aspect was hardly mentioned.'[81] Peacock's comments received fairly wide play in the press. Daly was 'absolutely disgusted' with the program, which he thought 'more dishonest than usual'.[82] He felt constrained to write to the ABC's general manager, Talbot Duckmanton, for the first time in his career to express his 'bitter disappointment'. The series of 'contrived situations' that were aired were

> designed to show the College as an 'anachronism' in what the commentator was pleased to refer to as the days of 'push button warfare' and the 'missile age', as an institution well behind the times, being dragged reluctantly into the 'seventies', and 'out of step' with the requirements of modern war... To sustain a picture of backwardness in a technological age, it was necessary to suppress any reference to the cadets' academic education... and to avoid scenes... of the laboratories, the computer centre or other places of instruction.[83]

As Daly also fairly pointed out, 'the Army has been engaged for the past twenty years, in Korea, Malaya, Borneo and Vietnam, in a type of warfare requiring skills additional to those needed for button pushing'.[84]

Aside from the disciplining of a number of senior cadets, the fullest brunt of responsibility was ultimately seen to be borne by the Commandant, Major-General C.A.E. Fraser. Daly had been strongly supportive of Fraser's responses once the scandal broke, noting his 'unenviable task in reconciling fundamentally opposing philosophies... [and] in reconciling the military and academic components of an officer's education'.[85] Fraser's posting as COMAFV was read as a criticism of his term as Commandant (although being preferred for the senior operational command in a major war might be thought a queer sort of chastisement for a senior officer), and the Academic Staff Association at Duntroon vehemently protested the move and expressed its full support for his handling of the affair, which he had initiated *before* it became public knowledge.[86] In fact, Fraser's posting as COMAFV had been proposed to the Minister for Defence in early August, and his intended replacement was to have been his predecessor in Phuoc Tuy province, Major-General R.A. Hay (a subsequent commandant in the mid-1970s). Major-General C.M.I. Pearson, who had commanded the 1st Australian Task Force in Phuoc Tuy in 1968–69, had recently returned to Australia and the position of Commander, 1st Division, but had been heavily involved in the Fox Committee in which role, as Peacock noted, 'he has acquired a close insight into the affairs of the College and has been party to discussions from which will stem recommendations for its future conduct'. Daly thus recommended, and his minister duly supported, that Pearson rather than Hay become Commandant, thus avoiding any break in the continuity of command at RMC and availing themselves of Pearson's 'prestige... and valuable experience as a member of the Fox Committee', which made him 'unquestionably the most suitable officer available for the appointment'. Daly also drew the recommendation directly to Malcolm Fraser's attention 'since I am anxious that the officers concerned should be warned as soon as possible'.[87]

The move to tertiary qualifications as an integral part of the RMC process reflected broader discussions within the army at this time, some of which were also allied to the deliberations of the Army Review Committee (also known as the Hassett Committee and dealt with in chapter 7). In July 1970 the Military Board considered a report on the standards of training and education required by army officers, which suggested, *inter alia*, the requirement in the long term for tertiary level qualifications for all general service officers before commissioning, the requirement for tertiary qualifications after 1980 as a prerequisite for promotion to lieutenant-colonel, the need for specialised degrees 'as a regular feature of career planning for permanent officers of the specialist category', and the reform of the Staff College curriculum to facilitate recognition for postgraduate tertiary qualifications.[88] Some of these issues – such as the quality of the Staff College course (now a tri-service one) – continue to the present, while the discussion overall reflected the long-standing argument about 'specialists' versus 'generalists'. The Canadians likewise had undertaken a wide-ranging study of these matters in 1967, and the whole issue in its turn suggested the realisation by Western armies of the need to meet expectations in the broader community from which they recruited. It is probably an argument without end.

Disorder had also marked the PIR in protest over pay and conditions and the difficulties – and hence delays – that the army experienced in formulating a decent pension plan for Pacific Island soldiers. By the second half of the 1960s there had been considerable further developments in the PIR, including the appointments of indigenous men as officers with the obvious implication by the beginning of the 1970s of a future role for the PIR in an independent Papua New Guinea. The Joint Intelligence Committee examined the implications of these developments in an extensive report in 1967, a copy of which Daly read. The strategic importance of Papua New Guinea for Australia was a given, in terms of maintenance of the lines of communication that would skirt a potentially hostile Indonesia and the value of the forward basing facilities that Australia maintained there. (This was, of course, the era of 'forward defence'.) Constitutional and political developments could have key influences on the army's continuing role in the country but were not properly part of the army's policy or activities. Race relations, economic development (and specifically the capacity of a post-independence national economy to sustain infrastructure and other national expenditure such as a national defence force) and the possible or likely future role of an indigenous army leadership in such circumstances were all issues that directly affected the army. Even after independence, whenever that might occur, 'in the foreseeable future an independent Papua and New Guinea could neither provide nor economically support a defence force capable of defending unaided the country against external aggression'.[89] In mid-1970 consideration had to be given as well to the call-out of the PIR 'in aid to the civil power' prompted by the occupation of government land by activists of the Mataungan Association on the Gazelle Peninsula, itself part of increasingly violent agitation by Tolai people in the context of the move to independence. Following a visit to Papua New Guinea by the Prime Minister, John Gorton, in early July 1970 the Australian cabinet confirmed the view that the PIR be available to assist the police 'to maintain peace and enforce lawful eviction'.[90]

The provision and development of indigenous officers was one that had concerned the army since at least 1960. While Daly was still at Northern Command, the Military Board had decided that the army's policy for the future in PNG 'should be to build up a force which, with its own indigenous leaders, would provide a stabilising influence in the community after self-determination is granted'. In 1966 the Defence Committee recognised that for the foreseeable future at least, the direction, leadership and training of indigenous forces would be the responsibility of Australian service personnel, but that alongside this there was a clear need for increased participation by native men at senior NCO and officer ranks. This would involve the broadening of access to secondary education for young men sufficient to enable their training and commissioning, involving additional resources and expenditure.[91] Indigenous officers would be produced through OCS Portsea, but even with the lower educational requirements for entry (relative to RMC) there was still a significant gap between them and the standard of Papua New Guinea secondary schools. A scholarship system existed for able boys to complete their secondary education in Australia: both Ted Diro and Patterson Lowa, for example, the first two indigenous officers to reach the rank of major, followed this pathway from Papua New Guinea high school to school in Australia, then to OCS.[92] The idea of a separate officer academy located in Papua New Guinea itself was considered, then dropped for practical reasons.

Relations with the Department of Territories remained antagonistic. In mid-1968 the Defence Committee conducted a review of 'the size, role, rate of development and disposition' of the PIR at the request of Territories, allegedly from concern that the PIR could pose 'a threat to internal security' and that the economy of an independent Papua New Guinea would be unable to sustain the force. The second battalion had been added to PIR in March 1965; a third battalion was talked about and never eventuated, but even raising the 2nd Battalion, PIR (2PIR), to its full strength met objections and obstruction from External Territories. As part of the expansion of the PIR the army had undertaken an extensive building program to modernise and expand facilities, which had raised the ire of Territories, which was under pressure through lack of provision of educational accommodation and facilities. Daly noted that External Territories' objection was couched 'in the form that the Army in PNG should be held at its present strength, and that surplus Army accommodation be made available to Territories'.[93] The Defence Committee had proposed a review in 1970 to look at the future structure of the forces in Papua New Guinea, a structure 'which might not conform to the Australian pattern and might point to the desirability of a unified defence force', with obvious economies. The army's proposals to raise another company for 2PIR in 1969 were met by the expected 'uncompromising attitude' from External Territories, which opposed the move and tried to substitute an increase of just ninety-nine men to include staff at the training facility at Goldie River, medical orderlies and other specialists; all these were needed, but in addition to the proposed company and not as a substitute for it.[94]

Pay and conditions had been the spark to ignite disturbances in the PIR in the past, and Daly was adamant that these needed to be regularised in the interests of fairness and the maintenance of discipline and to keep faith with soldiers who by 1969 had patiently waited more than three years for a resolution of outstanding claims.[95] At issue were such matters as the payment of service loadings and gratuities and trade pay, in order to bring soldiers into line with awards elsewhere in the Territory. Of equal, perhaps greater, concern was the continuing absence of a satisfactory pension scheme, despite the fact that Pacific Islands soldiers had been paying 5 per cent of their pay towards a pension scheme since 1966. There was no civilian Administration scheme in lieu, although one had been mooted for some time, and this was the problem: External Territories insisted that an army scheme must be comparable with the one for which they would have responsibility, but since it did not exist the army's proposed scheme was unable to proceed. This was a 'potentially explosive area', and Daly emphasised to the Secretary of the Department of Defence, Sir Henry Bland, that movement on the issue was 'urgently necessary'.[96] 'I am convinced', he wrote, 'that unless constant pressure is maintained at the highest Ministerial and Departmental levels, these matters could continue to remain unresolved indefinitely.'

The Whitlam Government would accelerate the move to independence after it came into office at the end of 1972, but the army, at least, was well advanced in preparing the PIR for service to an independent nation well before this occurred. In June 1969 Daly observed that the army had 'reached the stage when it has become a matter of urgency to produce a plan to provide a suitable political, operational and administrative structure for an indigenous Army in the Territory as it moves towards independence', and set up a planning cell staffed from Australia for this purpose.[97] The commissioning and promotion of native officers has been noted; initially they were deployed to the battalions of the PIR, but by January 1972 it proved possible to post indigenous officers to technical and support units such as signals, transport and the workshops as well, while in January 1973 Majors Diro and Lowa was selected to attend the Australian Army Staff College at Queenscliff. The force was being 'indigenised' in other areas, too: in August 1970 the last of the Australian RSMs left his position in 2PIR. At the regimental birthday parade in March 1972, the now-retired Lieutenant-General Daly in his new role as Honorary Colonel of the PIR received the salute. His appointment accurately reflected the sustained interest and support he had taken in the PIR and the men (and their families) who soldiered in New Guinea in these years. Three years ahead of the formal grant of independence, but with considerable internal political autonomy already under way, the PIR was for all intents and purposes the young national army of a nation-to-be.

The final issue for this chapter involves the development of army aviation. The dispute with the RAAF over operational issues in Vietnam will be discussed in the next chapter, but the expansion of army aviation in Australia continued separately as a process and one in which Daly took a close personal interest. Wilton had encountered concerted opposition from the RAAF to the idea, much less the expansion, of the army's aviation capabilities, and as CGS Daly was to encounter considerably more. Opposition to army aviation from the RAAF had an older history still; the then CGS, Lieutenant-General Sir Henry Wells was told in December 1958 that while 'the necessity for Army to own and operate light aircraft could be agreed in principle', nothing would be effected without 'full consultation with the RAAF' to ensure that expansion in army aviation did not come 'at the expense of higher priority requirements', i.e. RAAF ones.[98]

Shortly after Daly's appointment the Chiefs of Staff Committee decided to review the joint service implications of a proposed expansion in army aviation. One issue was numbers, the other was platforms. Put simply, the expansion of the army necessitated more aircraft while a better and more versatile performance was required than the modest Cessna 180 then in service was able to provide. The army was facing a greater range of tasks – not simply in Vietnam but also within Australia, elsewhere in South-East Asia (principally Malaysia, of course) and in Papua New Guinea.[99] At the same time the expansion of the RAAF, and especially the anticipated acquisition of the F-111, meant that the army's use of existing facilities at Amberley would be curtailed, necessitating the establishment of a new mainland home for the army's aviation assets.[100] The intention was to expand the current capability from fifteen fixed-wing and twenty-seven rotary-wing aircraft to thirty-seven and fifty-one respectively. Prompted by experience in Vietnam but separately from that was the whole question of close air support for ground forces since, as senior RAAF officers privately conceded, 'when the Sabre is withdrawn from operations the Mirage will not be used in the close support of forward troops'. As one senior air staff officer noted, if as a result the army acquired a capability of its own in this role – such as the acquisition of ground-attack helicopters – 'it will not be many years before they take over the responsibility for the entire tactical battle area – an area that they already state may extend to 40 miles beyond their forward troops'.[101]

The next step was the creation of an Army Aviation Corps, but this, too, was a fraught business. A proposal had been placed before the Military Board in March 1966 but was not proceeded with because of inter-service deliberations on the future of army aviation. The army's dissatisfaction with the RAAF's attitude to provision of air support was well founded, as even the Minister for Air, Peter Howson, admitted (in private, to his diary): 'army aviation . . . has been neglected for many years in Australia. I am not sure who is to be blamed, but I suspect the RAAF more than the army.'[102] The long and terminal illness of the previous Minister for Defence, Senator Shane Paltridge, might also have contributed, although it certainly did not cause it.[103] In September 1966 the Minister for Defence, now Allen Fairhall, ruled in favour of 'an enduring division of responsibility between the Army and Air Force for the control and operation of light aircraft'.[104]

Daly had a very direct involvement in this outcome. He regarded the RAAF's position as 'an all-out attack on the entire concept of the Army operating its own aircraft', and when Howson argued for a clean sweep of air assets under air force control ('Either Army will gradually duplicate air facilities, or we must provide them with the services they require'), the CGS used a somewhat irregular line of approach direct to the Minister for Defence.[105] While GOC Northern Command Daly had become good friends with Sir Theodore Bray, editor-in-chief of the Brisbane *Courier Mail*, and at a dinner in Canberra hosted by Bray he used the serendipity of the seating plan to argue the army's case with his dinner companion, none other than the Minister for Defence. After a lengthy (although doubtless amicable) discussion, Fairhall 'laughed and told me not to worry; the Army would retain its aircraft. He was as good as his word and the Air Force submission was rejected.'[106] This did not discourage the senior hierarchy of the RAAF from continuing to stymie the development of army aviation through, for example, delays in the implementation of pilot training for army aviators or the provision of aircraft in support of army training activities.[107] The latter had serious implications in the preparation of battalions for rotation to Vietnam.[108]

There were three further developments with which Daly was closely involved: the creation of the aviation corps, the establishment of the aviation regiment at Oakey in Queensland, and the breaking of the restriction on the types of aircraft that the army was permitted to fly. The need for a separate aviation corps was structural. In the early days of army aviation – up to 1960 – Regular Army officers were given pilot training then posted to flying duties for two or three years. The numbers needed increasingly exceeded the numbers volunteering (as we have noted already), and the army introduced a direct-entry pilot training program in which 90 per cent of those engaged in flying duties were enlisted specifically for that purpose (the majority) or, as we have also noted, were national servicemen. (The US Army's solution to this problem was to introduce the rank category of Chief Warrant Officer, Class 2 (CW2) as part of the warrant officer aviator program, with the result that the majority of army pilots were young senior enlisted men.)[109] The short-service commission met the immediate objective but not a longer-term requirement for permanent officers 'who, with their wider knowledge of the Army, could use their experience in command duties and, at the same time, pass on their experience to the short service commissioned officers to fit them for command'.[110] The manpower ceiling would be set at 909, with 160 officers, 84 NCOs and 268 rank and file in the aviation element (the remaining numbers to be filled from RAAOC and RAEME). The 1st Aviation Regiment would have two squadrons (Nos 16 and 17) and two workshops under command with other training and reconnaissance units being under command of the Army Aviation Centre.

The arrangement for shared facilities with the RAAF at Amberley was increasingly unsatisfactory; accommodation was substandard, it was difficult fitting in flying training for army personnel alongside the needs of the air force, and the impending acquisition of the F-111 and its basing would place these under even greater pressure.[111] Daly was made aware that the Department of Civil Aviation was looking to dispose of a small civilian airfield at Oakey outside Toowoomba in the Darling Downs; a wartime aircraft maintenance and construction facility had been located there and, while the surviving civilian strip was small and underdeveloped, it provided an excellent opportunity to establish a permanent home for army aviation. Daly argued that a simple book transfer of the facility was all that was necessary while the Treasury, predictably, wanted to dispose of it by public tender. Daly's opportunity came while the Minister for National Development, Reginald Swartz, was acting as Treasurer while the Treasurer himself was overseas (Swartz had held the civil aviation portfolio between 1966 and 1969). Swartz had been a CMF officer on the headquarters of Northern Command while Daly was GOC, and at this time remained a lieutenant-colonel on the Reserve of Officers (he had joined the AIF and been captured with the 8th Division during the war); he had entered parliament in 1949, and his own electorate was Darling Downs. As Daly later recalled,

> I rang him, explained the situation and suggested that as acting Treasurer he had a unique opportunity to dispose of Oakey to the mutual advantage of his Department, Civil Aviation and the Army. He was not slow to act, realising no doubt the value that an Army establishment would bring to the district, and within days we had our home for the Aviation Corps. In recognition of this signal service Reg Swartz was invited to become Honorary Colonel of the Corps, an appointment which he accepted and of which he was intensely proud.[112]

Oakey was handed over to the army on 1 July 1969, a ceremony at which Swartz presided in his new honorary role. A master plan for the redevelopment was prepared and costed at $20 million (in 1970 values), but the Secretary of the Department of Defence advised that the Defence Committee would baulk since the Estimates could not accommodate such a large figure in a single year. Daly agreed to halve the cost by reducing the immediate requirement to the basics and essentials, assuming that these could be expanded and upgraded in future years as funding became available. And so it proved.[113]

Army aviation operated *light* aircraft only, a category defined by a weight limit of 4000lb and a legacy of the British Army's similar restrictions that, by 1970, no longer made sense nor were applied in the United Kingdom but which the RAAF fought hard to maintain. Daly recalled that the air force retained control over the selection of aircraft for the army, and grudgingly replaced the Second World War–vintage Austers

Photo 27 The Minister for Civil Aviation, R.G. Swartz, inspects a guard from the 1st Aviation Regiment at the handing over of the facilities at Oakey to the army, 1 July 1969. (FAI/69/293/NC)

with the Cessna 180 and, subsequently, the Pilatus Porter. Daly argued for a more capable, twin-engine aircraft such as the Queenair for certain communication and supply missions, for survey tasks and to support operations in close country such as existed in Papua New Guinea. The RAAF offered some aged DC3s, an aircraft that the RAAF itself argued 'was getting past its useful safe life'.[114] The breakthrough came in what Daly later described as 'a piece of opportunism almost equal to the acquisition of the Army Aviation Centre at Oakey'.[115] Briefly, the Government Aircraft Factory (GAF) had established an expensive production line for its Nomad project, but the plane struggled to find customers. Concerned to maintain the stimulus to local aircraft production, the Department of Supply attempted to interest the RAAF in the plane but was rebuffed. Daly then offered to take some for the army. 'The Nomad was not quite what we wanted having, at least in the early models, a limited range but it was twin-engined and would represent the breakthrough we were seeking,' he wrote. 'The Government was determined to support the infant, home-grown aircraft industry, the civilian market was limited, the Air Force had no requirement and the Army provided the only opportunity to absorb a part of current production. So we got a twin-engine aircraft.'[116] The Nomad also provided the short take-off and landing (STOL) capability that the army had sought, but in most other respects the aircraft was a disaster, suffering thirty-two total hull-loss accidents resulting in seventy-six fatalities internationally before it was withdrawn from service with the army.

Horner has suggested that 'many Australian Army officers played a role in forming the Australian Army Aviation Corps', and that Wilton deserved a significant measure of the credit.[117] Wilton was vital, as CGS, in getting the army's aviation capability on a more or less firm footing. In his turn, Daly as CGS was equally vital in regularising and institutionalising aviation within the army, and seeing off several concerted attempts by the RAAF to throttle army aviation in its early years. Army aviation's current significant role at brigade strength owes much to both of them.

Daly's health was robust enough given his age (54 on appointment as CGS); his medical classification in 1960 was 1, although he had attended a medical board in Brisbane in late 1959 with a recommendation for further audiometric checks in twelve months time. But the pace was punishing and stress is a cumulative disorder; in early August 1968 he was hospitalised for a week. He put it down to 'general decrepitude and a couple of years of frustration... [that] caught up with me'.[118] The travel doubtless accounted for some of it; in 1968 he was in Vietnam in March–April, New Zealand in June July, Singapore, Hong Kong, Seoul and Tokyo in September–October and Vietnam again just before Christmas. The commitment to Vietnam was the major item of business for the army on his watch, and he was continually and deeply immersed in its course and conduct.

CHAPTER 6

DALY, THE ARMY AND THE WAR IN VIETNAM, 1966–71

Australia's war in Vietnam was largely an army affair, and within that commitment the largest, hardest and most dangerous part was played by the soldiers of the infantry battalions. Vietnam was the third largest commitment in Australia's history, the longest continuous deployment in a single theatre of operations, and arguably the most complex of Australia's wars at both the military and the policy levels. For Daly as for the army generally, it was the dominant issue on the agenda throughout his period as Chief of the General Staff. 'Vietnam colours all our thinking and influences practically everything we do', he wrote to a former subordinate from his Korean War days. 'It provides us with a clear purpose and to my way of thinking a good and rewarding one. This view is shared wholeheartedly by practically every soldier who has served in that unhappy country and has a first-hand knowledge of the issues and of the values at stake.'[1] The Vietnam commitment also demonstrated strains and shortcomings in the defence machinery and within the army and in its relationships with the media, some politicians and the wider Australian society.

The decisions over whether to commit forces to Vietnam and what size and shape they would be had been made before Daly became CGS, and he had no involvement in them. As he later recalled, at Eastern Command 'I wouldn't have known about it until I was informed that the battalion was actually going... I can recall the CGS ringing me one day to inform me that the battalion was going to Vietnam.'[2] Horner notes in addition that the Defence Committee, for example, did not discuss the Vietnam commitment until April 1965 while Daly himself had noted that the selection of officers and NCOs for service in the AATTV had been left largely to the heads of relevant corps.[3] Once the decision was made, the basis on which the Australians would operate in Vietnam under US aegis was negotiated between the Commander, United States Military Assistance Command Vietnam (COMUSMACV), General William Westmoreland, and the Australian Army's Director of Military Operations and Plans, Brigadier Ken Mackay, with the initial military working agreement being signed between Westmoreland and the new commander of Australian Army Force Vietnam, Colonel O.D. Jackson. This was the structure that oversaw the year-long deployment of 1RAR in 1965–66 and had in-theatre responsibility for the AATTV as well.

Daly visited Vietnam briefly in September 1965 while accompanying Wilton to the CIGS's annual exercise in Britain. He had visited 1RAR during its work-up before deployment, and now saw them in the field at Bien Hoa. The Australian battalion was operating in an American environment as the third battalion of the 173rd Airborne Brigade (Separate), and while logistically Daly found them to be 'extremely well looked after' by their much larger partner organisation, he nonetheless felt some 'reservations' about placing units 'into an American structure, trained to our own standards and according to our own ideas'.[4] Although the Australian battalion acquitted itself well on its first tour of Vietnam, the experience was not an altogether happy one precisely because of the need to work closely within the US system with its very different assumptions and approaches. It was also important to maintain the national identity of a much smaller force (which had been a factor in Korea as well). Drawing on his previous experience of working with the US Army, Daly thought that while 'we were very keen about security and deep patrols, information, knowing what was going on, and we liked to go on doing this', he also thought that the time spent at Bien Hoa meant that 'we had lost a little bit of our expertise in this field. We were rather more inclined to use firepower... than seek information and destroy whatever threat might be appearing before it really could manifest itself.'[5] Wilton felt similarly and, according to Horner, was determined to protect the Australian force from the consequences of 'capricious military operations'.[6]

Daly later observed that the army 'wasn't prepared for this kind of commitment – it never is. It wasn't prepared for Korea, but the army has to do these things when the government wants them to do it.'[7] The army's commitment to Vietnam possessed several overall defining characteristics. Commitments to Malaysia and Vietnam (and Papua New

Guinea), the National Service scheme and the reversion from the Pentropic to the Tropical establishment meant that increases to the army's commitment in Vietnam were piecemeal and episodic, reactions to pressure from the Americans for force increases and to concerns about the unbalanced nature of AFV rather than part of any rational force structure build-up. The army sent what it had when it could, cannibalising other parts of the organisation overall; this had obvious impact upon the CMF, as we have already noted. While still CGS, and as a result of the visit he and Daly had made to Bien Hoa, Wilton had resolved to expand the Australian force and provide it with an operational area of its own (while obviously remaining within the US structure in country), but the provision of a self-contained task force was beyond the army's means in July 1965. The Prime Minister, Harold Holt, was able to announce only the replacement of 1RAR in its augmented form with a two-battalion task force (comprising 5RAR and 6RAR) in March 1966.

The decisions concerning the establishment of what would become the 1st Australian Task Force (1ATF) were also made before Daly became CGS: 'I wasn't party to the decision to deploy the force in Phuoc Tuy in the first place'.[8] When 5RAR left Holsworthy for Vietnam in April 1966 Daly was still (just) GOC Eastern Command, and attended the parade in that capacity. Jackson became first Commander, 1ATF and Mackay was promoted to major-general and appointed COMAFV. The arrangements governing 1ATF's operations under overall US command were negotiated between Wilton, in one of his last acts before assuming the chairmanship of the Chiefs of Staff Committee, Westmoreland and their South Vietnamese counterparts. Although these command arrangements had been made before his time, Daly was confronted with several hard fights in the Chiefs of Staff Committee over them.

The expansion in size to a task force involved the provision of RAAF aircraft in the form of eight Iroquois helicopters and personnel in support, flown by the RAAF but under army control, as Peter Howson noted critically in his diary: this was 'a course recommended by CGS [Wilton] and CCOS [Scherger]' on which the Chief of the Air Staff 'had not been consulted'.[9] Given Murdoch's long record of intransigent non-cooperation in matters of air support for the army, this was perhaps just if not altogether fitting. AFV was joint in name but not really in organisation and, although the deputy force commander was an air force officer with the rank of air commodore, he was generally ill-equipped to play a useful role in anything other than RAAF matters.[10] Daly identified the problem succinctly: 'the whole situation was quite unsatisfactory. Because, if he

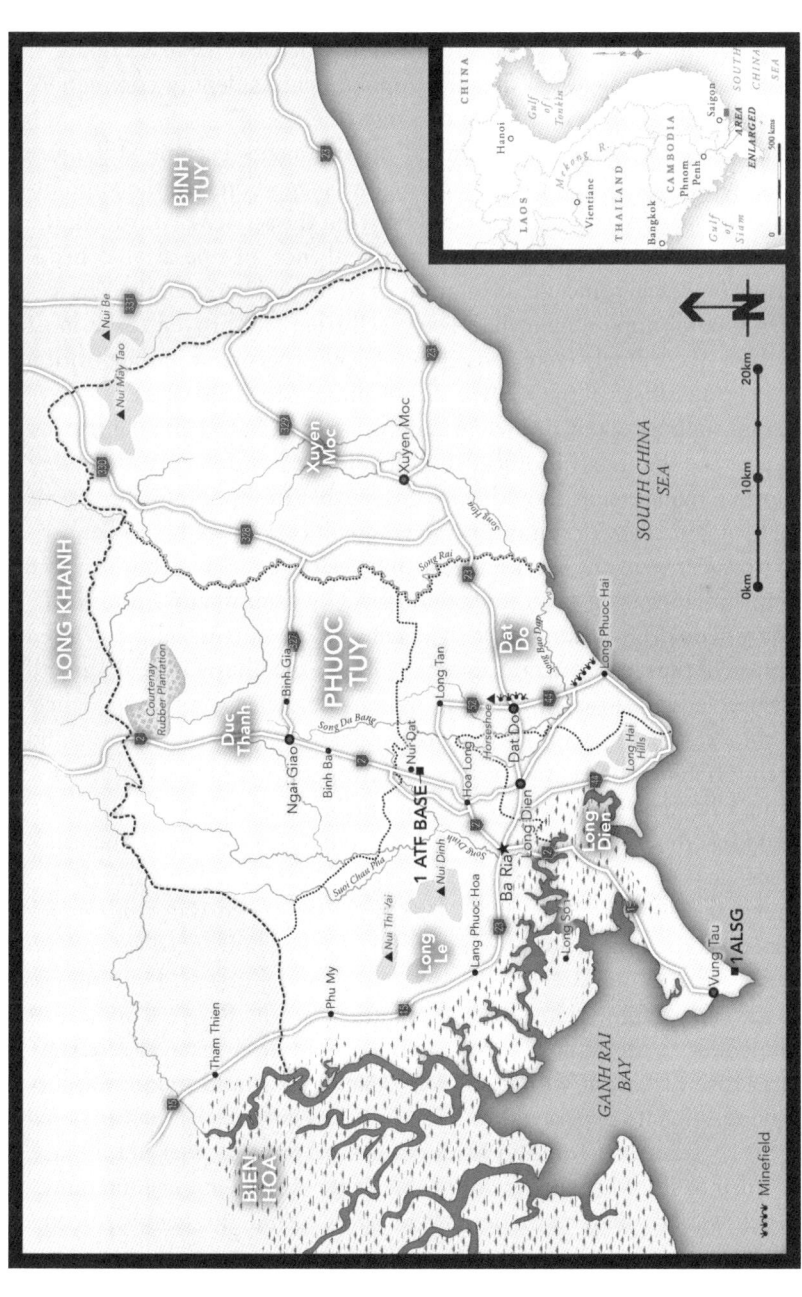

Map 7 Phuoc Tuy province, South Vietnam, 1966–71.

had to sub for the Commander in, say, a conference with COMUSMACV, he wasn't really in a position to represent the operational view of ground forces, which was of course the great majority of the force in Vietnam.'[11] He subsequently suggested that the appointment as deputy commander was effectively little more than 'a courtesy title'.[12]

The question of senior command appointments became still more pointed in the middle of 1967 following the suggestion that the appointment of COMAFV should be rotated between the services. Murdoch, the CAS, argued that HQ AFV 'was a national, not an operational headquarters [and] the principle of rotation of command between the Services in this type of appointment had been well tried and proved to be most effective'. Accordingly he proposed that the next occupant of the position should be an officer of the RAAF. Vice-Admiral McNicoll, the CNS, gave apparent support to the idea while making it clear that he had no intention of suggesting that a naval officer should hold the position and added that 'the prime requirement should be to ensure that the appointment... was filled by an officer with suitable personal qualities, knowledge and experience irrespective of the Service to which he belonged',[13] which was a nice example of appearing to straddle two mutually contradictory positions.

Daly would have none of it. 'Cogent arguments', he said, favoured retention of the current arrangement, including credibility in dealing with Westmoreland and the Americans, 'military knowledge and experience' and the fact that COMAFV had real operational responsibilities and was closely concerned with 'the day-to-day operations of the Task Force'. Although he strongly supported integration, he stated firmly that he 'could not support the rotation of integrated commands irrespective of the needs of the specific situation'.[14] Not surprisingly, COSC failed to agree on the matter and Wilton, as chairman, passed the matter to the Minister for Defence, Fairhall. In Wilton's opinion the CGS had 'advanced very sound reasons' for retaining COMAFV as an army appointment. Pointing out that the earlier agreement to the appointment of the RAAF Component Commander at the rank of air commodore had been reached to ensure greater ease of liaison with his USAF counterparts, and the desirability 'of giving Vietnam experience to a senior RAAF officer', he further noted that the argument for rotation as an established principle was not, in fact, true. Further still, the majority of problems thrown up in the command – logistics was a prime example – were overwhelmingly army problems because the personnel and systems involved were primarily army ones as well. Wilton's recommendation in favour of Daly's argument was accepted by the minister without demur.[15]

Admiral McNicoll might well have believed that the army 'thought that Vietnam was their war', but to a considerable extent this was actually the case. Murdoch appears not to have learnt anything from the argument over the COMAFV appointment, however, because in October 1968 he once again attempted to have an RAAF officer selected for what he now chose to describe as 'largely an administrative position'. On this occasion he nominated Air Vice-Marshal Colin Hannah, perhaps on the basis that Daly and the latter enjoyed warm personal relations and that this might overcome any objections the CGS might raise. It did not. More than a year previously, in July 1967 – not coincidentally just after the CAS's previous foray had been seen off – Daly had asked the then COMAFV, Major-General Vincent, about the performance of his senior RAAF subordinate. Expressing himself happy with Air Commodore Lush's 'determined and enthusiastic' approach to understanding the workings of the army at war, Vincent went on to note that Lush was firm in the view that 'an airman could not act as COMAFV unless there were significant change in the relationship between COMAFV and COMUSMACV... He appreciates the peculiar army aspects of the relationship... part national – part army in general and detail sense – part tactical.'[16] Murdoch's advocacy once again was frustrated (which did not stop him attempting it again the following year), but the issue further reinforced Daly's later reflection that 'we learned a lot of lessons about interservice cooperation in Vietnam'.[17]

On this issue the CGS was rather more than one among equals perhaps, aided no doubt by the fact that the chairman, Wilton, as a former CGS had a more than usually well-developed appreciation of the difficulties. The higher-level direction of the Australian effort in Vietnam lay with Wilton, notwithstanding that he did not have the sort of formal authority later vested in the Chief of the Defence Force. Deliberative authority at that level lay formally with the Chiefs of Staff Committee, of which Daly was a member, but on matters of doctrine, training, equipment, logistics and personnel the CGS, his staff and subordinate commanders were closely involved in the decision-making and implementation of policy and administration of army units in Vietnam. The command of 1ATF resided with the army's Promotion and Selection Committee, and Daly had a very clear view of what was required. In considering the succession to Brigadier S.P. Weir in early 1970, he noted the view of some of the committee members: 'In view of its great experience value the appointment should go to an officer who will unquestionably progress to higher rank. With this I could not disagree, but the overriding priority is to see that 1 ATF is led by the officer best qualified to do so.'[18] Similarly, when Brigadier S.C. Graham put the case for the appointment of a deputy task force commander to relieve him of much of the administrative load at the base at Nui Dat, Daly made the appointment.[19]

Suitable appointments to the Task Force were 'the first priority' in his view, and not only at the top. The 'fragging' incident in 106 Battery in December 1967, in which Lieutenant R.G. Birse was mortally wounded by one of his own soldiers, filled him 'with an unease that is not dispelled by explanations so far received'. The details of the particular incident were one thing (as he noted, 'all is not well with the battery concerned and perhaps with the regiment'), but responsibility for breakdowns in discipline, in his view, lay with the officers. The commanding officer's statement on Birse's officer qualities 'does not tally with his continued employment as a battery officer or with my own directions concerning officer standards for Vietnam'. The lives of soldiers depended on the capacity of their officers, among other things, and Daly directed the newly arrived COMAFV, Major-General A.L. MacDonald, to 'take steps necessary to weed out incompetent officers in this or any other unit'.[20]

The army's preparation of soldiers for deployment to Vietnam was extensive and rigorous within the limitations then existing in Australia. The experiences of 7RAR are illustrative in this respect. Newly raised (from a cadre of 3RAR) in September 1965, the battalion came together in Puckapunyal; quarters and facilities were suboptimal, and the extreme shortage of married quarters meant that most of the regulars as well as the national servicemen were single. Despite this, the commanding officer, Lieutenant-Colonel Eric Smith, thought that he had at his disposal 'training opportunities never previously available to any battalion leaving Australia for active service', especially in the provision of rifle ranges for individual companies.[21] The absorption of national servicemen was a critical part of the process, as was training at the subunit level. The preparation cycle involved two major unit exercises at Shoalwater Bay and a compulsory battle efficiency course at the Jungle Training Centre, Canungra, at which units were certified as fit for deployment.

The remaining shortcomings were important, however. There was no artillery or aircraft available to practice fire support missions, and no helicopters; in a move reminiscent of Daly's preparation of the 2/10th for Balikpapan, soldiers of 7RAR in 1966 practised boarding drills with chalk outlines on the ground. Smith nonetheless felt that when the battalion embarked for Vietnam 'everything that could be done to train the unit had been done'. Even so, the COMAFV, Vincent, noted in a long report to Daly in mid-1967 that at that stage of the war, at least, 'The skilful use of all means of support is lacking in commanders at all levels. This is understandable because it is not until reaching this theatre that the means are readily available and to make the best use of them the person concerned needs, after initial introduction, constant practice and up-dating in their use.'[22] The same had been true in 1941 when Australian battalions had reached the Middle East.

The 7th Battalion returned from Vietnam to Australia in April 1968, the national servicemen were discharged and many of the regulars received new postings. In effect the battalion was broken down and now rebuilt, a process that took about twelve months with 'most of the officers, NCOs and diggers having been posted elsewhere or discharged'.[23] Not only was the new training cycle intense but also the resources by this stage were more plentiful: the battalion trained regularly with 106 Field Battery, who would operate in direct support in Vietnam, and even with helicopters, which, while still not plentiful, were made available for a number of the major exercises towards the end of the pre-deployment period. Officers who did not measure up were transferred and replaced by those who did.[24] As on the first tour, the training cycle culminated with several large and testing exercises at Shoalwater Bay. As a general statement, all battalions destined for Vietnam service experienced this cycle, with those deployed later in the war benefitting from the greater resources and accumulated experience that a prolonged war brings with it.[25]

The emphasis on sustained and realistic training came from the top, with the CGS taking a close personal interest in the preparation of battalions and ancillary units under the complex 'build-up and relief' cycle with which the army managed the deployments to the Task Force and which Daly personally approved.[26] The size of the commitment itself had a significant influence on this, since the Task Force itself kept growing in response to the changing demands of the war the Australians faced and the environments in which they operated. As we have seen, the Australian commitment grew from a battalion group to a two-battalion task force between early 1965 and mid-1966, but the limitations of operating with two battalions rather than three quickly made themselves apparent: the Task Force base at Nui Dat drew off two rifle companies in a defensive role. As Daly told Vincent, the problems were appreciated 'but this is a fact of life and must be lived with', at least initially.[27] The possibility, even likelihood, of further expansion of the Australian ground commitment was well understood, evidenced by the deliberations of the CGS Exercise for 1967, which had as its aim 'the tactical and administrative problems associated with the mounting, lodgement and deployment of a divisional force in South Vietnam'.[28]

The needs of the Nui Dat base were one such problem. Daly later reflected that 'if we could have got rid of the problem of maintaining Nui Dat from Vung Tau, and of maintaining reserves in Nui Dat in case of the cutting of communications between the two areas, we probably could have increased our own capacity to maintain the force without too much of an increase'.[29] This meant that 1ATF worked with fewer companies actually available as maneouvre elements on operations than, theoretically, were available to it. Vincent made the point again in discussions with Daly during a return visit to Australia: 'The deductions are both self-evident and vary little from those which have always been accepted, namely a three-battalion force is necessary. As has been accepted it is not the size of the battalion that matters, but the number of manoeuvre elements.'[30] The government had imposed a manpower ceiling on the army, however, one geared to the Defence budget and which determined the size of the National Service intakes. One option Vincent suggested was to reduce the two Australian battalions by one company each which then, together with a company from the 1st Battalion, Royal New Zealand Infantry Regiment (1RNZIR) could be combined to form a third, reduced-establishment unit. This was not the only manpower problem Daly faced. 'The combination of the abnormal operational and climatic environment of the South Vietnam theatre place a considerable strain on the soldier', necessitating a 10 per cent unit increment to cover temporary shortages, which, in some circumstances, ran as high as 15 per cent of unit strength. As Fraser, the Army minister, advised Fairhall in a long letter on the issue, careful study revealed 'just how stretched the Army is in meeting its present commitments'.[31]

New Zealand's commitment to the Vietnam War was less enthusiastic at the political level than Australia's, and the contribution of infantry companies to 1ATF had to wait on the withdrawal of 1RNZIR from operational duties in Borneo as part of Confrontation. Two companies (V and W) were deployed and formed part of a composite Anzac battalion of five rifle companies (rather than the standard four); the justification was that the arrangement would 'suit local tactical requirements', but New Zealand historian Ian McGibbon has suggested that with 'a two-two company battalion, New Zealand would be more likely to seek a rotating command of New Zealand and Australian officers'.[32] The Australian component of the resultant Anzac battalions was therefore only three rifle companies and a saving of about 150 all ranks, which eased the pressure

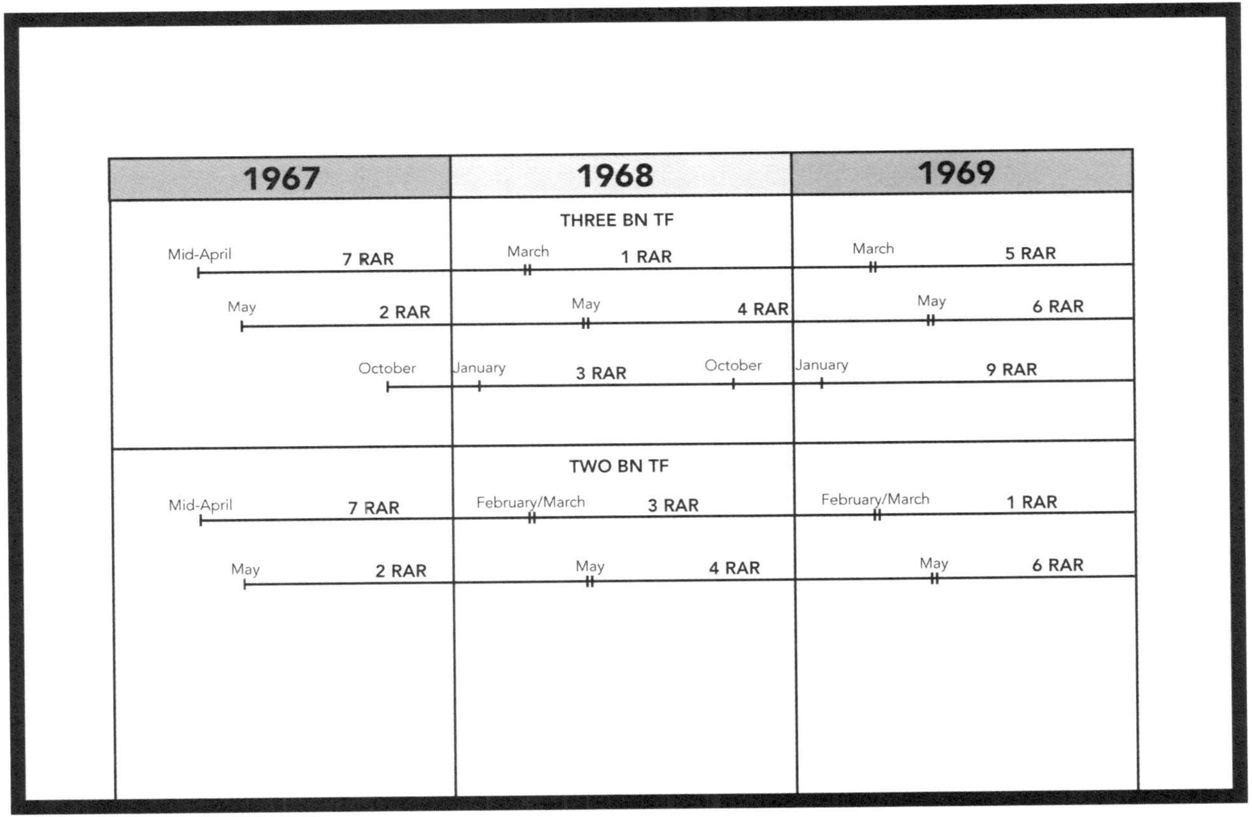

Figure 6.1 Build-up and relief patterns of Australian Force, Vietnam, 1967–69.
Source: Military Board Proceedings, 1967.

on the overall infantry establishment without solving it.[33] The integration of the infantry companies worked very smoothly, although there were occasional problems with the supporting New Zealand artillery battery that was also incorporated into the Task Force.

Relations between the two armies were close, as one might expect. Daly noted the warmth of his reception on an official visit in mid-1968 and the 'wealth of goodwill' that he encountered. He thought that his counterpart, Major-General R.B. Dawson, 'and some of his officers seemed a little on the defensive, and appeared to feel that they were not pulling their full weight as an Anzac partner. This, of course, is a matter of politics and economics and quite beyond their control but in spite of this they seemed quite unnaturally modest, even humble about their contributions in Malaysia and Vietnam.'[34] In Daly's view, however, New Zealand's contribution to 1ATF merely demonstrated again the pressing need for 'a greater degree of uniformity between our Armies', although he recognised at once that this was 'dependent on the New Zealand Government being prepared to make the necessary funds available', and this constituted 'a formidable obstacle'.

There was no single answer to the problems posed in Phuoc Tuy by manning levels and the types of forces deployed, and as such there was no single – much less simple – solution to them. A two-battalion task force was unbalanced, and there was no way round that fact. Increasing the commitment to three battalions would unbalance the army unless an additional infantry battalion was raised in Australia, since a three-battalion commitment implied a nine-battalion force structure such that a complete relief could be accomplished. Additional helicopter crews could be provided from RAAF and RAN resources (the latter despatched crews from the Fleet Air Arm who were integrated into a composite US Army helicopter company, the 135th), but the argument over the army's force increase came down to two fundamental issues: an increase in the numbers of infantry deployed and an increase in the Task Force's operational capability. The former required an additional infantry battalion while the latter involved the commitment of tanks for the first time since the Second World War.

The first step was to raise the overall manpower ceiling from the authorised 41 000 in June 1967 to 45 750 by June 1971; this would enable the raising of 9RAR, and the Minister for the Army, Malcolm Fraser, made the case to Fairhall and the Prime Minister, Harold Holt, in May 1967.[35] As Daly commented to Vincent when responding to the latter's case for the increases, deliberations over the Budget meant he

Photo 28 Chief of the General Staff Lieutenant-General Sir Thomas Daly is greeted by Lieutenant-General Tran Ngoc Tam of the Army of the Republic of Vietnam (ARVN) at Tan Son Nhut airport. (AWM LES/69/0445/VN)

was 'having to fight hard to sustain our current commitments... we are very much over-stretched at the moment and unless we can increase our manpower ceiling we will get into a bigger and bigger muddle as time goes by.'[36] He had already responded to Vincent's request for another battalion following his own visit to the Task Force in March: 'I can give you one if the pressure mounts too much but I cannot sustain it, so leave it as long as you can.'[37] The question of a third battalion was a political one, and it was decided by Cabinet on 6 September 1967 after discussion in the Chiefs of Staff and Defence Committees. Daly had already made the case in a separate submission to the Prime Minister in May in which he commented that if the ceiling increase was approved it could be met 'by a continuation of Regular Army recruiting at current levels' and that this constituted 'the most effective and economic way' of doing so.[38]

Daly in fact had foreseen the requirement to field an additional battalion since returning from his March visit to Phuoc Tuy and, notwithstanding the six months required in the manning and training cycle to ready a battalion for deployment, had already earmarked 3RAR as the additional battalion should one be called for in advance of and in addition to the planned reliefs of 7RAR and 2RAR (by 1RAR and 4RAR respectively) in March and May 1968. This might entail bringing 3RAR's originally anticipated departure forward from March 1968 to, perhaps, October 1967. Once the decision to expand the Task Force was made, moreover, another battalion, 1RAR, would need its training cycle brought forward rapidly if it, too, was to be deployed earlier than originally envisaged. Malcolm Fraser expressed concern that such a move 'could give rise to speculation' (presumably in the press), but the decision to accelerate the battalion's preparation was given by the Prime Minister in an informal discussion 'in the ante-room' of parliament house.[39]

There was a problem, however, in that 3RAR was not yet ready for war. The battalion was based in Adelaide, in Central Command, one of the smaller and more isolated territorial commands. The deployment to Vietnam was scheduled for November–December 1967, but its major pre-deployment exercise – 'Piping Shrike' – in the Shoalwater Bay area in late September revealed deep deficiencies in many areas of the battalion's performance sufficient to demand the close attention of the CGS. In a lengthy and handwritten letter the GOC of the 1st Division and recent former COMAFV, Major-General Ken Mackay, listed the deficiencies and some probable causes. The relative lack of resources in Central Command and the fact that the battalion had not trained at unit level before the exercise explained some things; so, too, did the fact that 'not one of the key officers appeared to have recent Vietnam experience [while] across the board the Bn [battalion] seems to have a below average selection of officers and in many cases the combinations are poor'.[40] The deficiencies were not only within the battalion, however; Mackay noting further that the supporting arms working with them in the exercise – 'guns, armour and APCs [armoured personnel carriers]' – were 'green... which did not help a green Bn'.

Questions were also asked about the suitability of the commanding officer, Lieutenant-Colonel Jim Shelton. Shelton was a gallant officer (who had been awarded the Military Cross in Korea for his actions as a company commander at the battle of Maryang San) and was widely liked. Acknowledging that 'it must have been a depressing experience for a CO to have so very many weaknesses brought out', Mackay reaffirmed that the training process 'was not helped by a number of his officers who are weak' and, that as CO, he 'must make some changes in [company] commands and he should be given a more forceful 2 i/c. (Personally I feel only one of the rifle coy comd passes muster.)' Such changes in key personnel 'together with intensive mentoring and training should see the battalion right'. Daly responded that 'we have done all that can be done at this stage to repair the training deficiencies of 3RAR and I would hope that the next month will see a significant improvement. The weakest of the officers have been replaced' and a mentoring team from the Headquarters 1st Division was working intensively with the remainder.[41] As with the disturbances in the Pacific Islands Regiment in 1957, there was a reluctance to remove a CO whose difficulties were in part systemic and over which he had little or no control. The battalion nonetheless was to be eased into its overseas deployment. Daly informed the new Commander 1ATF, Brigadier R.L. Hughes, that 3RAR 'will have to be handled fairly gently for the first few weeks', while in the planning for its move the battalion was afforded extra 'assistance and guidance in the preparation and despatch of its stores and equipment' by quartermaster cells provided from 5RAR and 6RAR.[42] Writing to COMAFV in late January the following year, Daly expressed himself 'delighted to hear that the arrival of 3RAR and its subsequent absorption into the Force proceeded smoothly'. While following the reports of their early activities 'with great interest', he nonetheless reminded Vincent that 'provided they receive a reasonably graduated introduction to the Vietcong, they will acquit themselves every bit as well as their predecessors', which indeed they duly did.[43]

The expanded task force structure brought the need for a modified program of build-up and relief and the raising of 9RAR to provide balance to the infantry structure of the Regular Army. In effect this would involve raising, training and deploying the battalion in only slightly more than a twelve-month time span. The experience with 3RAR highlighted the need for careful supervision of the new battalion's training; at a meeting to discuss the issues in mid-October 1967 the nomination of the new CO had not yet even been finalised. Lieutenant-Colonel A.L. 'Albie' Morrison was selected, and he and his nucleus staff took up their appointments before Christmas 1967. The progressive establishment of the battalion required most of the regular soldiers to be posted in by March 1968 with their National Service counterparts and remaining personnel taken on strength by June 1968. Deployment overseas on HMAS *Sydney* was assumed for November–December the same year. Infrastructure and facilities were a problem. The shortage of married quarters at Enoggera, Holsworthy and Puckapunyal meant that Woodside, in Adelaide, virtually self-selected as the battalion's new home (because it was vacant now that 3RAR was itself in Vietnam), even though at the same time it presented problems from a training viewpoint of precisely the kind already encountered. The decision was made to transfer 'a hard core of Vietnam veterans' to help alleviate potential training problems rather than posting such men to

5RAR where, as Daly noted, 'there is no immediate need'. Equipment deficiencies would be monitored closely and the training program would see cadre training at JTC, Canungra, in May 1968 with eight weeks of training to be completed there, six weeks given over to unit and Task Force training followed by a battalion exercise at Shoalwater Bay before final administrative preparation for embarkation.[44]

The other major addition to the Task Force's capabilities involved the deployment of tanks. Initially the conventional wisdom, shared by the US Army, was that Vietnam was an unsuitable environment for the operation of medium and heavy armour. In fact, as the US Army's post-war study of the deployment of armour noted, 'Vietnam is not a land totally hostile to armored warfare. When the terrain was examined in detail on the ground, as it was in 1967 by a team of US armor officers, it was found that over 46 per cent of the country could be traversed all year round by armoured vehicles.'[45] The COMAFV, Vincent, requested a reinforced tank squadron for the Task Force in June 1967. He summarised the arguments of a long letter to the Chiefs of Staff Committee in a short paragraph:

> A ground mobile weapon is needed. This weapon should: possess a day and night seeing capability with both black and white light; be capable of firing canister and high explosive rounds; be capable of moving over all nature of terrain, thickly or thinly wooded, with a speed and mobility superior to that of the VC [Viet Cong]; be relatively invulnerable to mines compared with the APC; be capable of withstanding substantial anti-tank fire. In short, the weapon should be a forty to fifty ton medium gun tank.[46]

Tanks provided both a defensive and an offensive capability that the Task Force at that stage lacked, and operations with US armoured units had demonstrated the absolute utility of deploying armour in the fight. As Vincent concluded, 'the medium tank is a two edged weapon; it can be the dominating factor ensuring victory in the infantry "eyeball to eyeball" fight; it can also force [enemy] main force units to flee to such a distance that the contact hinge between them and the provincial/guerrilla forces is certainly weakened and perhaps broken.'

Approval for the deployment of tanks was gained through the Defence Committee. Fairhall asked Daly for an unequivocal assurance that they were needed, which the latter had no hesitation in giving.[47] This was not the end of the matter. The army's Centurion tanks weighed 51 tonnes and were transported to Vietnam on board MV *Jeparit*, a general-purpose bulk carrier subsequently 'taken up from trade' and commissioned as an

RAN vessel. *Jeparit* made twenty-five trips between Australia and Vietnam carrying bulk stores and equipment; Vung Tau had no heavy lift equipment on the pier so on those occasions when Centurions were transported they were taken to and from the US facilities at Cam Ranh Bay.[48] Light armour in the form of the M113 (APC) and its various derivatives had operated within 1ATF from the outset but, however valuable these were, they lacked the mobility, firepower and protection provided by the Centurions. These were drawn from the 1st Armoured Regiment, based at Puckapunyal, and were deployed to Vietnam on a squadron rotation basis – although it took some considerable time to make the initial move of the four troops of C Squadron to Vietnam over the course of 1968.

The initial deployment in February 1968 involved two troops, two bulldozer and two bridge-laying tanks; three tanks had been positioned previously in country as a vehicle reserve while the armoured workshop had a further two recovery vehicles. The army had not deployed armour overseas since the Second World War, and there was some uncertainty about what would be required and how it should be organised. The CO of the Armoured Regiment, Lieutenant-Colonel I.J. Wilton, urged Daly to relieve on a squadron basis in the interests of morale and efficiency: 'a squadron launched into operations must be worked up as a squadron initially in Australia (and this includes training at squadron level with other arms), so that all officers, NCOs and men have trained together and understand each other'.[49] The CGS took the point, noting in reply that he was 'by no means certain that we have the right squadron organisation for Vietnam' but that he had initiated a further study of the issues.[50] He followed up with a letter to COMAFV, who was now Major-General A.L. Macdonald, asking for his views 'on the ultimate composition of the Armoured Squadron... as a result of your experiences to date and of further operations which may be undertaken before the wet season'.[51] The resultant report, forwarded to Daly in October, confirmed the efficacy of deploying tanks and the wisdom of the decision to do so. C Squadron's vehicles had 'been used on most operations [and] both in attack and defence the squadron has provided a significant contribution to the Force by the effective use of its firepower'. They were, MacDonald concluded, 'an asset of considerable value'. Daly noted to the Minister for the Army that 'in view of the controversy which was aroused by the proposal to introduce tanks into the theatre, and the support given to the proposal by the Minister for Defence, you may care to send him a copy'.[52] The tanks provided outstanding operational support until they departed in

September 1971 as part of the phased withdrawal of Australian forces. Some APCs remained until the Australian base area at Nui Dat was closed in March 1972.

The decisions concerning the placement of 1ATF in Phuoc Tuy province were made by Wilton, as were the decisions to place the 1st Australian Logistic Support Group (1ALSG) at Vung Tau and the 1ATF base at Nui Dat.[53] Vung Tau sat at the end of a peninsula, which meant that if things went bad the force – or the surviving parts of it – could be withdrawn by sea; the position also meant that the logistic build-up avoided the need to go upriver to the port of Saigon. Otherwise it had little to recommend it; it was sandy, open and windswept and required great quantities of engineering stores and construction work to turn it into an operable base. The RAE corps history summarises the challenges succinctly:

> Many of the early difficulties stemmed from the lack of a first key plan and the poor planning associated with the original deployment which adversely affected the ability of the sapper units to commence work until their equipment arrived. The area to be developed consisted of a series of sand dunes and low scrub and had been used at various times as a temporary transit area by US forces. It was dirty and covered with debris from previous occupation. Apart from one road cutting through the dunes it was undeveloped. The Vung Tau area has little or no rain from October to April and heavy southwest monsoon rains from May to August. On the back beach the worst period was in the dry season when the fine dune sand was stirred up by the northeast winds, seriously interfering with all activities, making life uncomfortable for soldiers and damaging equipment in use or parked in the open.[54]

The shortages and delays were exacerbated and mutually reinforced by the need also to construct facilities at Nui Dat, a decision that was criticised at the time and subsequently because of the demands it made on manpower resources to build, maintain and defend. As Daly remarked, 'once we were on Nui Dat, once we began to develop it, it just grew. And the more it grew the more we were stuck with it.'[55] The shortages within construction engineer units meant that sleeping accommodation at Nui Dat remained in tents, reducing the call on engineer resources 'as well as giving more protection' in the event of rocket or mortar attacks. But construction work at Vung Tau lagged through 1967, with Vincent noting that until it was 'in a stable condition the installations are not able to function efficiently with economy'.⁵⁶

The maintenance of two permanent bases led to duplication and wasted effort. Nui Dat was centrally located within the province but difficult to defend. ('On the face of it', said Daly, 'it was fairly easily defensible – in fact it wasn't – but looking at it in terms of a small force going in there, it could have been quite defensible.')⁵⁷ Vung Tau was a much easier and more formidable defensive option but was tucked in a corner of the province. Although Australian units would operate outside Phuoc Tuy at times, especially during 1968, the Task Force essentially remained anchored in the province. A suggestion made to Daly and Wilton on one of their visits that it might have been employed in the northern provinces with the US III Marine Expeditionary Force near the De-Militarised Zone was 'purely a kite, it was a straw in the wind – there was no substance to it and it never got off the ground'.⁵⁸ Given the tenor of the times and the political sensitivities of the war, it was 'inevitable' in Daly's view that 'we developed a Rolls Royce type base' with levels of amenity such as beer supplies and leave centres, 'which wouldn't have happened in, say, a campaign in World War II, where you would have lived in a hard-arsed sort of way and done the best you could'. The establishment of the logistic support area was improvised in the early days, however, with confusion on the docks at Vung Tau and difficulties in locating stores and equipment that had, in fact, been shipped to Vietnam, largely as a result of the short lead times in planning 'what was quite a substantial complex expedition'.⁵⁹ Notwithstanding the eventual size and diversity of the base at Vung Tau and the numerous support activities of 1ALSG, the Australians were still forced to rely on the Americans at times for various types of supply and support.

Vietnam is sometimes characterised as the 'helicopter war', reflecting the development and influence of the 'airmobility' concept in the US Army from the late 1950s, which received its first full testing during the 1960s.⁶⁰ Helicopter support of 1ATF was a fraught issue informed by the periodic fights in Canberra over the acquisition of an army aviation capability and the development of the Aviation Corps, as we have seen. These organisational squabbles did not originate over the apparent problems in army–RAAF cooperation in Phuoc Tuy province, but certainly came to be informed and influenced by them to such an extent that they continued to resonate in the 1980s when ownership of the new generation of tactical helicopters – the Black Hawk – was decided on by the Chiefs of Staff Committee.

The main workhorse of the helicopter war was the Iroquois – more properly the Bell UH-1, colloquially the 'Huey' – in all its models and variants. It entered general service with the US Army in 1962. The Australian Cabinet approved its acquisition the same year for service with the RAAF but as a battlefield helicopter to support ground operations. The Chief of the Air Staff, Air Marshal Sir Valston Hancock, was entirely uninterested in supporting the army and refused several requests for training support and for the deployment of the Iroquois of No 5 Squadron to Borneo in an operational role in 1964.[61] The helicopters that went to Phuoc Tuy were part of No 9 Squadron, eight aircraft with six on line at any time. When he was CGS, Wilton had suggested in August 1965 that the RAAF should send two aircraft and crew to operate with a US unit to gain experience in the tactics and techniques of airmobile operations. The CAS, who was now Air Marshal Alister Murdoch, again refused. Wilton's tersely pointed rejoinder summed up the poor relationship between the two services at the top and reflected the frustration and irritation that would manifest itself in Vietnam in 1966–67: 'Since the Iroquois helicopter was purchased primarily to provide support for the Army, I consider that the sooner they begin to learn how to provide this support in an operational situation the better.'[62] His request for the RAAF to reconsider its position was ignored. 'I believe that such action would be inadvisable', Murdoch minuted back. 'The experience to be gained in present conditions is doubtful and the complications of control would be difficult.'[63]

Daly's view of the attitudes at the senior level of the RAAF was pertinent: they had 'been brought up on victory through air power... there are some who would say that you can win a war without successful operations on land.'[64] The air power historian Alan Stephens has described the early months of RAAF–army interaction in Vietnam as 'an interservice disaster' and asserts bluntly that No 9 Squadron 'was not prepared for war when it arrived in South Vietnam'.[65] One officer at Headquarters 1ATF characterised relations as marked by 'conflict, friction, antagonism, ill-will, lack of cooperation... It was really very, very bad.'[66] Australian army officers looked at the American system with envy: army crew flying army helicopters in direct support of army operations (the US Army had felt the same way about US Marine Corps air support to Marine ground units during the Korean War). Daly's perspective was doubtless that of many army officers at the time:

you had a situation where the Army believed they knew a damn sight more about operating helicopters than the Air Force by virtue of their experience with the Americans, and the Air Force who had restrictive directives from their own Department of Air as to what the rules were. They were operating on much the same basis as aircraft or air support has always operated – that was that the army asked for a task to be done, described the task, and the air force decided whether in fact it could be done and if done, how.[67]

The Air Staff in Australia, on the other hand, appeared to look upon the American example with disdain: 'The US tactics employed in Vietnam for the use of Iroquois helicopters are unacceptable to the Air Staff' summed up the position pithily.[68] No one has ever suggested that the problem was with the pilots or crews, whose courage and skill was widely acknowledged. Historian Ian McNeill points out that 'few in the Air Force even understood the requirements of the helicopter' and, at senior levels, had never evinced any desire to learn. A perfect example of the 'peacetime mentality' that ruled in the Air Board was provided by the Minister for Air, Peter Howson: 'we heard that three Iroquois helicopters have had engine trouble seriously, two of them in Vietnam. This means that we have grounded all the helicopters for the time being until we find the cause.'[69] The situation was so bad that in early 1967 Army Headquarters was trying to obtain 'drawings of the Iroquois UH1D helicopter as used by US forces in Vietnam so that we can have mock-ups made for training'.[70]

This situation did not last, and it needs to be reiterated that the helicopter support given by No 9 Squadron was generally exemplary, especially after the number of aircraft was doubled to sixteen in July 1968. In addition, the posting of RAN pilots to the squadron and the creation of the US Army's composite 135th Assault Helicopter Company jointly with RAN personnel, and which flew regularly in support of the Task Force, helped to break down the early, 'restrictive practices' attitude that prevailed in 1966. From a 'whole of war' perspective Daly, again, undoubtedly reflected the views of many army personnel: 'I would think there were more difficulties in Canberra than there were in Saigon; there were more difficulties in Saigon than there were in Nui Dat; and there were more in Nui Dat than there were out in places like Xuan Loc and Long Tan where the operations were taking place.'[71] Between 1967 and 1969 the army also attached a small number of army pilots to US Army aviation units in both helicopter and command or liaison fixed-wing aircraft.[72]

Senior army officers were frustrated by the apparent lack of RAAF performance precisely because they appreciated the tremendous advantages that rotary-wing aviation presented in support of the ground war in Vietnam. In his lengthy report on the Task Force sent to Daly in July 1967, Vincent made a number of observations along these lines. The RAAF squadron (effectively at this stage a half squadron) was 'light on' for crews and maintenance men, and additional personnel were needed since 'the use of helicopters rises with activity... I consider that the quick responsive airlift and associated gunships should be of company lift size and anything less is not making the best use of the troops or the opportunity to exploit success.' The SAS had enjoyed some notable successes on recent operations 'but we do not have the Iroquois lift and gunships' to increase the number and range of such operations.[73]

The following month Vincent, as COMAFV, attended the British Army exercise 'Unison' and briefed the conference on helicopter use in the Task Force. His comments received a hostile reaction from the senior RAF members present ('it was made clear that the RAF were not prepared to entertain any lessons from Vietnam that were contrary to their current views and that was that'), but in response to questioning from the British CGS, Field Marshal Sir James Cassels, Vincent responded that 'the most singularly significant weapon in the Vietnam War' was the helicopter gunship.[74] In response to his earlier request Daly was able to reply that the extra RAAF crews, together with the RAN crews operating with the 135th AHC, 'will provide 1ATF with an additional capacity for immediate response'.[75]

However much the CAS, Murdoch, irritated Daly with his attitudes and seemingly wilful lack of cooperation, the CGS was nonetheless active in seeking RAAF input to the army's deliberations. This was clearly demonstrated at the annual CGS Exercise in August 1968 at which the AOC Support Command, Air Vice-Marshal Colin Hannah, was the senior RAAF officer at the head of a 'strong' representation of air force officers. In Daly's view this was 'a great step forward... [and] I hope that perhaps next year it may be even stronger, if only for the purpose of enabling people to get alongside each other and talk to each other for a week. I know you will agree with me that we are still only scratching the surface of this problem. We have a long way to go but at least we have made a start.'[76]

Like Vincent, Daly had become a great proponent of armed helicopters, 'gunships' in Vietnam parlance to distinguish them from the troop-carrying helicopters, or 'slicks'. The Chiefs of Staff Committee had looked at the provision of an aerial fire support system for the army in

1966, and the request was examined in turn by the Land/Air Warfare Committee and the Joint Warfare Committee in the course of 1966–67. The Chiefs of Staff requested expediting of the matter in July 1968, and Daly found himself writing to Murdoch in April 1969 with the findings of a further army report on the provision of aerial fire support and the request for the inclusion of gunships in the RAAF's equipment acquisition program.

The Chiefs of Staff recommendation had included the purchase of four 'gunship kits' to modify existing Iroquois frames – three for use in Vietnam and one in Australia for training purposes.[77] By April 1969 the kits had been purchased but had yet to be fitted to aircraft serving with 1ATF. Daly wrote that he 'regarded the purchase of these gunship kits as a stop-gap to meet an immediate operational need', and his irritation at the repeated delays imposed in consideration of the gunship issue was clear. Furthermore, the RAAF 'shopping list' of equipment acquisitions forwarded to the Chiefs of Staff Committee in February 1969 (i.e. more than two years after the committee had first considered the matter) 'makes no provision for gunships'. Gunship kits of the kind purchased (but not yet utilised) were designed for older-model aircraft and did not in any case meet the army's requirements as repeatedly defined.[78] Additionally, the modified Iroquois would involve the diversion 'of our meagre stocks of troop-carrying helicopters from their primary role', hence the need for acquiring purpose-designed gunships such as the Huey Cobra. The converted helicopters, designated 'Bushrangers', gave good service once the conversion was actually undertaken, further emphasising the need for such a capability. Daly made the point to Murdoch again in May; the three-battalion Task Force then operating in Phuoc Tuy needed a capacity to lift a company group at a time 'in order to function effectively'. 'I would emphasise the need', he wrote, 'for the acquisition of gunships and medium lift helicopters to be expedited in order that the Iroquois type helicopters may be reverted to their normal role. Until medium lift helicopters become available, a company group lift will not be attainable.'[79] Murdoch clearly regarded the army's needs with contempt, privately advising his staff that anything the army needed had a lower priority 'than anything we now have on our "shopping list"'.[80] That disregard for the army's needs was reflected right back: the acting Deputy CAS responded that he could not understand 'how the acquisition of gunships and medium lift helicopters will alter the current position in Vietnam'.[81]

The command relationships for Vietnam were complex, and evolving; Horner has shown how Wilton as chairman of the Chiefs of Staff attempted to persuade the government of the need for more sophisticated joint machinery precisely as a result of the unsatisfactory nature of the command arrangements with which he had to work.[82] Some of this was aided (and, depending on your point of view, some hindered) by the new secretary of the Department of Defence, Sir Henry Bland, who assumed the role in January 1968. Bland had spent a long period as secretary of the Department of Labour and National Service, was strongly of the view that the Defence Department was dysfunctional, and had the backing of the minister, Fairhall.[83] What Defence really needed was the kind of root-and-branch reorganisation that the Morshead Committee had recommended in 1957 but which Menzies had declined to act upon and of the kind that Arthur Tange would institute when he became secretary in succession to Bland. Daly thought Bland both tough and charming by turns, but that his lack of background in Defence was reflected in his apparent belief that the CGS was akin to the general manager of a large corporation.[84]

The lack of coherent command arrangements helps to explain the most significant mistake of the Australian conduct of the war in Phuoc Tuy: the construction of the barrier minefield. The subject itself is something of a minefield, one that arouses intense feeling on both sides of the argument.[85] Briefly, the minefield was Graham's response as 1ATF's commander to the problem and limitations posed by a two-battalion task force. The operations officer on the headquarters, (then) Major S.J. Maizey, observes that 'our first option was not the minefield, but for additional troops and tanks. This request was rejected by Army headquarters in Australia.' Maizey wrote the appreciation for Graham, and the decisions surrounding the minefield were made in conjunction with the Vietnamese province chief and his US adviser. Maizey had an engineering background, had served in Korea after the ceasefire in 1953 and had been second-in-command of 5RAR in 1966, including six months during the battalion's first tour in Vietnam. He was well aware of the problems posed by establishing the minefield, and had a close and personal experience of operational conditions in Phuoc Tuy at the time. The purpose of the minefield was to protect the rice harvest and the population, especially around Xuyen Moc, which had been isolated from the enemy. Maizey notes that his appreciation 'considered the need to protect the locals; prevent free movement of the VC; cut off the VC sources of money, food and information; force the VC to react to our activity rather than vice versa. We found troops to task impossible to reconcile.'[86] Vincent observed to Daly that 'our task is to keep the enemy from filtering back down to the population, and we set up Horseshoe Hill and built the wire and mine barrier to assist in this purpose'.[87] The intelligence officer of 5RAR, Captain R.J. O'Neill, noted of the arrangement that 'A barrier fence and minefield would present a formidable obstacle, provided that it was patrolled daily to check for breaches or attempted breaches. The patrolling commitment required for the maintenance of the fence and minefield would be far less than the activity needed to close the area off entirely by a moving fence of men.'[88] Maizey (and, by extension, Graham) fully appreciated this point, and the eastern side of the minefield was to be patrolled by a specific ARVN unit designated for the purpose and in place by April 1967.[89] In fact, 5RAR incurred casualties in an incident on 9 March 1969 at RF (Regional Forces) Company Post 609; briefly, the Australians were fired upon by Vietnamese soldiers as they, inexplicably, proceeded to move through a section of the minefield for which the RF Company was responsible.[90]

To be successful the minefield and fence needed to be covered by fire and actively patrolled, and this was where the process broke down. Maizey notes further that 'after Op Portsea patrolling took place on the eastern side of the minefield by the Australians and the western side by the ARVN. Route 23 was reopened to Xuyen Moc. At every opportunity battalion activities took place in the Long Green.' During Graham's tour in command the Task Force was not to operate outside Phuoc Tuy, but when he was succeeded by Brigadier R.L. Hughes this changed and much of the Australian force was moved north, for a time. As Maizey, again, comments, 'it was only when we [the Australians] failed to honour our agreement to patrol the eastern side that trouble began. The VC were able to approach the outer edge and lift the mines because we were not doing our agreed task.'[91] The consequence was that the enemy was able to infiltrate the minefield, lift a significant number of mines (a reliable estimate suggests as many as 3000 of the 22 000 sown) and use them against the Australians (and, presumably, others), inflicting a significant proportion of the casualties in 1ATF as a result.[92]

Wilton and Daly had both served in Korea and understood the uses and hazards of mines; Graham and Vincent had not, although this is scarcely definitive. Maizey comments that 'Commanders at all levels above the Task Force were informed of the plan – and none objected', and this is clearly the case.[93] As Horner states baldly, the minefield 'raised serious questions about who was responsible for approving it, and particularly the extent to which higher commanders should become involved in tactical decisions'. He concludes: 'Although it is easy to be wise later, Vincent, Daly and Wilton had all acquiesced in Graham's decision, and must share at least some of the responsibility.'[94] The problem was not possession of some sort of 'imperial mindset', but rather observance of the principle that the tactical commander should be trusted to make decisions on the ground without undue interference from above.[95] The high-level micromanagement of any and every issue through the minister's office that too often characterises operational and administrative issues in the Australian Defence Force today was largely unknown in the 1960s. Daly enunciated his command philosophy in this regard quite clearly: 'It's very easy to reach... decisions at a distance of 6000 miles without considering all the factors involved; and the commander on the spot has got to be given credit for being a highly professional officer who is there, who understands the situation, who is absolutely infused with the environment and the atmosphere and who knows what has to be done – and what's more he has to take some very courageous moral decisions.'[96]

It is worth noting in passing that the enemy recognised the minefield and fence as a significant threat intended 'to cut our liaison corridor... in order to enable the puppet army [i.e. ARVN] and authorities to carry out pacification in the strategic hamlets'.[97] This was precisely Graham's intent as he made clear in a later minute to the secretary of the Department of the Army, Bruce White: 'I was not naive enough', he wrote, 'to think that the fence would prevent infiltration of the VC... The basic purpose of the fence was to control the previously unrestricted flow of supplies by vehicle, oxcart and sampan, by channelling their movement through a few check points'.[98] Horner again has noted 'the absence of any strong direction being given to the fighting in Vietnam',[99] itself a consequence of the ill-defined roles and relationships between the chiefs of staff, the Defence Committee, individual ministers and senior officials. Soldiers paid the price.

Daly felt all the casualties in 1ATF keenly and was always sensitive to the risks that his soldiers ran. 'It's not easy to order an operation which you know is going to be sticky, difficult and dangerous and you don't do it unless you feel it's absolutely necessary.'[100] He could not share the risks his soldiers ran directly, but he made certain that he had a firsthand feel for the conditions they faced and the broader political and allied environment in which they operated. Notwithstanding that he had continuous access to 'fine intelligence reports' from a variety of Australian and US sources, he visited Vietnam twice a year throughout his tenure as CGS, usually spending a week to ten days there. Clearly he found the visits informative, as he noted in a letter to A.L. MacDonald. The more often he visited Vietnam 'and the better I get to know the various key figures, the easier it is to talk with them and, by and large, the more

Photo 29 The CGS talks to a soldier from 6RAR manning the perimeter of Fire Support Base Discovery, November 1969. (AWM BEL/69/0808/VN)

profitable it becomes. I think I finished with a sound impression of the over-all situation, and most of the points I made to my masters on my return have since been confirmed from other sources.'[101] He had found this particular visit especially useful because it enabled him to

> dispel some of the scepticism that exists in quite surprising places concerning the results of the Tet offensive, but it is remarkable how difficult it is to persuade otherwise reasonable and responsible citizens that the Americans are not entirely a pack of blundering amateurs. This idea is a fixation with my World War II contemporaries and is the result of a deep prejudice originating in the New Guinea campaigns, some queer ideas on the kind of war being fought in Vietnam, and some very loose thinking on how to deal with an insurgent situation.[102]

As well as spending time with the units of the Task Force, he made a point of travelling around Vietnam to see members of the Training Team, who were scattered in small detachments all over Vietnam working within the US advisory effort with the South Vietnamese (visits that were greatly facilitated by access to US aircraft to get him to the more isolated posts). This gave him a much wider perspective on the war than was possible in Phuoc Tuy alone or receiving briefings in Saigon and made him (along with Wilton) one of the best informed Australians where the progress of the wider war was concerned. He also met officials and other senior figures on both the US and Vietnamese sides; the latter, he felt, tended to give 'optimistic appraisals of operations and outcomes. One could be sceptical, but one didn't have any solid evidence to dispute their appreciation in a quick visit there.'[103] On the other hand, after visiting in late 1969 he wrote to COMUSMACV, who was now General Creighton W. Abrams, that he had found 'the situation in Vietnam more encouraging than on any of my previous visits',[104] as a result of the greater emphasis on pacification in the countryside and the undoubted blows that the enemy's main force units had suffered in the fighting in the first half of the previous year.

The visits were physically demanding, as consideration of one such schedule demonstrates. On his first visit as CGS, in September 1966, he flew via Singapore (in the days before 747s or A380s) to the enormous military air base at Tan Son Nhut, just outside Saigon. He went straight to a briefing at Headquarters AFV, thence to a series of meetings with senior Vietnamese figures such as the Foreign Minister, the Prime Minister, Nguyen Cao Ky and the chairman of the National Leadership Committee (aka the President), Nguyen Van Thieu, before a reception hosted by COMAFV. The following morning involved a call on the Australian ambassador before leaving Saigon to spend the day with the Task Force. Another day followed with 1ALSG and the RAAF at Vung Tau before flying to Da Nang by US aircraft and a round of meetings, briefings and field visits with the US Commanding General of I Corps, III Marine Amphibious Force and the 3rd US Marine Division. From there he visited the local AATTV personnel and US 5th Special Forces Group. The last full day in country was spent at An Khe with the US 1st Cavalry Division (Airmobile) before returning to Saigon, a further meeting with COMAFV, then departure from Saigon. Travel within Vietnam was largely by jeep, car or helicopter. All this in seven days, and with just one 40-minute period designated 'free time' while in Da Nang.[105]

His visits to the war were obviously an important part of staying in the picture, supplemented by the regular reports and often very frank personal

Photo 30 The CGS talks to soldiers from C Company, 7RAR at the Horseshoe, 1970. (Author's collection)

letters he received, and sent, to successive Australian commanders in Vietnam. The CGS was not the only visitor the Task Force and other components received, of course, and Daly was careful not to be thought to intrude too closely into his subordinates' command space. Following the Tet offensive he wrote to MacDonald that he had 'not intended coming up until later but in view of the goings-on in the past month I think it is high time one of the chair-bound warriors appeared on the scene'.[106] As well as the various ministers, successive prime ministers and senior service officers, Australian Force Vietnam received a galaxy of other visitors including journalists and occasional academics whose visits at least to the Australian units and areas were fairly tightly controlled. Sometimes Daly would interpose on the latter's behalf, as with a visit soon after the Tet offensive by the noted historian of counterinsurgency, Geoffrey Fairbairn of ANU. Daly signalled the then Australian commander that Fairbairn's 'views on [South-East Asia] are very sane and his writings in the more serious journals do something to offset the lunatic hallucinations of the daily press which have achieved transcendental levels in the past week. Please help him if you can.'[107] During his own visits, Daly eschewed formal press conferences either on arrival or departure or upon his return to Australia, seeking rather to stress 'that his visit is routine'. On the other hand, 'CGS has no intention of avoiding press and will talk to them informally if interview is sought'.[108] His final visit to 1ATF took place in April 1971, just weeks before his retirement.[109]

Daly was not enamoured of the press, at least when it came to its treatment of the army and the war. Neither were many of his ministers or his predecessor, Wilton. In early 1966 the latter noted that the emerging problem of press coverage 'stemmed from the present environment in which the army was called upon to conduct operations under the spotlight of public interest. In this unique situation the army had to observe security but there was no real censorship of reports or comments. The whole army must therefore be made PR conscious and aware that all its actions had both PR and political implications.'[110]

Individual journalists were another matter, especially those whom Daly had known for years – in some cases going back to the Second World War as war correspondents. John Hetherington, who was at that time with the *Age* in Melbourne, had been a correspondent in North Africa and Europe and wrote to Daly (on a first-name basis) in late 1966 suggesting an interview, 'something authoritative and coherent about the Vietnam war from the military viewpoint'.[111] Daly saw the merit in the proposal – 'an authoritative and coherent up-to-date statement might be of considerable use to many people who unquestionably support involvement but who have vague misgivings as to where we are going' – but, in the aftermath of the reporting of Bruce White's remarks, 'the Government has some misgivings about officials bursting into print on controversial subjects such as this', and so declined.[112] White's mild and well-informed criticisms of some aspects of US conduct of the war had attracted press attention, although he himself suffered no penalty as a result. Even fairly innocuous and balanced comment could expose sensitivities in ministers like Malcolm Fraser.[113]

Daly saw his major role as being 'the overall organisation of the effort for Vietnam, of which I suppose the most important part was to try to keep the government off the soldier's back'.[114] The government 'was extraordinarily sensitive to any kind of criticism of the administration of the army that affected national servicemen', and this made life difficult the longer the war went on and the more controversy and opposition it elicited at home. The CGS was clearly increasingly frustrated by the climate of domestic opinion and the fact that in many respects the government ceded the argument to the opponents of the war and Australian involvement; there was in no sense an information campaign aimed at informing the electorate about what Australian soldiers were actually doing (some things don't change). The activities of 1ATF tended to hit the front pages only when they incurred casualties while the main picture of the war conveyed through the media was of the US and South Vietnamese. In part the army itself was to blame for this, since it imposed extensive restrictions on journalists' freedom of movement in the 1ATF area that were in marked (although not necessarily unfavourable) contrast to the extreme *laissez-faire* regulations overseen by the US forces. Daly's feelings were made clear, however, in a letter to Air Chief Marshal Sir Frederick Scherger, Wilton's predecessor as chairman of the Chiefs of Staff and now in an active retirement; greater restrictions on press comment 'would not only relieve me of some of my worries but would allow the Australian soldier to feel that he could get on with his task without being kicked in the guts and stabbed in the back by a few of his fellow countrymen'.[115]

Press reportage of Vietnam in Australia has received insufficient attention from historians.[116] Denis Warner, noted journalist with many years experience as a war correspondent and with extensive knowledge of South-East Asia, wrote in 1969 that 'the Australian government needed an informed public [but] it deliberately sought to seal off the channels of information to the point where Australian soldiers, with important stories to tell, were afraid to speak'. Analyst Trish Payne confirms the point: 'officially, no Australian military commander was allowed to speak to the press without permission... Even Sir Thomas Daly spoke of the personal public restrictions he himself faced.'[117] Daly's own feelings were mirrored by one Australian correspondent, Hugh Lunn, who covered the war for Reuters in 1967–68. 'I was isolated by my consuming interest in a subject that rarely entered the thoughts of people in Australia,' he later wrote. 'What was even worse was their ignorance.'[118]

Daly's motivation was always the interests of his soldiers and his army, which was reflected in a letter to Sir William Morrow, leading physician and president of the Australia Club who had served in the Middle East and the Pacific during the Second World War. The letter was prompted by the imminence of Anzac Day. 'In World War II we were virtually all in it and there was no dissension at home', Daly wrote. 'This made a great difference. The surprising thing is that the nonsense that goes on back here, the politics and the moratoriums etc, don't seem to register to any extent in Vietnam. There, values are more obvious and the perspective very much clearer.'[119]

Before his term as CGS ended Daly would be thrust into the middle of a political crisis that was both caused by and was a reflection of the disfunctionality of the higher political and military relationships and structures with which Australia fought the war in Vietnam.

CHAPTER 7

THE CIVIC ACTION
CRISIS, 1971

Like many soldiers before and since, Daly believed firmly that a national government should not commit the armed forces to war unless they were willing to win it. 'You should never get involved in a war that you don't intend to win', he stated, and a war could not be won 'on the defensive'. Like many critics of Australian involvement, he came to the view that Australia had no direct strategic interest in Vietnam and that Australia's contribution was 'very minor' in comparison with the vast forces fielded by the Americans and the South Vietnamese themselves.[1] The progress in Phuoc Tuy itself was clear enough, with the enemy presence (or, at least, enemy activity) having fallen away 'to fairly negligible proportions' towards the end of the Australians' time there, at least according to the intelligence briefs provided to the Chief of the General Staff.[2] (In point of fact this was not entirely true, and the movement of elements of the North Vietnamese 33rd Regiment into the province in the course of 1971 led to some serious fighting. Daly's more conservative reading of the situation was, in fact, more accurate.) Australian policy in Vietnam was reactive, in the sense that its primary drivers had always been the US alliance and decision-making in Washington (rather than in Saigon) and, with Richard Nixon becoming President on a platform of 'peace with honor' (and disengagement from the war), Australian policy faced some sharp, although entirely predictable, challenges.[3]

Timed to the US presidential election, in November 1968 the Joint Staff had been tasked with a study of the implications of withdrawal. Wilton had made the 'lock step' nature of Australian planning clear in his discussions with US General Abrams in Saigon during a visit in October: 'our decisions are dependent on US decisions and . . . it was essential that we be kept informed and consulted before decisions were made'.[4] The second problem concerned the nature of any withdrawal: immediate or phased? The Australian Task Force had been built up in phases (although, as we have seen, this was not the most desirable way to achieve the outcome intended) and was now a balanced and self-contained force. The arguments that had been made in favour of a three-battalion structure presumably meant that reducing 1ATF to a two-battalion structure again were, at least, undesirable. Daly and Wilton, on behalf of the chiefs of staff, advised the government in December that in the circumstances 'and as long as the current level of enemy activity continues and their capability to launch large-scale attacks anywhere in South Vietnam remains – which is likely until Hanoi agrees to a mutual withdrawal – we consider that a balanced three-battalion Task Force is required in Phuoc Tuy province. We therefore could not make progressive reductions to match progressive American withdrawals and maintain our present deployment without endangering our forces.'[5] While stating that 'prospects for an agreement are not good', the Chiefs of Staff Committee also noted that 'Vietnamisation' was an uneven process and that a withdrawal of US and allied forces would leave '171 RVNAF [Republic of Vietnam Armed Forces] battalions [with] sole responsibility for tasks at present undertaken by them plus 100 Free World/United States battalions'. Daly's considered view was simply that 'there was no way that the [South] Vietnamese could conduct the war on their own'.[6]

The chiefs of staff initially recommended no reduction, but Daly subsequently altered his view to favour a phased withdrawal, partly in response to intelligence briefings that showed the enemy threat to Phuoc Tuy to be less than he had thought, and partly due to 'political pressure'.

> The Americans were reducing gradually on a phased withdrawal. They had no choice because their force was so large it would have been a logistic impossibility for it to be withdrawn other than over a period of time. I think that politically it was felt that it would be undesirable for us to run out and leave the Americans still withdrawing on a phased programme: it was equally undesirable politically to leave our whole force in the theatre, while the Americans were withdrawing.[7]

In April 1970 the Prime Minister announced the decision that 8RAR would complete its tour in November and would not be replaced. Some difficult decisions followed.[8] Rather than pulling the Task Force back from Nui Dat and creating a garrison force in Vung Tau 'protecting itself and its base and not doing much else', as Daly put it, responsibilities within the province were reconfigured. Phuoc Tuy was divided into two operational areas, east and west, and a battalion was assigned to each; this 'allowed each battalion to build an intimate knowledge of the ground and establish firm relationships with its corresponding district officials'.[9] Reflecting the new political realities of winding down the war – or at least, the US part in it – in April 1969 the US commander of II Field Force, Lieutenant-General Julian J. Ewell, directed COMAFV to focus on pacification and Vietnamisation tasks within Phuoc Tuy. This was further underpinned by the 1970 operational plan issued by Abrams in late 1969, and which emphasised as its primary tasks: (a) participation in the 1970 South Vietnam Government Pacification and Development Plan; (b) organise, train, equip and modernise RVNAF to achieve a maximum state of combat effectiveness; (c) employ RVNAF in accordance with their assigned missions and capabilities; and (d) replace, on a selective basis, regular force units assigned to Pacification and Static Territorial Security Missions, with regional forces.[10] At the same time the decision was conveyed to COMAFV that Australian activities were to be confined to Phuoc Tuy, meaning no further 'out-of-province' operations,[11] while the training team was expanded and consolidated in the province and given a series of training missions with Regional Force/Popular Force (RF/PF personnel) and, subsequently, with the Khmer military, the *Forces Armée Nationale Khmer*.[12]

Daly had been very much in two minds about a phased drawdown even as he accepted the political necessity. The concentration of Task Force activities within the province proved highly successful, which was as well because he felt that the alternatives were unpalatable:

> if we had to withdraw somebody, I was in favour of it being the Civic Action people rather than the combat troops... it wouldn't have made any sense to have withdrawn the combat troops and left the civic action elements unprotected; it would be the same as leaving the Training Team exposed – although the Training Team was more secure than the Civic Action Teams. It was at least attached to South Vietnamese military units whereas the civic action Teams were operating to a large extent in unprotected hamlets.[13]

The criticism of the army's position on withdrawal from within the Prime Minister's Department – that it was 'argumentative, impudent and in some sense wilful' and that 'it is [the] prospect of losing face in dealing with the problems of [the] province that the military are most deeply concerned about' – was grossly unfair to Daly and the Military Board. It also suggested that the rest of government was ignorant and out of touch with Australia's war effort in Vietnam.[14]

'Civic action' or 'civil affairs' was the mechanism through which the Task Force organised its pacification tasks within Phuoc Tuy. Australian thinking and practice in this area owed a great deal, at least initially, to experience of the 'hearts and minds' approach in Malaya during the Emergency. The effort in 1ATF began in 1966 with a civil affairs section which, while it did its best, was overwhelmed by the extent and volume of tasks facing it. As Brigadier Graham recorded in January 1967, 'there is a tremendous amount of work to be done in the civil affairs field. With our present resources and limited finance we are barely scratching the surface of the problem.'[15] The creation of the 1st Australian Civil Affairs Unit (1ACAU) followed shortly thereafter. The unit's tasking came from the senior province adviser, however, who was an American officer, and civil affairs activities were not really focused as a result until the shift in emphasis in US conduct of the war under Creighton Abrams from 1969, although it also enjoyed close links operationally with Task Force headquarters. Teams from 1ACAU worked at the local and district level building infrastructure and facilities, making medical and dental visits and generally assisting the South Vietnamese Government in its pacification efforts. Its structure included engineer, medical, agriculture, education and liaison detachments and also coordinated civic action efforts by other units elsewhere in country. All of this was in keeping with Australian doctrine as enunciated in the relevant 'counter-revolutionary warfare' pamphlet issued through Army Headquarters.[16] The Military Board had confirmed the importance of civic action in early 1966 when Wilton emphasised that it went 'hand in hand with operations'.[17]

Fairhall retired from parliament at the election in October 1969, and Gorton appointed Malcolm Fraser to succeed him in the Defence portfolio in November. Daly and Fraser had enjoyed a good relationship when the latter was Minister for the Army, and during that period the minister had taken an increasingly close interest in civic action as a concept and an activity.[18] Fraser's style then had been to demand more and more information in a quicker manner, a characteristic he continued when he moved to the Education and Science portfolio thereafter. As Army minister he issued a monthly statement on army activities in Vietnam (750 copies distributed to MPs, the press gallery and Australian diplomatic posts overseas), most of which was devoted to civic action operations. At the minister's direction, in mid-1968 the Military Board requested that the despatch of information to be fed into these statements was to be sped up.[19] This put additional pressure on the staff process for no obvious operational purpose other than to satisfy the minister's desire to appear in control.

That characteristic had not changed with Fraser's elevation to a senior ministerial role, but a number of other things had. Bland had retired as secretary of the Department of Defence and been replaced by Sir Arthur Tange in March 1970. Tange and Fraser saw eye to eye on a great many matters, while Tange was to be regarded in some uniformed quarters as a 'prince of darkness' figure because of the centralising reforms he oversaw in the second half of the 1970s and which Defence, as a whole, had badly needed for a quarter of a century.[20] Given their personal rapport (they shared a love of trout fly-fishing), Tange's summation of Fraser as Defence minister provides some useful insights into what was to follow.

> He had opinions about most things, and was sometimes impetuous in forming them. He expected his advisers to disagree with him and some found his personality hard to endure. He was not always considerate enough to recognise the pressures felt by some. Setting short timetables for production of results by his subordinates maintained his reputation for vigour as a Minister, but it sometimes made for unreasonable demands on those serving him. Sunday night had to be accepted as a normal working time if it happened to suit him.[21]

Tange himself was a demanding individual with a healthy appetite for work and a low tolerance for those who did not share his appetite for work, yet even he thought that some of the things over which Fraser could be most demanding 'are not big issues' and that Fraser was unreasonable 'in respect to things that could have afforded to wait'.[22]

The political context was also shifting. Holt was replaced by Gorton as prime minister on the former's death by drowning, and many of the rancorous jealousies that are never far beneath the surface in any political party, but which Menzies had been able to manage astutely for the long term of his own prime ministership, increasingly came to public view. Gorton had numerous enemies – of whom Fraser initially was *not* one – especially on the conservative wing of the parliamentary Liberal Party, but his political inclinations to moderate reform and greater centralisation *vis-à-vis* the states together with his increasingly wayward personal behaviour did not help him; some of his opponents on his own side held that there was 'not much to pick and choose between Gorton and Whitlam'.[23] It was also readily apparent that others, principally the Treasurer, William McMahon (famously described by Gough Whitlam as 'Tiberius with a telephone'), relentlessly stoked the fires in the furtherance of their own ambitions. This did not make for stable – much less happy – government.

Daly was scarcely immune from any of this, and in mid-1970 had a significant falling-out with Fraser that almost certainly cost him promotion and advancement to the position of Chairman, Chiefs of Staff Committee in succession to Wilton and for a while soured what had otherwise been a good working and personal relationship. The issue was a significant one coloured by incipient rivalry between Fraser and the Minister for the Army, Andrew Peacock, who had succeeded Menzies in the seat of Kooyong and who was touted as a younger and more stylish face of the Liberal Party; his leadership ambitions were obvious, although many wondered whether there was much substance behind them. Fraser and Peacock had already clashed earlier in the year over declining enlistments in the CMF;[24] the fact of decline in the CMF was indisputable but was a symptom, as we have seen, of a much wider malaise that no tinkering with recruitment advertising would affect. This was a good example of Fraser's apparent inability to differentiate between the important and the immediate.

Accommodation and facilities, or the inadequacy thereof, had long been a theme with Daly. With the withdrawal of the Task Force from Phuoc Tuy now a matter of timetable only, the basing of the army in Australia once again became a more pressing issue. Tange noted that 'Treasury intrusion into Defence management had reduced the Department's standing in the eyes of Service personnel', and that one of Bland's last achievements before his retirement had been to get 'Treasury out of controlling the works programs of the Services in their various bases and establishments. It took time to wear down Treasury's parsimony over the housing provided for other ranks', a fight that had consumed a lot of Daly's attention over the years.[25] A new base had been completed at Townsville in 1968, and appropriate facilities existed at Holsworthy in Sydney and Enoggera in Brisbane, although the latter needed work. Battalions had also been based at Woodside in South Australia. In November 1969 Fraser directed that the army consider basing one of the three task forces that would initially make up the post–Vietnam Army in Western Australia. The argument in favour was essentially political: three of the nineteen seats lost to Labor in the 1969 election had been in Western Australia, and Federal 'neglect' of defence in the country's western third is an old theme. Characteristically, Fraser wanted answers immediately and Tange noted the 'typically slow response' from the Department of the Army to the request. In this case the complaint seems justified; Daly directed that the feasibility study be undertaken only in July 1970 and that it should 'determine, fairly and realistically, any increases in costs and manpower arising from such a deployment. In the event of there being significant increases, they should be so set out as to be capable of explanation to a layman in simple and convincing terms.'[26] The CGS's exasperation with the Minister for Defence was not well hidden.

The remote basing of substantial elements of the army poses a variety of problems, both in terms of soldier and family welfare (no small consideration in a volunteer force) and the inefficiency and expense of duplicating facilities and bringing widely scattered units together for higher-level training. Peacock supported the advice provided from his portfolio while Tange likewise saw the merit in the army's response, thus ensuring that his own relations with Fraser entered a frosty period, albeit short-lived. In a meeting with Fraser to discuss the army's recommendations, Daly's irritation clearly boiled over; the Chief of Naval Staff, now Vice-Admiral Sir Victor Smith, describing his approach as 'undiplomatic'.[27] As the CGS later recorded, 'the entire idea filled [me] with dismay. Heaven knows it was enough to have to run an Army with the resources available, to fight a war in Vietnam with the need to relieve a force of up to seven thousand annually and to cope with the demands of the Malayan Emergency [*sic*] without this added commitment for which there was no military need.'[28] His blunt defence of common sense and the interests of his service were to have consequences.

Daly had been extended as CGS once already, to May 1971 by Cabinet decision in 1968 that had seen Wilton extended as well. The relevant Cabinet submission in fact made clear that of the three Services the Army was easily the best placed in terms of talented senior officers available to fill the role of professional head of the Service. It would be practicable to extend Lieutenant-General Daly as CGS without loss of a potentially good successor through retirement as a Major-General. On the other hand there is no Army reason to extend Daly as the quality of candidates for selection to CGS is high.[29]

The RAN likewise had a viable succession plan, but the RAAF was in a more parlous position: there was 'a significant and serious drop in the quality of RAAF officers' below a small pool of eligible seniors, and in the circumstances then pertaining 'prospects for a good quality CAS in 1975,

Photo 31 The CGS inspects a guard from the Grenadier Guards, Whitehall, 1970. Behind is General Sir Geoffrey Baker, UK CGS (1968–71). (Daly family)

and probably in 1978, are poor in any event'. Daly had also been knighted, as was customary for the chiefs of the services, in his case in the Queen's birthday honours in June 1967.[30] In August 1970 the appointment of a successor to Wilton came before Cabinet. Tange declined to put his views on paper but conveyed them 'separately' to Fraser, suggesting at the same time that consideration might be given to further extending Wilton.[31] Peacock argued for Daly while his counterpart Minister for the Navy, Jim Killen, argued hard, and successfully, for the appointment of Sir Victor Smith.[32] It was, in any case, the RAN's 'turn', although this was not, supposedly, a consideration. Daly had seen the difficulties that confronted Wilton in the job at first hand; 'it is not a position of power', he recalled telling Peacock. 'It is a token uniform within the system.'[33] He had developed a heart condition over his period as CGS, and after dealing with politicians, press and a major war for five years he had had enough: 'When I retired I was absolutely wrung out. I was absolutely, to put it coarsely, I was buggered.' He also firmly believed that Fraser did not want him; clearly there were limits to Fraser's self-proclaimed desire to have senior officers and officials who were willing to argue with him.[34]

The virtual breakdown in relations between the CGS and the Minister for Defence, allied to the decline in the government's standing electorally and growing tensions between Fraser and the Prime Minister, Gorton, provide the context for the political crisis that broke in March 1971. Tange characterised it as 'a crisis of misunderstanding and distrust', which adequately describes the events but does not necessarily provide an explanation for them. Fraser's second biographer records his subsequent ruminations on John Gorton: he was 'a sad character in many ways, he was certainly his own worst enemy, but I think this was just the way he was made, I don't think it could have been any different'.[35] Of Daly Fraser is on record as saying (today) that he was 'without doubt a most honourable and admirable man' but one who would place the army and its interests ahead of the interests of his minister.[36] On top of all this, moreover, the media played a critical role in fomenting the crisis and exacerbating it once it began. As one commentator has observed, the media of the day 'was no passive observer of the Prime Minister's sudden demise'.[37]

The timetable for withdrawal of the Task Force from Phuoc Tuy presented Daly with both options and problems. His concern over leaving parts of the force unprotected if the emphasis was on withdrawing combat units first has already been discussed. As he commented later, the South Vietnamese authorities 'did not want to be left with the responsibility for carrying on a [civic action] task that we had left unfinished and for which they would not have the resources, either technical or material, to complete'. The provincial administration wanted 'to take over certain of the civic action programmes while at the same time I was wanting to reduce our commitment to civic action. The two things were nicely matched.'[38] Not only did Fraser take a particular interest in civic action activities but also the program was a regular source of 'good news' stories about Australian involvement in the province. Accordingly, when an ABC journalist filed a story saying that the army was shutting down involvement in civic action programs it produced a response from the minister very quickly indeed.

As is so often the case, the truth was both different and more complicated. Colonel John Salmon had arrived in Saigon in early January as chief of staff to COMAFV, Major-General Colin Fraser; the job had been vacant for some weeks due to the medical evacuation of his predecessor in early December. At Major-General Fraser's direction he produced a series of guidelines for the civic action program for 1971/72 (i.e. the following financial year) in order that these could be factored into the army and Defence estimates and in the context of an anticipated withdrawal from

Phuoc Tuy. There was not, at any stage at this level, any intention of cutting out the civic action program except in so far as it would clearly end when the army's presence in the province did so.[39] Equally clearly, COMAFV sought a managed conclusion to the program; 'he clearly did not wish the need to hastily complete military civic action projects to inhibit his successor's planning nor did he wish to leave semi-completed monuments to Australia's incompetence throughout the province'. In view of criticism from subordinate commands that documents issued by AFV Headquarters were unnecessarily lengthy, Salmon deleted the contextual preamble since, as he knew full well, those on the distribution list were well aware of its contents already. This decision 'was a mistake which I now regret'.[40]

It became so only because the document was leaked to an ABC correspondent, Andrew Swanton, who filed a report alleging that the army was cutting out the civic action program.[41] As Daly recalled, this 'created a tremendous amount of excitement in the Government and the Minister... was greatly concerned'. Daly and an official from the Department of the Army spent a full Sunday afternoon on 21 February with Malcolm Fraser, going through all the signal traffic that dealt with civic action in order to help prepare a statement for the House of Representatives. As Daly observed, 'this should have laid the matter to rest', although he also thought the minister 'was over-sensitive to press criticism' and that the matter should not have been invested with an importance that, in his opinion, it did not merit.[42] The CGS then went to the Northern Territory for a scheduled round of unit visits. He returned on Sunday 28 February to a story by Alan Ramsay in the *Sunday Australian* that, in Daly's words, was a mixture of 'more than normal journalistic distortions, half truths and untruths'. Ramsay's story alleged that the army was deliberately intransigent and providing false information to the Department of Defence and therefore, by extension, to the minister. It was 'a vicious and vituperative' attack.

Daly consulted the secretary of the Department of the Army, Bruce White; the minister, Peacock, was in hospital in Melbourne and Fraser was in his electorate in Victoria; neither was easily contactable, Peacock probably not at all so in an age before mobile phones and Facebook pages. Daly himself then provided a background brief to two journalists well known to him – Ian Fitchett of the *Sydney Morning Herald* and Max Hawkins of the *Brisbane Telegraph* – 'a most unusual step for me'. Fitchett had been a correspondent in North Africa during the Second World War, and Daly had known both men for years. His first inclination was to release a press statement through the minister, but the latter was unavailable and the CGS would not, as a matter of course, release one in his own name. Tange notes in his memoirs his clear impression that Fraser 'was conducting his own unacknowledged briefing of selected media, making clear his disapproval of Army actions in Vietnam over civic action', with a clear implication that this had been going on for some little while. Tange's biographer adds that by early 1971 'Fraser was particularly suspicious of the Army's attitude to the civic action programme' and that he 'began "off-the-record" press briefings on his intention to use Defence's intelligence machinery to check on the Army's performance'.[43]

Gorton now further muddied the waters by asking to see Daly. This was unusual in those days, not exactly improper but generally 'not done' in the absence of Daly's own two ministers, who would normally have been included.[44] Gorton's biographer notes that the Prime Minister began the year in a strong position, his performance in a number of areas over the previous six months having gone some way to temper the criticisms of all but his most inveterate or intemperate critics: 'John Gorton was at his best in early 1971.'[45] Perhaps this renewed assertiveness was the final contributory cause of his unmaking. In what Tange characterised as 'another imprudent entry in Fraser's domain', Gorton assured Daly of his support and clear determination to officially refute any further allegations made against the army. The next day a story appeared in the *Daily Telegraph* by Robert Baudino alleging, among other things, that Fraser had directed the Joint Intelligence Organisation to report to him on the army's activities in South Vietnam in respect to civic action. This story was followed on 3 March by another piece by Peter Samuel in the *Bulletin*, which claimed to provide further detail on the tensions between the minister and the army. That same day, Alan Ramsay spoke to Gorton asking for confirmation of a report that Daly had accused Fraser of disloyalty to the army and to its minister, Peacock. Here Gorton made a cardinal error by declining either to confirm or to deny 'a private conversation with a third party', and Ramsay duly published the following morning.[46]

The tangle of claims, counter-claims, accusations and explanations whirled around parliament, press and bureaucracy for some days and riveted the electorate, or at least the media. Fraser made a statement denying that JIO was spying on the army, which was literally true since JIO was an analytical organisation without a field intelligence-gathering capability. This statement was promulgated throughout units in 1ATF, as was the Prime Minister's earlier statement of full confidence in and support for the army and the CGS.⁴⁷ Daly had spoken to Tange after the appearance of the Baudino piece, and Tange had said 'he was less concerned with the accusations against the Army than with the silly story about JIO, an organisation that fell within his area of responsibility'.⁴⁸ The problem was that Fraser *had* been briefing journalists on his dissatisfaction with aspects of the army's reporting; the fact that journalists and editors then used what he gave them in their own manner and for their own purposes should have been entirely predictable and reflects upon his own judgement.⁴⁹ Samuels' article carried the ridiculous headline, 'The Australian Army's "Revolt" in Vietnam', but Fraser had been shown the original story by its author before publication. Although he subsequently refuted its wilder claims in a joint statement issued with the CGS, the fact remains that it 'was the (partly garbled) product of his own briefing'.⁵⁰

The increasingly frenzied business now moved firmly into the political realm and the darker depths of party politics frequently seen in governments that have lost their way and are on the path to electoral defeat. Fraser decided that he would resign, but in a manner calculated to inflict maximum damage upon the Prime Minister; Gorton attempted to reconcile with him, offering a way out that would preserve everyone's position, but on some evidence Fraser had previously cleared his desk and was committed mentally to the outcome already.⁵¹ Paul Ham describes him as 'a proud, sensitive man with a leviathan ambition [and] a tendency to obscure honourable intentions in the dark arts of subterfuge and intrigue'.⁵² He duly resigned while famously declaring that Gorton had forfeited the right to the prime ministership through his 'intolerable' disloyalty.⁵³ When Gorton was put on the spot in parliament, he dissembled; equally famously Ramsay, sitting in the Press Gallery, interjected 'You liar' in response to the Prime Minister's statement.⁵⁴ Fraser's resignation provided the opportunity that Gorton's internal opponents had been waiting for, and they moved quickly and concertedly. In a party room meeting on 10 March, with the vote of confidence in the Prime Minister evenly divided at 33 all, Gorton cast the deciding vote against himself and resigned the prime ministership.

As Hancock notes, 'In just nine days a disagreement between the Army and the Minister for Defence had escalated into a political crisis which ended with the resignation of the Prime Minister'.⁵⁵ There are a number of conclusions to be drawn from this extraordinary episode. Open clashes between the armed forces and the government are rare in Australian politics; respect for civil control of the military is very deeply ingrained. Daly thought the whole thing 'a miserable affair', and years later was still 'at a loss to explain the *raison d'être*' for it.[56] Fraser and Gorton were ultimately the victims of their own misjudgements. Fraser found himself 'forced on the one hand to show loyalty to an Army he felt had not kept him properly informed, and on the other to wrestle with the hazardous and unforeseen consequences of briefings he himself had initiated'.[57]

Gorton recognised, in his reply to Fraser's resignation speech, that his failure to kill Ramsay's story (with a clear denial of the claim that Daly had charged his minister with disloyalty to the army) was a serious error of judgement. Whether Daly did, in fact, say this at the meeting on 1 March is a matter of contention: he was emphatic that he did not, and told Fraser so in a letter shortly thereafter, a position reinforced by Gorton both at the time and again after he had nothing further to gain or lose; Fraser's second biographer claims to know the identity of Ramsay's informant for the damaging story (but refuses to identify them other than to concede that it was 'a third-hand source'), and claims that the account 'of what Daly said to Gorton was probably accurate'.[58] This is less than compelling.

The 'civic action crisis' highlights several major issues in civil–military relations, in military–media affairs and in the command and control of Australian forces deployed overseas. Although now recently retired, Wilton wrote to Fraser in the middle of the emerging political furore to make a couple of simple but fundamental points:

> The allegations about 'sabotage' attributed to unnamed ministers are not true and the same applies to the Army's attitude to civic action. Secondly and more importantly, is the fact that the Army and its leadership are being publicly attacked and cannot publicly refute the allegations. I believe someone in the Government should defend the Army... As you and I know, the Army initiated the military civic action program some years ago and to the best of my knowledge has continued to support civic action ever since. I am particularly concerned about the morale of the Armed Forces as a whole and the Army in particular if these attacks continue.

And 'with some diffidence' he concluded by reminding Fraser that 'loyalty must go down as well as up'.[59] Relations between Defence and the army were very tense in 1970–71, for both understandable and less good reasons.

Fraser's second biographer asserts two reasons for Fraser's resignation: 'the failure of Daly to share his concerns about civic action... and the way in which Gorton dealt with Daly, apparently using the civic action affair for political purposes, to attack Fraser'.[60] As Wilton's contemporaneous letter makes clear, the army – and by extension the CGS – had no 'concerns' with civic action *per se* and was seeking through the COMAFV directive to ensure that these programs continued on a sustainable basis in a context of gradual withdrawal from Phuoc Tuy. This was not something that required referral to the Minister for Defence. The internal politics of the Liberal Party were no business of the army or the CGS, and Daly sought assiduously to distance himself from them. Perhaps, as well, a boil-over at some stage was inevitable given frustration in the army (including its senior civilian officials) with the climate in which they were fighting a war that was neither of their making nor an existential national crisis. Bruce White had appended a handwritten note to Major-General R.A. Hay, who was then COMAFV, in August 1969 hoping that Hay might soon 'be able to go back to running the war undisturbed while we turn our attention to preparing for the elections on 25 October... and perhaps a change of Minister?'[61]

The failure of successive governments to explain the Vietnam commitment to the electorate in concise and coherent terms – to mount an information campaign, as it would now be styled – created increasing political difficulties for them as public opinion turned against the war (and the government) in the late 1960s. Daly regarded the attacks on the army in the press and parliament as intolerable, and the muzzling of the army as an aspect of government policy both frustrating and counter-productive (a view that Wilton clearly shared). 'It is not for Service officers to engage in public controversy', Daly said later, 'but this should not prevent officers speaking on subjects of public interest on which they are particularly well informed', especially in the absence of informed commentary from the relevant ministers. The result was that 'over the years the army has become conditioned to not talking to anybody'. Even the CGS was required to clear public remarks with the minister (and, on one occasion during Holt's prime ministership, with the Prime Minister himself). As we have seen, Daly generally declined speaking invitations thereafter, explaining that he would not 'submit myself to the humiliating business of having everything I said vetted by all these people before I spoke. So perhaps I was largely to blame if a group of influential people were denied a firsthand view of matters of great public interest.'[62]

Relations between the army and the press were generally pretty poor (Daly characterised them as 'not good... some [journalists covering the war] were reputable, some were quite disreputable').[63] Daly saw two problems; one was the very open system that MACV operated with regard to accreditation of correspondents while the other was the way in which their movement around the country was facilitated from US sources, such that any attempt by Australian authorities to regulate Australian journalists more closely was largely a waste of time. Daly strongly disliked the way in which the press covered the war, especially the Australian part in it (and as he himself fully realised, this reflected, in part, a generational perspective), but on the other hand recognised that while it was not 'the Army as much as the Government that was being attacked... the Army was always the meat in the sandwich'.[64] Denis Warner, a journalist for whom Daly had considerable regard, wrote in 1969 that 'the Australian Government needed an informed public'.[65] This must have made for considerable frustration for those journalists who tried to cover the war and government policy towards it in a responsible fashion; it cannot have helped the process when politicians attempted to manipulate coverage for their own purposes, either.

The involvement of the Packer media organisation in the destabilisation of Gorton as Prime Minister did nothing to reassure the army about the media's intentions towards it. Sir Frank Packer's outlets included television stations in Melbourne and Sydney as well as the *Bulletin* and the *Daily Telegraph*, both of which played a key role in the 'civic action crisis' (and not merely its reportage) in March 1971. Packer did not directly instigate this, obviously, but his most senior journalist within the Press Gallery, Alan Reid, 'exploited it for all it was worth'. In the view of one analyst, Reid believed 'that Gorton had to go' and he and Peter Samuel of the *Bulletin* 'were engaged in skulduggery for most of Gorton's period of office'.[66] Daly and the army were indeed the meat in the sandwich on this occasion as on numerous others, but in general there was little they could do to counter the 'complete, utter nonsense' that was sometimes published and which provided 'something with which to ridicule the Army, and indirectly, to discredit the Vietnam involvement'. Admiral Smith thought Daly took criticism of the army 'personally', which is probably true but does not undermine Daly's own belief that the morale of the soldiers engaged in operations of war was too precious and important a commodity to become the plaything of journalists and politicians.[67]

The lengthy commitment to Phuoc Tuy exposed serious weaknesses in the command of Australian forces from Australia. As Horner puts it succinctly, 'the most obvious fact about the Canberra command post was that it did not exist'.[68] Centralisation and integration of the civilian and military sides of the Defence group of departments was a slow, almost agonising process; Howson recorded as early as May 1966 that integration of the services was a goal 'we should move slowly towards'.[69] There was a linear progression of reviews and recommendations that ran from Morshead (1957) through Wilton (1966–71) to Tange (1973–76) on the issue of major reorganisation of Defence, one that would reach its culmination only after Daly (and Wilton, for that matter) had retired. These changes were driven to a considerable extent by the perception of weaknesses and shortcomings in the higher direction of Australia's Vietnam commitment.

Organisational change that flowed from the Vietnam experience was not confined to the highest levels, however. The war had demonstrated weaknesses in the army's structures and ways of doing business while developments in comparable armies elsewhere suggested that the army's basic organisation was increasingly behind the times. The army's leadership also recognised that the end of the Vietnam commitment, whenever it might come, would bring with it some necessary contraction and that this needed to be planned for and managed, especially if it included (as it ultimately did) the end of the National Service scheme.[70] On a personal level Daly regretted the ending of National Service, although he saw full well that the Vietnam War had destroyed any consensus over its retention.[71] In a paper for the Military Board in September 1970 the DCGS, Major-General Stuart Graham, had argued not merely for the retention of the National Service scheme but also for its expansion, yet the political and social realities of the time meant that this was never likely.[72] It built, however, on an initial review a year previously that examined the size and shape of the army after Vietnam, and the ratios likely to pertain between troops in the field and those in support. (On this occasion, Daly recommended to Peacock that he 'seek the agreement of the Minister for Defence to proceed, as a matter of urgency, with the provision of the balance of the accommodation and training requirements to support a Regular Army of nine battalions with appropriate combat and logistic support units. Its organisation as a division or as a number of task forces can then be decided in the light of future needs.')

In the middle of 1969 Daly initiated a review of the future organisation of the army that would constitute one of his longest-lasting and most significant legacies. It began when Lynch was Army minister and Fairhall held Defence, and would be bedded down only under a Labor government in the mid-1970s and alongside the most far-reaching review of the CMF undertaken in decades. After discussions with both Daly and the secretary, Bruce White, Lynch wrote to Fairhall in August 1969 recommending a high-level and 'really thorough-going' review, to be chaired by a major-general, examining 'our administrative structure and procedures which would be most rewarding in terms of economy and efficiency in the use of Army manpower'.[73] (Then, as now, a justification in terms of 'economy and efficiency' often proves more persuasive than more rational explanations for a course of action within government.) A review of this kind was possible not least because the government had placed a figure on the size of the post-Vietnam army, which in turn permitted rational forward planning.[74] The most telling part of the minister's recommendation, obviously originating with the CGS and the secretary, observed that the review, to be meaningful, 'must not be circumscribed by traditional organisational or procedural beliefs. I believe the review should not disregard the practicability of quite fundamental changes, even though these have been found inexpedient in the past. For example, whilst not necessarily suggesting a complete departure from the long-standing geographic basis of Army organisation, the examination in depth which I believe necessary would encompass this as well as other avenues for streamlining our administration.'[75] In order to avoid 'premature repercussions' from state governments the review process was to be kept on a 'need to know' basis.

The officer selected to head the review was Major-General Frank Hassett, who was then GOC Northern Command.[76] Although his appointment was not announced by the new Minister for the Army, Andrew Peacock, until March 1970, Hassett began thinking his way through the major problems that the review would confront before the end of 1969. In particular, he recognised the long-standing problem posed by the CMF in its severely run-down form, noting that if his proposed committee was to give the CMF only 'minimum attention' he hoped that 'somebody else is working on this aspect'. (The 'somebody' would be the Millar Committee, which undertook its review of the CMF and school cadets in 1974.) The continuation, or otherwise, of National Service was also an important imponderable; 'this is a tricky one', he wrote to the DCGS.[77] As he added in a further letter to Daly, the review's outcome should be 'recommendations which will produce not only a worthwhile military result and, of course, this is the most important thing, but will also be politically attractive'.[78] Final approval came from Malcolm Fraser who, characteristically, attached a senior officer from Defence as an observer, and annotated on the foot of his letter to Peacock: 'No publicity till Defence statement.'[79]

The fundamental problems with the existing organisation that the Hassett review addressed can be summarised succinctly. The state-based organisation fractured the functions of the army such that no headquarters other than Army Headquarters in Canberra had full responsibility for any single function within the organisation. Training, for example, was a responsibility located within each regional command.[80] In a sense Australia possessed seven little armies rather than a single one. This situation reflected the old assumptions and methods of business that assumed that the CMF was the mainstay of Australia's land defence, which had not been true for several decades at least. Daly suggested that the geographic system of commands 'was a relic of the pre-Federation era' while the organisation of Army Headquarters 'had grown piecemeal, with the result that not only were there gaps in the structure but in some areas responsibility was divided and even duplicated'.[81]

The review recommended, and the government accepted, a system of functional commands that brought the army into line organisationally with both the RAN and RAAF and saw the creation of Field Force, Logistic and Training Commands. The regional commands continued but with greatly reduced responsibilities largely tied to the CMF. Army Headquarters was likewise substantially recast, as was the Military Board, designed to allow greater concentration on policy formulation through reduced administrative loads and the delegation of policy execution.[82] In recognition of the increased size of the army and the workload carried by senior officers, Defence agreed reluctantly to the creation of a position of Vice-Chief of the General Staff in addition to the existing position of DCGS. Peacock argued that the position was 'long overdue', but Defence succeeded in making a temporary appointment in the interests of parity with the other two services, and indeed the role proved short-lived and was abolished in 1975.[83]

By now Daly's retirement was in close prospect. Although his successor, Major-General Mervyn Brogan, had been identified for some time, the usual delays and loose ends came into play as they had done when Daly had taken over from Wilton. Brogan was GOC Eastern Command and wished to visit his counterparts in the major partner armies in the UK, the USA and New Zealand, but as late as October 1970 the CGS was experiencing difficulties trying to have him relieved from his current

Photo 32 Military Board, 1970. (Army History Unit)

posting 'some weeks' before he was to take up his new appointment. Daly suggested to Brogan as well that the latter's first visit to Vietnam was perhaps best made after he was 'wearing three stars' in terms of dealing with both the Americans and South Vietnamese in Saigon.[84] His own retirement date was set down as 18 May, and at his last Military Board meeting a few days earlier the minister conveyed 'the deep sense of appreciation and gratitude' felt by all those present.[85] With the end of the Vietnam commitment approaching, Daly also formed a small military history cell to assist the Australian War Memorial in identifying material for transfer to the museum collections and to begin the process of collecting and organising records implicitly for an official history should that eventuate.[86]

The retirement age for lieutenant-generals was 60, and Daly was only 58. He might, as he later said, have prevailed on the government to extend him to mandatory retirement age 'but I had little desire to do so'. He had been extended once already and had turned down the offer of a state governorship because, with the army at war, to accept 'was not to be contemplated'. Furthermore, an extension would force Brogan's retirement as a major-general on age grounds and thus deny the army his services as CGS. It was time to go: 'I was tired, less than completely fit and when the time came, ready to make way for my successor.'[87] His journalist friend, Max Hawkins, noted 'the tremendous affection within the Army' with which Daly was regarded, but if attempts were made to change his mind they were unsuccessful. He was placed on the Supernumerary List for a couple of months while he received treatment for the heart ailment he had developed while CGS, and his retirement became formal on 10 July 1971.

Daly had served the Australian Army for forty-two years. The army he joined was close in organisation, culture and function to that created in the decade or so between Federation and the outbreak of the Great War from which it had emerged greatly enhanced and as a repository of national identity and values. That from which he retired was in a process of wide-ranging and fundamental change, uncertain of its place in Australian society at the end of a divisive, unpopular and lost war but with many of its institutional fundamentals nonetheless intact. He now embarked upon a long and active retirement, one that permitted him to remain an observer of the fortunes of an institution he loved and, in the manner of retired senior officers, to retain formal and informal links with it.

CHAPTER 8

Epilogue

It would be a little melodramatic to suggest that Daly's final advancement in the profession of arms – to chairman of the Chiefs of Staff Committee – was one further, and perhaps the final, casualty of the 'civic action crisis'. As we have seen, Daly himself was mentally exhausted and physically unwell by the time he left the post of Chief of the General Staff and the army in the middle of 1971 and had made it clear that he lacked the desire to take on the top job in any case. In Vice-Admiral Sir Victor Smith there was, as well, an able alternative choice who had the advantage of being from a different service, and he held the post until November 1975. Speculation as to how Daly would have discharged further high office serves little useful purpose, although he might have found working with the Whitlam Government as challenging as anything he had experienced in the political domain of the second half of the 1960s.

His final meeting of the Military Board convened on 14 May 1971. As was customary, the Minister, Andrew Peacock, spoke of the achievements of the retiring CGS in what seems to have been a lengthy and genuinely effusive tribute. It was, said Peacock, 'a period characterised by the innumerable problems and difficulties associated with an operationally committed and expanding Army', and Daly's carriage of his duties had been characterised by 'his fine qualities of wisdom and perceptiveness and... the very human manner in which he had always discharged the onerous responsibilities of his position'. His had been 'a most distinguished and dedicated military career... [of] outstanding service to the Nation, as well as the Army as a whole'. Daly in turn expressed his thanks and characteristically paid equal tribute to 'the corporate wisdom and experience' of the board itself and spoke of his 'immense pride and satisfaction' at his association with it.[1] A newspaper comment on the selection of a successor to Wilton the previous year had noted 'the tremendous affection within the Army' in which Daly was held, and the farewell tribute from his most senior colleagues certainly reflected this. Peacock greeted his successor, Lieutenant-General M.F. Brogan, to his first Military Board meeting a fortnight later in much the same manner as Fraser had welcomed Daly back in 1966: he would find 'the duties of his new office both challenging and stimulating'.[2]

Daly left the army in a strong position, and far healthier than it might have been, given the organisational and institutional stresses imposed by the war in Vietnam and the social and political climate in the country in the early 1970s. Outside his family, the army occupied the central place in his affections, and he had bent his every effort as CGS from the very beginning to protect it as an institution and to safeguard its members, both collectively and individually, wherever possible. He felt the slights and attacks directed at it in a personal sense, and his distress at the casualties among his soldiers, which were an inevitable part of the war in Phuoc Tuy, was genuine, just as he had felt the same way about the losses incurred by the 2/10th Battalion or within the units of the 28th Commonwealth Brigade. The army faced important challenges as Daly retired – Peacock identified the 'significant problems brought about by the current financial restraints, the changeover to a functional organisation and a reduction of commitment in Vietnam' – and worse was to come in the course of the 1980s and 1990s as the army was further reduced to feed the seemingly insatiable demands of major capital acquisition projects for the navy and air force; but all this was in the future and was beyond Daly's responsibility or capacity to influence.

Daly's retirement was slightly delayed, notwithstanding his departure from office, because of his health. Originally slated to retire on 18 May and be transferred to the Regular Army Reserve, he was instead placed on the Supernumerary List – presumably in order for his heart condition to be assessed and dealt with. His retirement in fact took effect on 9 July.[3] With an eye to life after the army, on 11 June Daly had applied to the Military Board for permission to accept a company directorship with Associated Securities Limited, a necessity while he remained, technically, still in the service.[4] He continued to live in the house he had built in Yarralumla until early in 1973 when he and Heather moved to Sydney and a house in Bellevue Hill where he was to remain for the rest of his life.[5] He was

58, his health would improve substantially after he retired, and he was far too young, active and with too much to contribute to simply vegetate.

He was to enjoy a long and active retirement. His involvement with the army he loved was perpetuated through appointment as Honorary Colonel of the Pacific Islands Regiment and Colonel Commandant of the Royal Australian Regiment (both 1971–75), and he served as well as a trustee of the Infantry Museum at Singleton, while in 2001 the officers mess at Lavarack Barracks in Townsville was named in his honour. He added a number of directorships to his portfolio – with Jennings Industries from 1973 to 1985, Fruehauf Trailers Australasia Ltd between 1974 and 1989 and the Associated Merchant Bank of Singapore in 1975. He served on the National Council of the Australian Red Cross Society between 1971 and 1974 and as a councillor of the Royal Agricultural Society of New South Wales from 1972 until standing down in 1985 after which he was an honorary councillor. He remained active in returned service affairs and was a regular participant in Anzac Day marches in Sydney and elsewhere over the years. His long-standing involvement with the Board of Trustees (subsequently Council) of the Australian War Memorial gave him enormous satisfaction, and he played an important part in the modernisation of that institution.

His direct involvement with the War Memorial went back to the mid-1960s, in fact. As remains the case today, the service chiefs were members of the council *ex officio*, and although some or all are often precluded from attending meetings by the demands of their day jobs (and one or two perhaps have had little active interest in the role), their membership constitutes an important and continuous link between the armed forces and the principal institution charged with commemoration of earlier generations of soldiers. The AWM has supported successive series of official histories of Australia's wars (and more recent peacekeeping and stabilisation operations), while the cooperation of the services has always been critical to the Memorial's ability to expand its collections of equipment, records, illustrations and sundry other items from both our own side and our opponents'. A small instance of this was provided by Daly in his last weeks as CGS, writing to the director, W.R. Lancaster, to inform him of the creation of a 'small Military History cell' to be sent to Phuoc Tuy to assist in the selection of items for possible display and to gather and preserve materials and records to support the writing of an official history, whenever that might eventuate.[6]

As with everything else he did, Daly took his duties as a trustee very seriously and attended meetings of the board when he was able. The

Memorial of the 1960s was a very fusty institution reflecting the emphases and concerns of C.E.W. Bean and its founding and early directors and seemingly had moved on little since that time. It was under-resourced, out of touch and out of date, understood little of contemporary museological practices, which put its vast collections at serious risk, and in some respects showed little inclination to change its ways of doing business. Older Australian historians of war such as Dr Bill Gammage (author of the seminal *The Broken Years*), who first worked there in the 1960s, remember the old institution with nostalgia. This author recalls being sent off to sit on the floor of the stacks with boxes of original documents around him, happily rifling through papers without a skerrick of supervision, as late as the mid-1970s. It was wonderfully innocent and it could not possibly last, but while it did it was glorious.

The historian of the Australian War Memorial (and of much else besides) and a former deputy director, Dr Michael McKernan, notes that Daly had so impressed the chairman of the board, Lieutenant-General Sir Edmund 'Ned' Herring, that when he retired as CGS – and thus left the board *ex officio* – Herring sought his return as an appointed member, an office in the gift of the minister.[7] Appointment in his own right was made with effect from 1 July 1972.[8] Daly was elected chairman in 1974 and served in that capacity until his retirement in 1982. Of his tenure as chairman McKernan comments that he was 'the first Service professional' to occupy the position and thus 'made even more pronounced the position of the military in the Memorial'. Countering this mild implied criticism, however, McKernan further observes of Daly that 'he was a man who respected professionalism and he came to rely heavily on the contributions of other Board members with broader backgrounds than his own':

> He was also keen to develop the young, professional staff now being recruited and it was not unusual for him to drop into the offices of various staff to discuss issues. Where Herring appeared remote and out of touch, Daly gave confidence to the curators and the conservators that he understood their concerns for the collection and that he wanted the memorial to develop to communicate its message more effectively. His was a sensible appointment for a period of change because, while he accepted the need for change, his high military rank and prestige would allay the fears of those afraid of change.[9]

As one of those 'young professional staff' recruited in 1981, McKernan developed a warm relationship with the chairman despite their differences in age and outlook.

Something of Daly's style and approach as chairman is conveyed in one of McKernan's anecdotes. In late 1981 the director of Theatre ACT, George Whalley, 'came to us with an idea for a version of the "Broken Years" to be performed in the courtyard in the days leading up to Anzac Day':

> Professional actors, Woden Valley Youth Choir, Band of the RMC. This was novel for the AWM if not audacious. I floated it with Bryan Gandevia, a good friend on Council, who was enthusiastic. He suggested I talk it through with TD because if he was onside it would definitely be a goer... TD was interested, but wary. A long conversation and he warmed to the idea... Whalley appointed Michael Boddy as writer. Innocuous choice, it seemed to me with runs on the board and best yet a local. TD was appalled, an impossible man, he thundered, left-wing, totally inappropriate. He came to the first rehearsal full of apprehension. I introduced him to Michael Boddy beforehand and he seemed most reluctant even to shake his hand. Very formal, Mr Boddy etc. Up to the show [which was] moving and brilliant. TD thereafter couldn't have enough of Boddy's company. Why, he asked me, at some point in the few nights' entertainment, do we form judgements of people on the basis of what other people say? The point was, having backed me on it he was never going to pull the rug. His conservatism worried him for the 'sanctity' of the courtyard but when it was a triumph his pleasure in having trusted his people shone through. And he could quickly re-assess a flawed character judgement because he had the kind of mind that was flexible enough to move quickly.[10]

Under the old *Australian War Memorial Act* the chairman was elected by the other trustees and served 'during the pleasure of the Board' or his retirement from it. This was what happened to Daly's predecessor, the wartime soldier, former Liberal Member for Henty (1946–55) and former ambassador to Greece (1965–68), H.B.S. 'Jo' Gullett. He had been elected to succeed Herring in April 1974, but was not reappointed by the minister at mid-year; if there was an ulterior motive to this (which seems unlikely) it is not recorded, and since he was recuperating from serious injury suffered in an accident someone might have felt they were doing him a kindness. Progressive rejuvenation of the board was an established pattern in any case,[11] and although Gullett was keenly disappointed at his forced retirement given his own and his family connections with the Memorial, and Daly expressed himself 'distressed' at Gullett's termination,[12] generational change and institutional renewal were clearly called for.

At its meeting on 15 August 1974 the board unanimously elected Daly chairman. Expressing regret only at the circumstances in which he was elected, the board under his chairmanship now grappled with a number of serious problems. At the same meeting Daly introduced the secretary of the Department of the Special Minister of State, who spoke of the Pigot Committee appointed by the Whitlam Government to look into Australian museums and national collections – the AWM was by no means the only institution seriously behind the times in terms of display, conservation and collection management.[13] The biggest need institutionally was not only for better-qualified staff but also simply for more of them – the Memorial was still operating under a staff ceiling of just eighty: 'Modest but rational demands for additional staff and for the reclassification of some of the existing positions have been made to the Department over a long period of time. Some of the submissions have been examined and apparently agreed to in principle by Department officers, but further action has not been forthcoming.'[14] Failure to act on these requests led to the loss of some staff through frustration and the absence of career paths within the institution. This situation would not be resolved quickly.

Soon after Daly assumed the chairmanship, the board included in its annual report for 1974–75 an overview of the Memorial and the changes and targets it needed to achieve in order to enter 'the last quarter of the 20th Century' in good health. It was a long list and it, too, took time to achieve, although, by the time Daly retired as chairman, a number of the 'big ticket' items – such as the storage and conservation annex in the industrial suburb of Mitchell – had been attained. The greatest single change, however, was the passage of a new *Australian War Memorial Act 1980*, which overhauled and modernised much of the management of the institution. The Board of Trustees was replaced by a council, and Daly was again elected its chairman.[15]

The council enjoyed greatly expanded powers, in particular involving direct control over funding and staffing. It also defined and allocated specific powers relating to the collections and education programs. The enhancement of the council under the new Act also meant that it was now

Photo 33 Chairman of the Board of Trustees escorts the Lord Mayor of London, Sir Murray Fox, on an official visit to the Australian War Memorial, September 1975. (AWM 043470)

able to push government harder for increases in staff numbers and for renovation and expansion of accommodation and facilities, while henceforth the director was appointed as a statutory office-holder by the Governor-General.[16] Daly had worked assiduously as chairman to help bring all this about. He remained equally persistent, and effective, as an advocate with the government for the resources the Memorial needed to fulfil its roles and missions, especially the increase in the staffing ceiling and the recruitment of new, younger professionally qualified staff in response to the much greater numbers of visitors and greatly increased demands on the collections by historians and researchers.[17] Like the army, the Memorial would realise the fruits of many of Daly's efforts after his retirement.

His devotion to the Memorial as an institution and his characteristic willingness to state his position on an issue clearly and uncompromisingly are well illustrated by an incident of vandalism at the Memorial in August 1980. Spray-painted slogans on the external walls prompted the council to offer a $1000 reward for information leading to the apprehension of the culprits, and the following letter to various newspapers from the chairman concerning 'this infamy': 'That the memories of so many brave Australians, who gave their lives that these depraved wretches might enjoy comfort and security, should be besmirched in this manner makes me feel ineffably sad. There must be hundreds of thousands of my fellow countrymen who will be equally sickened.'[18]

Daly's hard work on behalf of the institution and his willingness to defend it were part of what prompted the feelings of warmth and regard in which the staff held him.[19] In October 1981 his term came up for renewal but the responsible minister, Ian Wilson, offered him only a single, twelve-month extension on the grounds of age – Daly was then 68. Michael McKernan had driven him over to parliament to see the minister and waited in the car. Daly returned after perhaps fifteen minutes, looking grave.

> He said (words to this effect): 'The Minister told me he couldn't reappoint me for a full term as I was approaching 70. I said to him, if you think I'm too old for a full time appointment you probably think I'm too old for a half-term so I think I'll go right now.' But in fact I think he saw his term out to end June 1982. He was not angry with Wilson, more bemused as I think he saw himself as a fit, vigorous person with much, still, to offer.[20]

One wonders, had he been extended, whether the War Memorial might have avoided the period of internal turbulence it soon encountered.

Thomas Joseph Daly died on 5 January 2004, aged 90, after a period of serious illness. His requiem mass was held at St Mary's Cathedral, Sydney, on 14 January with the Governor-General, Major-General Michael Jeffrey, reading a lesson and more than 800 mourners in attendance. The eulogy was delivered by the Chief of the Defence Force, General Peter Cosgrove, with the Chief of Army (as the CGS was now called), Lieutenant-General Peter Leahy, as Chief Mourner. Obituaries all noted his warmth and humanity, his concern for soldiers and the influence he had exerted upon '*his* Army'.[21]

There were three facets to the life of Tom Daly: the army, his family and his Catholic faith. This book has said much about the first and has touched upon the second in places. After his retirement from the council of the War Memorial, family affairs (especially those pertaining to grandchildren), occupied much of his time, although he remained active in the community

Photo 34 Sir Thomas is carried from the cathedral to the hearse on the way to his final resting place, 2004. The coffin is borne by warrant officers class I of the Australian Regular Army. (Department of Defence 2004 5024-001)

in various capacities. His religious faith informed everything he did but was never allowed to intrude upon his professional functions.

Monsignor Eugene Harley, a former principal chaplain to the army, had first met Daly on exercise near Holsworthy in the early 1960s.[22] Appointed as staff chaplain to Army Headquarters in Canberra after service in Vietnam, Harley regularly encountered the CGS and was often called into his office for a few minutes of 'spiritual thoughts and reflection'. Daly affirmed his faith publicly, but never ostentatiously. 'Even when he attended Mass in the [RMC] chapel in full uniform he never sought precedence but took his place along with the cadets at the altar rail.' When visiting units in the field, and in Vietnam, he would always ask when and where Mass would be celebrated and would line up among the soldiers, sometimes offering to serve the Mass himself. His faith was a considered one; he observed to Harley that the crucifix in the RMC Chapel (a work executed by the artist Tom Bass) was a fitting representation for a soldier with strong and upright stance and direct gaze, 'freely giving his life'. In retirement in Sydney he volunteered at the Matthew Talbot Hostel, washing and feeding the indigent guests who sought shelter and sustenance and introducing himself simply as 'Brother Tom'. On one occasion, in conversation with a young fellow-volunteer who lived in the parish of Mosman, he asked that his regards be passed to her parish priest, Monsignor Harley. When she asked how Daly knew him the latter replied simply, 'We were in the Army together.'[23]

His family life was the other rock on which he built a distinguished career as a soldier. Two of his three daughters ultimately gave him five grandsons (one currently serving in the Australian Army) and two granddaughters (one of whom predeceased him). He imparted to his daughters the fundamental importance of rugby and the mysteries of cricket, along with an appreciation of ballet, opera, symphony concerts and art, which he collected with an assiduous and informed eye. He also imparted his senses of duty, discipline and humour; when asked what he would have done had he had a son, he replied, 'Strapped his right arm to his side. Australia desperately needs a left-hand bowler.' He continued to play golf into old age, and to ski at an age when many would have given it away.[24]

He could never have achieved all that he did without the pillars of faith and family, but it is as a soldier that he is best known, as a soldier that he is most important outside his own intimate circle and as a soldier that he had the greatest influence. How then might his influence be assessed and summarised?

Daly idenitified strongly and personally with the army. It is no exaggeration to say that he regarded it as *his* army, a precious asset held in trust and to be defended, nurtured and enhanced in any and every way open to him. His own bearing and conduct were beyond reproach, and he insisted on similarly high standards from others; he was sometimes disappointed but never dissuaded nor discouraged. His great personal rectitude covered, although rarely hid, great personal warmth and concern for soldiers and their families. He demonstrated this throughout his career, in his attention to detail in order to safeguard the lives of those under his command in Borneo or Korea; in his long-running belief in the worth of the Pacific Islands Regiment and the indigenous men in its ranks; or through his wrangling with civilian authorities to improve the shabby standards of service accommodation allotted to soldiers' families, standards of housing that few civilians at the time would have tolerated. He inherited an army at war when he became CGS, and guided it through the political shoals and the operational pitfalls inherent in a commitment made for strategic political reasons (the maintenance of the US alliance) but which the army was called on to fight while under-resourced and without clear political directives from the governments of the day. Towards the end of his stewardship he initiated a root-and-branch organisational reform that remained in place until the early years of the following century and which reflected the needs of a modern army.

In the final analysis it was his soldiers who had first claim on his attention, as he pointed out in an address at RMC Duntroon many years after retirement: 'It is a leader's job to do all in his power to alleviate the hardships inseparable from a soldier's life.'[25] His soldiers knew this; as one veterans' magazine put it, 'Paternal and patrician, Daly embodied the caring virtues of the best type of senior officer in any army. He had the endearing gift of remembering soldiers' names and making them feel embraced in an extended military family that looked after its own.' He would not have had it any other way.

'It is doubtless fitting', as the *Edinburgh Review* commented in 1841, 'that there should be some among us who propose to prepare men's minds for that happy time when war shall cease among men. It is also proper that there should be others who, regarding the world in its present state of hostility, seek to raise, as much as our nature will permit, the character of that necessary institution, an army.'[26]

Given the 'present state of hostility' that helps to define Australia's strategic landscape, the army is as necessary a national institution as at any time in its history. Like armies anywhere – even those with longer and more complicated lineages – it remains very much a work in progress. The army that Daly joined at the height of the Depression was very different from the one that he bequeathed to his successors, and the current organisation is significantly different again. The roles, tasks and challenges that it faces, however, have changed little, if at all. So long as that remains the case – so long as war remains a human activity – the insights and experiences and lessons of the past can, will and must continue to inform the decisions and developments of the present and function as a guide to the future.

NOTES

1 Regimental soldiering

1. Carver, *The Seven Ages of the British Army*.
2. I have written about the growth of the army as an institution elsewhere: Grey, *The Australian Army*.
3. The development and experience of the Australian Army over the first two generations of its existence forms the backdrop to Grey, *Australian Brass*.
4. McGregor, 'An army at dusk'.
5. Details from his attestation form, CRS B2455/1. In his retirement Daly also compiled a short family history, 'The Daly Brophy Family', a copy of which is in the family and used by permission.
6. The 9th LH was to be unlucky in its COs, losing two killed in action on Gallipoli, including Miell.
7. Daly, interview with Breen, 11 March 1991. Copy in author's possession.
8. Darley, *With the Ninth Light Horse in the Great War* provides a full and detailed account of the regiment's activities. Other details are drawn from his service dossier.
9. Gullett, *The Australian Imperial Force in Sinai and Palestine, 1914–1918*, p. 766. This was the only enemy colour captured by Australians in any theatre of the war.
10. Daly, 'The Daly Brophy Family', p. 14.
11. Daly, interview with Breen, 8 April 1991.
12. Coulthard-Clark, *Duntroon*, pp. 104–8.
13. Lee, *Duntroon*, pp. 87–8.
14. Ibid.
15. The mechanics of the relocation are covered in Coulthard-Clark, *Duntroon*, pp. 115–22.
16. Daly, cadet file, RMC Duntroon archives.
17. This might not have been as impressive as at first appears; see Coulthard-Clark, *Duntroon*, p. 129.
18. *RMC Journal*, April 1934, pp. 43–50.
19. Daly, cadet conduct sheet, cadet file. Daly, interview with Breen, 8 April 1991.
20. Captain C.W. Huxtable, memorandum to HQ, 1 Cavalry Division, 1 May 1933. Daly, cadet file.
21. 'Report on graduates: T.J. Daly, 12 December 1933', Daly, service dossier.
22. Confidential report, July 1934, Daly, service dossier.

23 Daly, interview with Breen, 8 April 1991.
24 Confidential reports, 1935–39, Daly, service dossier.
25 Confidential report, 4 May 1939, Daly, service dossier.
26 Minute, CGS to Secretary, Military Board, 28 February 1939, Military Board agendum 60/1939. NAA A2653/1, 1939/1.
27 For discussion of mechanisation in the Australian Army in this period, see Grey, *Australian Brass*; Morrison, *Mechanising an Army*.
28 Confidential report, 4 September 1939, Daly, service dossier.
29 Allchin, *Purple and Blue*, provides a detailed account of the battalion's doings throughout the war.
30 Daly, interview with Pratten, 26 October 2000. Copy in author's possession.
31 Daly, interview with Breen, 11 May 1992.
32 'Training Instruction No 8', 31 December 1940. War Diary, 18th Brigade, appendix B. AWM52, 8/2/18.
33 Daly, interview with Breen, 11 May 1992.
34 Ibid.
35 War diary, 18th Brigade, 21 January 1941, AWM52, 8/2/18.
36 Ibid., 31 January 1941. See also training instruction No 9, 5 January 1941.
37 Daly, interview with Breen, 11 May 1992.
38 I have no intention of providing a full account of the siege, even in summary. There is an excellent one by the official historian: Long, *The Six Years War*, pp. 75–7, 78–80, 97–9, 100–1. The classic contemporary account, still well worth reading, is Wilmot, *Tobruk 1941*. The relevant volume of the official history is Maugham, *Tobruk and Alamein*. A thorough, and thoroughly readable, account is Lyman, *The Longest Siege*.
39 Long, *To Benghazi*, pp. 287–304; Richardson, 'The siege of Giarabub, December 1940–March 1941', unpublished paper courtesy of the author; Wootten, 'Report on Giarabub Operation' [n.d.], TNA CAB106/836; War Diary, 18th Infantry Brigade, March 1941, AWM52, 8/2/18; Daly, interview with Breen, 11 May 1992; Daly to Gavin Long, letter, 11 April 1950. AWM67, 3/94.
40 Daly, letter to Long, 11 April 1950.
41 Daly, interview with Breen, 11 May 1992, p. 14.
42 Wootten, 'Report on Giarabub Operation', p. 5. TNA, CAB106/836.
43 Long, *To Benghazi*, pp. 303–4.
44 Daly, interview with Breen, 15 June 1992, p. 1.
45 Daly to Gavin Long, letter, 11 April 1950.
46 Gavin Long, notebook interview with Lieutenant-Colonel T.J. Daly, n.d. [mid-1945]. AWM67, 2/86.
47 An excellent example of excessive treatment is provided by Peter Fitzsimons, *Tobruk* (HarperCollins, Sydney, 2006), a book that can be recommended on no other grounds. If the iconic status of the 9th Division be doubted, consider the fact that it is the only infantry division from either world war to have a specific monument among the avenue of national commemorative sculptures on Anzac Parade in Canberra.

48 Daly, interview with Breen, 11 May 1992, p. 18.
49 War diary, 18th Brigade, March 1941.
50 Daly, interview with Breen, 11 May 1992.
51 Daly, interview with Pratten, 26 October 2000.
52 Daly, interview with Breen, 11 May 1992.
53 Ibid., 15 June 1992.
54 Ibid., 15 June 1992.
55 Wootten, 'Report on operations', 9 May 1941. 18th Brigade war diary, May 1941, AWM52, 8/2/18. Daly also offered comments in the war diary at the conclusion of the monthly narrative for May.
56 Maugham, *Tobruk and El Alamein*, p. 332. A further consequence of the failed attack is reflected in Wootten's brigade instruction of 12 May, which reflects the division commander's views perhaps more closely than those of the brigade headquarters. 18th Brigade war diary, May 1941, appendix 35, AWM52, 8/2/18.
57 Daly, interview with Breen, 24 June 1991.
58 This author's grandfather was one such.
59 See Grey, *Australian Brass*, p. 111.
60 Final report, Major T.J. Daly, service dossier.
61 The Japanese had no such intention, nor the capacity to carry through such an ambitious operation even if they had wished it. Stanley, *Invading Australia*.
62 War diary, 5th Infantry Division, appendixes, July 1942, AWM52, 1/5/10.
63 Daly, interview with Breen, 24 June 1991.
64 Daly, interview with Pratten, 26 October 2000.
65 5th Division Training Instruction No 4, 2 August 1942. War diary, August 1942. AWM52, 1/5/10.
66 'Lieutenant-General Sir Thomas Daly', in Pratten & Harper (eds), *Still the Same*, p. 16.
67 Daly, interview with Pratten, 26 October 2000. Daly, interview with Breen, 17 August 1992.
68 Horner, 'Staff Corps versus militia'; Horner, *Crisis of Command*; Horner, *General Vasey's War*; Grey, *Australian Brass*; Keating, *The Right Man for the Right Job* all cover the ground from various perspectives and are representative of a wider literature.
69 Daly, interview with Breen, 17 August 1992.
70 Ibid.
71 In many ways Wilton and Daly came to dominate the post-war army, and there would be wide agreement that they were the two outstanding regular senior officers of their generation. Wilton had been in 1st Class at RMC when Daly arrived in 1930, and graduated into the British Army because of the reductions in the Australian regular establishment. As we will see, Wilton followed Daly in command of the 28th Brigade in Korea and Daly succeeded Wilton as CGS, but the two do not appear to have been close.
72 Daly, interview with Breen, 17 August 1992.
73 Daly to Dexter, letter, 20 May 1952, AWM93, 50/2/23/417.
74 Recommendation for periodic award of OBE, n.d. Daly, service dossier.

75 The army also produced its own doctrine in the form of the *Army Training Memorandums* (*ATM*s), written by Australian officers for conditions specifically encountered by Australians, for the first time.
76 Daly, interviews with Breen, 24 June 1991, 17 August 1992.

2 *Balikpapan, 1945*
1 Allchin, *Purple and Blue*, p. 351.
2 Ibid., supplement, p. 48.
3 Pratten, *Australian Battalion Commanders in the Second World War*, pp. 194–6.
4 Brune, *A Bastard of a Place*.
5 Allchin, *Purple and Blue*, p. 345; Brigadier Sir Frederick Chilton, interview with Bob Breen, 12 May 1992, p. 3. Chilton was coy about the reasons for Geard's removal, as he was also in a later interview with Garth Pratten on the same topic.
6 Pratten, notes of interview with F.O. Chilton, 25 October 2000; R. Cundell to Pratten, letter, 21 January 2004. Courtesy of Garth Pratten.
7 TX2013 Geard, Charles John, 2nd AIF personnel dossier, NAA B883. Geard's dossier has clearly been 'weeded', since no efficiency reports or any other correspondence relating to his relief are contained in it.
8 Gullett, *Not as a Duty Only*, especially pp. 1–12. Gullett's description of an Australian infantry battalion at war has been much admired and much cited in the literature.
9 Hay, *Nothing Over Us*, p. x.
10 Pratten, *Australian Battalion Commanders in the Second World War*, p. 3.
11 Ibid., p. 28.
12 Gavin Long, diary, 20 June 1946, AWM67, 1/11.
13 Discussion based on Pratten, *Australian Battalion Commanders in the Second World War*, passim.
14 Three others received unit commands after him: L.J. Loughran (8th Battalion), J.L.A. Kelly (31/51st Battalion) and D.D. Pitt (37/52nd Battalion).
15 Gavin Long, notebook, 'Aitape April 1945 and Morotai August 1945', AWM67, 2/86.
16 Daly, interview with Breen, 24 June 1991, p. 9.
17 Ibid., p. 11.
18 Chilton, interview with Breen, 12 May 1992, pp. 3–4.
19 2/10th Battalion, war diary, appendix 10, October 1944, AWM52, 8/3/10.
20 Daly, interview with Pratten, 26 October 2000, pp. 13–14.
21 Ibid.; appendix 11, 24 January 1945, War Diary, 2/10th Battalion, AWM52, 8/3/10.
22 Routine orders No 58, 27 November 1944, War Diary, 2/10th Battalion, AWM52, 8/3/10.
23 Routine orders No 59, 28 November 1944, ibid.
24 War diary, 2/10th Battalion, 21 December 1944, AWM52, 8/3/10.
25 Daly, interview with Breen, 24 June 1991, p. 11.

26 A common saying held that 'lieutenants may not marry, captains might marry, and majors should marry'.
27 War diary, 2/10th Battalion, 29–31 May 1945, AWM52, 8/3/10.
28 Daly, comments for Gavin Long, 11 April 1960, AWM93, 50/2/23/417.
29 Long, *The Final Campaigns*, especially chapters 2 and 16. See as well Horner, *High Command*.
30 For a discussion see Grey, *The Australian Army*, pp. 149–50; see as well Grey, *A Military History of Australia*, p. 188.
31 Derrick had enlisted in July 1940 and had fought in the 9th Division through the campaign in North Africa and the Sattelberg–Finschhaffen campaign in New Guinea. Grey, *The Australian Army*, pp. 158–9.
32 Gavin Long, notebook interview with Lieutenant-Colonel T.J. Daly, n.d. (mid-1945). AWM67, 2/86.
33 Daly, interview with Pratten, 26 October 2000, p. 15. He told Gavin Long in 1960, 'I would hold, quite categorically, that never throughout the war did we have so much information about the enemy and his positions or such opportunities for disseminating it.' The point is further reinforced by the divisional intelligence review: AWM52, 1/5/14, June 1945.
34 Daly, interview with Breen, 14 September 1992, p. 12.
35 Long, *The Final Campaigns*, p. 502. The seizure of the Philippines and the fighting on Okinawa were both largely completed, and Rangoon had fallen to the British Fourteenth Army in early May.
36 Chilton, interview with Breen, 12 May 1992, p. 8; Long, *The Final Campaigns*, pp. 509–10; Intelligence summary No 1, 2/10th Battalion, 10 June 1945, war diary, 2/10th Battalion, AWM52, 8/3/10.
37 Long, *The Final Campaigns*, pp. 505–6.
38 Operational order, 13 June 1945, war diary, 2/10th Battalion, ibid.; Daly, comments on chapter 21, to Gavin Long, April 1960. Long papers, AWM93, 50/2/23/417.
39 Allchin, *Purple and Blue*, p. 372. 'The only fire from the enemy was from anti-aircraft guns, and their shells exploded too high to do any serious damage to assault forces.'
40 Long, *The Final Campaigns*, pp. 514–15. The 2/10th war diary notes that 'several Alligators appear to be having trouble in keeping direction' as the first wave went in at 8.40am.
41 A point explained at some length by my US Marine Corps students in February 2002 during a battlefield tour of the Dardanelles, to my considerable advantage.
42 Daly, comments, Long papers, AWM93, 50/2/23/417.
43 Long, *The Final Campaigns*, p. 536.
44 Daly, interview with Breen, 14 September 1992, p. 20.
45 Ibid., p. 22; Daly, comments, Long papers, AWM93, 50/2/23/417.
46 Allchin, *Purple and Blue*, pp. 374–80.
47 Daly, notes for Gavin Long, AWM67, 50/2/23/417.
48 Daly, comments, Long papers, AWM93, 50/2/23/417.
49 Ibid.
50 Daly, interview with Pratten, p. 35.

51 Daly, interview with Breen, 14 September 1992, p. 22; Daly, comments, Long papers, AWM93, 50/2/23/417; Long, *The Final Campaigns*, p. 519; 2/10th Battalion, war diary; Allchin, *Purple and Blue*, pp. 381–2.
52 Daly, interview with Breen, pp. 22–3; 2/10th Battalion war diary; Long, *The Final Campaigns*, p. 521. Daly thought that Chilton's decision reflected his tendency to being 'a little bit cautious and wanting to have all the facts'.
53 Long, *The Final Campaigns*, p. 519.
54 Ibid., p. 521.
55 Daly, interview with Breen, 14 September 1992, p. 24.
56 2/10th battalion, war diary, 3–4 July 1945.
57 Long, *The Final Campaigns*, p. 521.
58 Daly, interview with Breen, 14 September 1992, p. 27.
59 Ibid.
60 Daly recalled that at the end of the war he had a photograph taken of the '39ers (those who had enlisted in that year) still remaining in the 2/10th. 'I suppose we had thirty, something of that order, forty maybe, of an original 800. And they were all either officers or senior NCOs.' Daly, interview with Breen, 14 September 1992, p. 27.
61 Gavin Long, notebook interview with Lieutenant-Colonel T.J. Daly, n.d. [mid-1945]. AWM67, 2/86.
62 Daly, interview with Breen, 14 September 1992, pp. 29–31.
63 General Sir Thomas Blamey, Commander-in-Chief, AMF, letter to Hon J.M. Fraser, acting Minister for the Army, 5 April 1945. CRS MP729/8, 40/431/2.
64 Long, notebook, AWM67, 2/86.
65 Sergeant Les Peterson, 2/10th Battalion, interview with Garth Pratten, 10 February 2001. I am grateful to Dr Pratten for making his notes of this interview available to me.
66 Chilton, interview with Breen, 12 May 1992, p. 5.
67 Pratten, notes of interview with Daly, 26 October 2000. Unless noted otherwise, the following paragraphs draw on Pratten's notes and the transcript of the interview concerned.
68 Chilton, efficiency report on Daly, 21 January 1946. Daly, service dossier.
69 Long, *The Final Campaigns*, p. 531.
70 Daly, interview with Breen.

3 'He could fill any appointment with distinction'

1 Daly, interview with Breen, 12 July 1993.
2 Fitzgerald was director and general manager (administrative) of Consolidated Zinc, a Collins House company that controlled the silver, lead and zinc mines at Broken Hill and owned Comalco, an early Australian foray into the aluminium industry. It merged with Rio Tinto to form ConZinc Rio Tinto (CRA) in 1962.
3 Bond, *The Victorian Staff Army and the Staff College, 1854–1914*.
4 Norman Alan Mark Nicholls, b. 1917, RMC Class of 1939. Nicholls had served in the Middle East and New Guinea, had instructed in the Junior Wing of the Staff School at Duntroon in 1943, and had held the GSO2

Planning job in the Directorate of Training at AHQ in 1945 before being posted to Camberley. He held the Directing Staff position for one year (1945–46) before returning to Australia and a long career in a variety of postings, including as army attaché in Pakistan (1959–61) and Washington DC (1964–66).
5 Daly, interview with Breen, 12 July 1993, p. 3.
6 Ibid., pp. 5–7.
7 Annual confidential report, August–December 1946. Daly, service dossier.
8 Daly, interview with Breen, 12 July 1993, p. 10.
9 Annual confidential reports, 1947, 1948. Daly, personal dossier. The assistant commandants were both brigadiers. Brigadier R.W. Macleod had commanded the SAS Brigade in the latter part of the war, while Brigadier W.H. Lambert had commanded 13th Infantry Brigade at the war's end.
10 Daly, interview with Breen, 12 July 1993, pp. 14–15.
11 Daly, confidential report, n.d. [1948]. Daly, service dossier.
12 Coulthard-Clark, *Duntroon*, p. 163. An earlier history of RMC, Lee, *Duntroon*, has been used as well in capturing this brief portrait of the college during the war years. In style the latter is very much of its time.
13 Coulthard-Clark, *Duntroon*, p. 165.
14 Ibid., pp. 182–5.
15 Daly, interview with Breen, 12 July 1993, pp. 15–16.
16 As an army brat, the author well remembers the amount of time, effort and money required to make successive quarters fully habitable during his childhood. This was the case in the 1960s (when many quarters were still early postwar constructions), and must have been even more the case in the late 1940s as a result of wartime neglect and lack of resources for maintenance or new construction.
17 'Military notes', *Mercury* (Hobart), 7 July 1910, p. 7. The Director of Drill was to 'instruct and supervise the drill of all arms, riding and driving, musketry and machine-gun practice, physical training and signalling'. The Director of Military Art's initial salary was £800, the Director of Drill's £700.
18 Coulthard-Clark, *Duntroon*, p. 160.
19 'Annual Confidential Report – Officers', Major-General H. Wells, 26 July 1950. Daly, service dossier.
20 Daly, interview with Breen, 12 July 1993, p. 18.
21 Coulthard-Clark, *Duntroon*, pp. 198–9.
22 'Annual confidential report – Officers', Major-General R.N.L. Hopkins, 20 July 1951. Daly, service dossier.
23 It is difficult to generalise or extrapolate about housing costs between the 1950s and today, not least because there is little comparative data with which to work (the House Price Indexes issued by the Australian Bureau of Statistics have been kept only since 1989). An advertisement in the *Argus* in July 1950 listed a six-room brick villa with a 70-foot frontage for £5000 ('Owners ready to sell vacant homes at auction', the *Argus*, 24 July 1950, p. 7). On one set of measures, the growth in Sydney property prices was less than 3 per cent between 1880 and 1950 (it grew, on average, 9 per cent in

the fifty years after 1955). Stubborn Mule, 'Australian property prices', 30 June 2009, http://www.stubbornmule.net/2009/06/property-prices.
24 Daly, interview with Colonel David Chinn, Canberra, 10 July 2001, p. 4; Daly, interview with author, Sydney, 12 October 1984, p. 1.
25 Daly, interview with author, p. 3.
26 Ibid., p. 3.
27 Grey, *The Commonwealth Armies and the Korean War* provides a full discussion of the issues at policy and administrative levels.
28 In a minute concerning the deployment of 1RAR the Minister for the Army, Josiah Francis, noted that British battalions in Korea were rarely more than 600 all ranks while the war establishment for the Australian battalions was held at 960. The 3rd Battalion then serving 'was by far the strongest Infantry unit' in the Commonwealth Brigade. 'Further unit for Korea', n.d. [early March 1952], NAA MP729/8, 37/431/122.
29 Daly, interview with Colonel David Chinn, Canberra, 10 July 2001, p. 4. In this interview Daly recalls himself as having been Director of Military Operations and Plans at this stage, but this is one of the few occasions when his memory played him false in interview. He held the position of Director of Infantry until he went to Korea in mid-1952 and assumed the position of Director of Military Operations and Plans only upon his return, in July 1953. Officer's Record of Service, Daly, service dossier.
30 The reasons for this were historical, and lay in the agreement that command of the British Commonwealth Occupation Force in Japan after the war was vested in Australia. When the Korean War began, Australia was the only remaining Commonwealth country with a presence (albeit vestigial) in Japan, and this became the structure on which the administrative, logistical and non-operational command arrangements were built.
31 Minute, Director of Military Operations to Chief of the Imperial General Staff, 20 March 1952, TNA, WO308/68.
32 HQ 28th Brigade, 'Standing orders for Brigade HQ in the field', 5 June 1952, TNA, WO281/150.
33 28 British Commonwealth Brigade, 'Staff List', TNA, WO281/711. The remainder of the staff continued to be drawn from the British Army.
34 28 British Commonwealth Brigade, 'Composition of Tac, Main and Rear Hqs', Standing order No 2, TNA, WO281/150.
35 Daly, interview with Chinn, pp. 5, 16.
36 Derek Sharp, letter to author, 8 August 2011.
37 The Australian Chief of the General Staff, Lieutenant-General Sir Sydney Rowell, drew this Great War comparison explicitly in his memoirs: Rowell, *Full Circle*, p. 180.
38 Daly, interview with Breen, 1 December 1993, p. 5.
39 Subsequently Daly's MA when he was Chief of the General Staff.
40 Daly, interview with author, 12 October 1984, p. 6.
41 Daly, interview with Chinn, p. 8.
42 Views drawn from interviews with Breen, Chinn and Grey. 'That's the trouble, you see. You get chaps who are brave but not particularly skilful, you can have a lot of casualties' (Daly, interview with Chinn, p. 11).

43 Cassels was a noted cricketer, playing first class for the army, the Egyptian national side and in India. A right-arm fast medium off-spinner, his best figures were 6/51 while playing for Punjab Governor's XI in 1928.
44 West was allegedly the model for General Liddament in Anthony Powell's *Dance to the Music of Time*. In retirement he was friendly with both Bob Dylan and Mick Jagger; the latter wrote several songs with West's socialite daughter as the object.
45 Daly, interview with author, p. 16.
46 Johnston, *A War of Patrols*, pp. 317–18.
47 Grey, *The Commonwealth Armies and the Korean War*, pp. 137–49, discusses the different operational styles of the two sides and the command arguments involved.
48 Daly, interview with Chinn, p. 13.
49 Ibid., p. 11. This could just as easily be determined through interrogation of enemy deserters. See 28 Britcom Inf Bde INTREP 95, 15 June 1952. TNA, WO281/150.
50 Pratten & Harper (eds), *Still the Same*, p. 34.
51 Brigadier T.J. Daly to battalion COs, 'Personal memorandum to commanders, No 11', 30 June 1952, TNA, WO281/150.
52 'It was a very, very uneconomical way of getting information' (Daly, interview with Chinn, p. 23).
53 O'Neill, *Australia in the Korean War*, p. 253; Grey, *The Commonwealth Armies and the Korean War*, pp. 150–1.
54 Johnston, *A War of Patrols*, pp. 316–19.
55 Daly, interview with Breen, 1 December 1993, p. 5.
56 Horner, *Strategic Command*.
57 Command of the 25th Canadian Brigade was always twelve months, while with the 29th British Brigade it varied.
58 General Sir John Wilton, diary/memoir (unpublished), entry for '1953', Wilton papers, AWM, PR82/119.
59 Citation, CBE, 29 January 1953, Daly, service dossier.
60 28th Brigade training instruction, 2 February 1953, TNA, WO281/711.
61 'I expected that they keep their positions in perfect order, that their weapons, gear, equipment and so on should be well cared for and in good repair, that their ammunition and weapons be clean, and that they themselves be clean. That was the sort of thing I looked for. I inspected them fairly regularly' (Pratten & Harper (eds), *Still the Same*, p. 35).
62 Daly, interview with Breen, 1 December 1993, p. 5.
63 Palazzo, *The Australian Army*, p. 226. Succinct and clear descriptions of the organisation of Army Headquarters over time are difficult to find. Palazzo's excellent book provides much more detail, and clarity, on the changes to the field army and the evolving relationship between the regular and citizen forces than on developments in the machinery for their higher direction.
64 Daly, interview with Breen, 1 December 1993, p. 7; Murphy, 'History of the postwar army'.
65 Horner, *Defence Supremo*, p. 237. There is no satisfactory history of the committee structures within the Defence organisation.

66 Andrews, *The Department of Defence*, p. 140.
67 Horner, *Defence Supremo*, p. 320.
68 Daly, interview with Breen, 1 December 1993, p. 8.
69 Lieutenant-General Sir Thomas Daly, letter to author, 5 September 1986, author's papers.
70 Ibid.
71 Churchill was Secretary of State for the Colonies at this point, but he chaired the Cabinet committee tasked with implementing the Geddes Report.
72 Gray, *The Imperial Defence College*, p. 2.
73 Horner, *Defence Supremo*, pp. 23–9. The 1928 course included Lieutenant-Colonel E.K. Squires, subsequently Chief of the General Staff and Inspector-General of the Australian Military Forces in 1938–40.
74 Rowell, *Full Circle*, p. 180.
75 Horner, *Strategic Command*, p. 143.
76 Gray, *The Imperial Defence College*, pp. 15–21.
77 Class list for 1956 course kindly supplied by Brigadier A.J. Lennard, Chief of Staff, Royal College of Defence Studies, 11 May 2011.
78 The Comet was the great hope of postwar British civil aviation. It suffered a series of fatal crashes in 1952–54, and has the dubious distinction of being the first jet passenger liner to be involved in a fatal accident (at Karachi in March 1953). A revamped aircraft returned to commercial passenger service in 1958 but had been overtaken by such American designs as the Boeing 707, and it rapidly faded from commercial use, although variants kept flying in more specialised roles for several decades.
79 Betty-Ann Daly, emails to author, 9 May 2011, 20 February 2012; Horner, *Strategic Command*, p. 142.
80 These two lines and the ships they ran were well known and much loved by several generations of older Australians, and by thousands of British immigrants who came to Australia after the Second World War to pursue new lives.
81 Daly, interview with Breen, 15 June 1992, p. 22.
82 Coombes, *Morshead*, p. 216.

4 The challenges of senior rank

1 These changes and developments are discussed in Palazzo, *The Australian Army*, passim.
2 Ibid., pp. 128, 221–5.
3 There was just one university in the state in the 1950s, and the university sector in Australia was generally much smaller than would become the case in successive expansions in the 1960s and 1970s.
4 Appendix A, Northern Command memo 12625, 3 August 1950, CRA BP129/1, NCCR 174/1/212. The organisational details in this earlier document remained largely unchanged by the time Daly became GOC.
5 Horn, 'Australia's development of the Pacific Islands Regiment', p. 13.
6 'Report on Inspection New Guinea 18–30 Aug 52', GOC Northern Command to Army Headquarters, 5 September 1952, NAA MP729/8, 37/431/114.

7 The postwar PIR is a largely untouched subject. In addition to Horn's sub-thesis, cited above, the major sources are Sinclair, *To Find a Path*, Vol. II: *Keeping the Peace 1950–1975* [hereafter *Keeping the Peace*], and an unpublished PhD thesis, Colebatch, 'To find a path'. The army receives only occasional mention in the larger literature on Australia's administration of TPNG. There was a wider contemporary discussion of the future prospects and likely development of the nascent PNG Defence Force (PNGDF) after independence: see, for example, O'Neill, *The Army in Papua New Guinea*.
8 Sinclair, *Keeping the Peace*, pp. 44–5.
9 Minute, GOC Northern Command, Major-General Secombe, to Army Headquarters, 9 November 1951, NAA MP729/8, 37/431/120.
10 Minute, Secombe to Army Headquarters, 15 August 1952, ibid.
11 O'Neill, *The Army in Papua-New Guinea*, p. 3.
12 The civil administration in postwar PNG is exhaustively, if somewhat selectively, treated in Downs, *The Australian Trusteeship*. Discussion of defence is confined to less than five pages.
13 Subsequently Governor-General of Australia, Hasluck held the Territories portfolio for the remarkably lengthy period 1951–63.
14 O'Neill, *The Army in Papua New Guinea*, p. 4.
15 Sinclair, *Keeping the Peace*, pp. 60–1.
16 Sinclair, *To Find a Path*, I: *Yesterday's Heroes, 1885–1950* [hereafter *Yesterday's Heroes*], pp. 273–84.
17 Sinclair, *Keeping the Peace*, p. 62.
18 Sinclair, *Keeping the Peace*, states that the incident occurred on 7 December; Daly's report states that it happened on 12 December. The particulars as reported in the two sources have some differences, and it is possible that two separate incidents are described. Report, GOC Northern Command to Adjutant General, Army Headquarters, 20 December 1957, NAA MP927/1, A5/1/132.
19 Sinclair records that 'European Army officers tried to intervene but got beaten up themselves' (*Keeping the Peace*, p. 63). This clearly did not happen.
20 Daly, report, 20 December 1957; 'extract from letter from Captain I.G. Ford, 1 Psych Research Unit, n.d. [late December 1957], NAA MP927/1, A5/1/132. This file contains Daly's report on the December incidents together with other, related correspondence.
21 Sinclair, *Keeping the Peace*, p. 67.
22 Major Don Barrett, Rabaul, letters to Daly, 20 December and 31 December 1957, NAA MP927/1, A5/1/132. Barrett was a company commander in the PNGVR, a former elected member of the Legislative Council and a long-time resident businessman and plantation owner in PNG. Barrett was a supporter of the PIR, and stated bluntly that 'the underlying attitude of many officers of the Administration to Pacific Islands Regiment is one of hostility'.
23 Hank Nelson, 'Cleland, Sir Donald MacKinnon', *Australian Dictionary of Biography Online*, http://adb.anu.edu.au.
24 Daly, letter to Adjutant-General, 7 March 1958, NAA MP927/1, A5/1/132.

25 Major-General I.T. Murdoch, Deputy CGS, memorandum to Minister for the Army, 2 January 1958, ibid.
26 Secretary, minute to Minister, 3 January 1958, ibid.
27 Breen, notes of interview with Lt Gen Sir Thomas Daly, 19 January 1994. Unfortunately the interview itself has been lost, and no transcript appears to have been made or, at least, cannot now be located despite extensive searching. Copy in author's possession.
28 Additional correspondence concerning the structure and roles of the PIR during Daly's period as GOC can be found at NAA A6059, 21/441/15.
29 Major-General [then Lieutenant-Colonel] J.W. Norrie, CO 1PIR, 1959–62, cited in Sinclair, *Keeping the Peace*, p. 71.
30 A copy of the document is contained in Fruhling (ed.), *A History of Australian Strategic Policy Since 1945*, pp. 199–245.
31 For a full discussion, see Palazzo, *The Australian Army*, pp. 240–9.
32 Pentropic took its cue from the American 'Pentomic' organization, a short-lived reorganization intended to disperse US divisions on the atomic battleground, thus ensuring their survival. For the US experiment see Bacevich, *The Pentomic Era*; for the Australian variant see Blaxland, *Organising an Army*.
33 Breen, notes of interview with Lt Gen Sir Thomas Daly, 19 January 1994.
34 McCarthy, *The Once and Future Army*, p. 103.
35 Cooke, 'One army', p. 77.
36 Betty-Ann Daly, email to author, 10 January 2012.
37 Phillips, Heritage Homes of the Australian Defence Force, p. 62.
38 Sharp, letter to author, 8 August 2011. 'Baptism of sweat for 4000', *Courier-Mail* (Brisbane), 17 April 1959, p. 2; Pratten & Harper (eds), *Still the Same*, pp. 35–6.
39 Palazzo, *The Australian Army*, pp. 287–93.
40 Daly, minute to CGS, Melbourne, 23 July 1958. NAA MP927/1, A240/1/606. The chief of staff system was introduced later, very much in light of the problems that Daly had highlighted here.
41 Minutes, Minister's Conference held at AHQ Canberra, 13–14 May 1960, AHQ File A65/1/813, Australian Army History Unit. The observation was the minister's, who at this time was J.O. Cramer. Daly did not attend this meeting, for reasons that are now lost.
42 Minutes, Command and Staff Conference, AHQ, 20–21 January 1960. Military Board Secretariat, Notes of Conferences 1958–60, vol. 1, AHU.
43 Conference notes, CGS Conference, 25 January 1960. Military Board Secretariat, Notes of Conferences 1958–60, vol. 1, AHU.
44 The point is made by comparing the minutes of successive CGS conferences through the decade. See, for comparison with the above, 'Report on CGS Conference 1952, 10–11 July 1952', NAA MP729/8, 12/431/185.
45 Various sources describe this process in detail. For a brief introduction to the issues, see Feuchtwanger & Philpott, 'Civil–military relations in a period without major wars, 1855–85'.
46 Bizarrely, there is no biography or serious study of Hutton and his important, if often contentious, roles in colonial empire defence, in Canada

and Australia. For a good, succinct discussion of developments in the period, see Stockings, *The Making and Breaking of the Post-Federation Australian Army, 1901–09*, especially pp. 29–54.
47 There is a lengthy discussion of the early evolution of the Military Board in Wood, *Chiefs of the Australian Army*, pp. 50–73.
48 Bolton, *The Middle Way*, p. 90.
49 Adjutant-General's report, Briefing at AHQ attended by the Military Board and GOCs/COMDs of Commands [hereafter AG's report], 23 March 1961, Military Board Secretariat, part 1, p. 16, AHU.
50 AG's report, 27 September 1963, Military Board Secretariat, part 1, p. 33, AHU.
51 Ibid., 28 June 1963, part 2, p. 10.
52 McNeill, *To Long Tan*, p. 26.
53 AG's reports, 23 July 1962, part 1, p. 36, AHU; 29 March 1963, part 2, p. 7; 28 June 1963, part 1, p. 29.
54 AG's report, 15 November 1962, part 2, p. 11, AHU.
55 AG's report, 30 April 1962, part 1, pp. 33–4, AHU. The decline of the CMF in this period is well analysed in McCarthy, *The Once and Future Army*, pp. 105–28.
56 For a discussion of the process by which doctrine evolved in the Australian Army context in this period, see Welburn, *The Development of Australian Army Doctrine 1945–1964*.
57 Breen, notes on interview with Lt Gen Sir Thomas Daly, 19 January 1994.
58 Handy figures for this, as for so much else, are difficult to find easily. See Vamplew, *Australia: Historical Statistics*, p. 344; Gerald Burke & Andrew Spaull, 'Australian schools: Participation and funding, 1901–2000', *Year Book Australia 2001*. http://www.abs.gov.au/Ausstats.
59 AG's report, 27 September 1963, part 1, p. 35, AHU; Breen, notes.
60 AG's report, 28 June 1963, part 2, pp. 12–13, AHU.
61 Very little serious work has been done on the post-war Australian women's services. The best discussion of the reintroduction of the three women's services remains Vincent, '"Women have come to stay"'. Substantive work on the WRAAC consists of Ollif, *Colonel Best and Her Soldiers*, and Bomford, *Soldiers of the Queen*.
62 Bomford, *Soldiers of the Queen*, p. 32. Equally revealingly, Ollif comments that 'a true appreciation of the value of the WRAAC was developing' in the early 1960s, although she rather undercuts the observation by noting that 'it was stressed that all members had a responsibility to the community, both as soldiers and as women. This was apparent in the amount of charitable work undertaken throughout Australia by members of the WRAAC' (Ollif, *Colonel Best and Her Soldiers*, p. 123). It is hard to imagine a corps or regimental history of any other part of the army making such a comment.
63 *Army*, 9 February 1961, cited in Bomford, *Soldiers of the Queen*, p. 53.
64 Bomford, *Soldiers of the Queen*, p. 59.
65 Breen, notes of interview with Lt Gen Sir Thomas Daly, 19 January 1994.
66 A good discussion of the early development of rotary-wing aviation in the army is provided in Lamerton, 'An asset to the Army'.

67 Ibid., p. 9.
68 See as well Horner, *Strategic Command*, pp. 294–304, and Stephens, *Going Solo*, pp. 313–22.
69 Stephens, *Going Solo*, p. 316.
70 AG's report, 29 June 1961, p. 16, 27 September 1963, part 1, p. 34, AHU.
71 Betty-Ann Daly, email to author, 10 January 2012.
72 GOC E Comd, Briefing at AHQ attended by the Military Board and GOCs/COMDs of Commands [hereafter GOC E Comd, Briefing], 10 December 1964, p. 7, AHU.
73 GOC E Comd, Briefing, 28 August 1964, p. 8, AHU.
74 Breen, notes of interview with Lt Gen Sir Thomas Daly, 19 January 1994.
75 GOC E Comd, Briefing, 11 June 1965, pp. 5–7, AHU. Breen, notes on interview with Lt Gen Sir Thomas Daly, 19 January 1994.
76 Lieutenant-General Sir Thomas Daly, interview with Ian McNeill, Sydney, 22 November 1974, Army Historical program, AWM 107, 707/R2/38 (5) (hereafter Daly, interview with McNeill).

5 Chief of the General Staff

1 Military Board minute 175/1966, 27 May 1966, Military Board Proceedings, 1966/2, AHU.
2 J.O. Cramer, Minister for the Army, minute to Athol Townley, Minister for Defence, 18 February 1960, NAA A1945/28, 19/4/9.
3 'Higher army appointments', n.d. [1963], NAA A1945/28, 19/4/9.
4 Recommendation for honours and awards, January 1965, Daly, service dossier.
5 'Future succession of Chief of the General Staff', 26 July 1961, NAA A1945/28, 19/4/9.
6 This was a process underway in the United States, Britain, Canada and New Zealand after 1945, at different rates of development and with some alternative features.
7 Horner, *Strategic Command*, pp. 267–71.
8 Hancock, *John Gorton*, pp. 82–98; Hyslop, *Aye Aye, Minister*, pp. 51–2.
9 Grey, *The Australian Army*, pp. 198–200. There is no equivalent for the army of Hyslop's excellent two volumes on the history of Australian naval administration.
10 Edwards, *A Nation at War*, pp. 129–30; Ayres, *Malcolm Fraser*, pp. 108–11.
11 McCarthy, *The Once and Future Army*, p. 218.
12 Horner, *Strategic Command*, pp. 265–6.
13 Ibid., p. 264.
14 Frame, *Where Fate Calls*, pp. 149–50; Frame, *The Cruel Legacy*, gives a similarly unsympathetic and unflattering portrait of McNicoll.
15 A.W.R. McNicoll, *Sea Voices* (self-published, 1932); Alan McNicoll (sel.), *Odes of Horace* (ANU Press, Canberra, 1979).
16 Wilton, memoir, p. 89, AWM PR82/119.

17 Daly, interview with Breen, 22 April 1994, pp. 1–2. Daly was also of the view that the relationship was improved by the greater integration of the services into the Australian Defence Force after his retirement.
18 Ibid.
19 Sue Langford, 'The National Service scheme, 1964–1972', in Edwards, *A Nation at War*, appendix 1, pp. 355–80.
20 Lieutenant-General Sir Thomas Daly, interview with Ian McNeill, Sydney, 22 November 1974, pp. 15–17, Army Historical Program, AWM107, 707/R2/38(5).
21 Ayres, *Malcolm Fraser*, pp. 109–11; Horner, *Strategic Command*, pp. 244–5.
22 Wilton, memoir, '1964–65', pp. 73–4, AWM PR82/119.
23 Daly, interview with Breen, 22 April 1994, p. 12.
24 Horner, *Strategic Command*, p. 245.
25 Daly, interview with Breen, 22 April 1994, pp. 14–15.
26 Ayres, *Malcolm Fraser*, p. 111.
27 Fraser, letter to Daly, 7 March 1968, p. 3, NAA A6876/1.
28 'The Australian Army', n.d. [January 1967], AWM101/11.
29 CGS remarks, Briefing at AHQ attended by the Military Board and GOCs/Comds of Commands [hereafter CGS remarks], 9 June 1966, p. 39, Military Board Secretariat, AHU.
30 CGS remarks, 2 December 1968, p. 48, AHU.
31 CGS remarks, 2 March 1970, p. 46, AWM 98/772.
32 Ibid., pp. 49–50.
33 It was a factor again for the British Army in Northern Ireland in the 1980s, with senior NCOs facing multiple repeat unaccompanied tours in the province and which led to increased levels of resignation or failure to re-engage.
34 Daly, 'National service', p. 9. This article contained the text of an address Daly gave to the national symposium of the RSL in August 1972, following his retirement.
35 Strachan, *The Politics of the British Army*, pp. 214–23.
36 Patterson, GOC 17th Division, letter to Daly, 21 August 1967, NAA A6836/2.
37 Minute 134/1967, 28 April 1967, Military Board Proceedings 1967/3, AHU.
38 Donnelly, *The Scheyville Experience*, p. 141.
39 Ibid., pp. xiii, 166.
40 Lieutenant-General Sir Thomas Daly, 'Major-General Sir James Harrison memorial lecture, 10 November 1982' (privately published, Canberra, 2000), p. 6.
41 Daly, 'National service', p. 14.
42 Minute 220/1967, 'Re-engagement rates – National Service', 23 June 1967, Military Board Proceedings, AHU.
43 Palazzo, *The Australian Army*, pp. 272–3.
44 Military Board minute 180/1966, 27 May 1966, Military Board Proceedings 1966/4, AHU.
45 Military Board minute 256/1966, 22 July 1966, Military Board Proceedings 1966/4, AHU.

46 CGS remarks, 9 June 1966, p. 44, AHU.
47 CGS remarks, 2 December 1968, p. 48, AHU.
48 CGS remarks, 2 March 1970, pp. 52–3, AWM98/772, AHU.
49 *Parliamentary Debates*, House of Representatives, Vol. 53, 27 September 1966, p. 1328.
50 McCarthy, *The Once and Future Army*, pp. 146–8.
51 Daly, interview with McNeill, 22 November 1974, pp. 8–9.
52 Baker, *Paul Cullen*, p. 186.
53 Daly, letter to Cullen, 27 July 1970, NAA A6835, 3.
54 Daly, letter to Reverend E.B. Phillips, 30 February 1968, NAA A6876/1, 3: 'I saw a lot of our mutual friends when I was in Adelaide last Anzac Day. It was the 28th Anniversary of the raising of the 10th Battalion at Woodside in 1939 . . . altogether it was a memorable weekend.' Daly, letter to Brigadier F.O. Chilton, 6 February 1967, NAA A6836/2: 'It is very encouraging, therefore, to hear your views on our troops in Vietnam and Malaysia because I value your opinion very highly.'
55 Daly, minute to Minister for the Army, 18 July 1969, NAA A6835, 2.
56 Blair, *There to the Bitter End*, pp. 12–15, recycles the idea that the JTC establishment was 'new' and that Serong was the instigator of training oriented to jungle warfare in the post-war Australian Army. The same line is given in Blair, *Ted Serong*, pp. 39–46. The biggest problem with both books is that their primary source is Serong himself.
57 The attribution to Serong of 'founding' Canungra distressed McDonald, who was by now an elderly man, and Daly wrote to the *Sydney Morning Herald* in reply to an article along these lines seeking to correct the record. Daly, letter to *SMH*, 17 October 1969, NAA A6835, 2.
58 Correspondence, Daly and Pollard, 7 April, 21 April, 26 April 1967, NAA A6836, 2.
59 Daly, letter to Lieutenant W.G.S. Boyd, 23 June 1970. NAA A6835, 3. In another letter to a former subordinate in Korea he noted that 'my subalterns of those days seem to be commanding battalions in Vietnam' (Daly, letter to Colonel R.E. Scott, 9 April 1970, NAA A6835, 3).
60 Pollard, letter to Daly, 26 May 1968, NAA A6836/1, 3.
61 QX39522 Captain John Ahearn Torpie, AAChD ANGAU (1910–2000), ordained 1934, Bishop of Cairns 1967–85.
62 Daly, letter to Torpie, 22 May 1968, NAA A6835, 1.
63 Daly, letter to HE Sir Edwin Hicks, High Commissioner to New Zealand, 9 July 1968, NAA A6835, 1.
64 Daly, letter to Brigadier F.O. Chilton, 6 February 1967, NAA A6836/2.
65 Colin Gurner, letter to Daly, 23 August 1968, NAA A6876/1, 3.
66 Briefing at Army Headquarters for Military Board and Commands, 26 October 1970, AWM98, R128/1/3/1.
67 By way of example, Andrew Peacock, Minister for the Army, letter to Fraser, 20 November 1969, NAA A1946, 1969/2269 pt 1.
68 The relevant statistics for 1966–67 are useful. Army strength stood at 43 548, of whom 15 435 were married; 9528 were serving overseas, together with 1446 families (the majority of these in Malaysia or Papua New Guinea). There were 7407 married quarters in Australia (and a further

660 in AAF FARELF), with 1422 service families awaiting a quarter in Australia (and, tellingly, no waiting list in FARELF). This latter figure was in addition to the 7368 families living in private accommodation. In that year 35 620 posting orders were issued, of which 28 298 involved movements.

69 Discussion derived from Military Board minute 439/1967 and supporting submission from Adjutant General, 15 December 1967, Military Board Proceedings 1967/5, AHU.
70 AG's remarks, Briefing at AHQ attended by the Military Board and GOCs/Comds of Commands, 23 July 1962, part 1, pp. 38–9, AHU.
71 CGS remarks, 18 July 1967, p. 67, AHU.
72 There is no documented source for this that I know of, but the point has been made to me by a number of individuals. When I asked him about it in conversation Daly flatly denied it.
73 Military Board minute 450/1969, 19 December 1969 and submission 73/1969, 2 December 1969. Military Board Proceedings, 1969/7, AHU.
74 In particular, the extensive, well-documented and thorough discussions of the phenomenon in two of the standard histories of the college: Coulthard-Clark, *Duntroon*, pp. 219–39, and Moore, *Duntroon*, pp. 347–96. See as well Dennis, 'The Duntroon affair'.
75 Daly, letter to Major-General C.A.E. Fraser, 31 October 1969, NAA A6835, 2.
76 Moore, *Duntroon*, p. 275.
77 Bryan, letter to Daly, 26 August 1968, NAA A6836/1, 3.
78 Dennis, 'The Duntroon affair'. The article is not paginated.
79 *Parliamentary Debates – HofR*, vol. 65, 25 September 1969, pp. 1359–62. Lance Barnard, a subsequent Defence Minister in the Whitlam Government, noted in his response to Lynch's statement that 'the Minister acted promptly and correctly in appointing the Board of Inquiry. He has wasted no time in getting the inquiry finished and taking appropriate action... Quite frankly, I believe there is little political capital in a matter of this nature.'
80 Daly, letter to Lynch, 31 October 1969, NAA A6835, 2.
81 *Parliamentary Debates – HofR*, vol. 67, 7 May 1970, p. 1784.
82 Daly, letter to Major-General L.E. Beavis, 11 May 1970, NAA A6835, 3.
83 Daly, letter, to Talbot Duckmanton, 6 May 1970, A6835, 3.
84 Ibid.
85 Daly, letter to Fraser, 31 October 1969, NAA A6835, 2.
86 Dennis, 'The Duntroon affair'.
87 Peacock, Minister for the Army, letter to Fraser, Minister for Defence [n.d., 5 December 1969]; Daly, letter to Minister for Defence, 4 December 1969, NAA A1976, 68/1137.
88 Military Board minute 403/1970, 21 August 1970; Military Board Proceedings 1970/5, AHU.
89 'The effect on Australia's defence requirements of developments in the Territory of Papua and New Guinea' (unpublished report), JIC (Aust) (67)54, July 1967, NAA A6836/2.

90 Downs, *The Australian Trusteeship*, p. 477; Cabinet minute 484, 19 July 1970, NAA A5873, vol. 2.
91 Military Board minute 444/1966, 9 December 1966; Military Board Proceedings 1966/5, AHU.
92 Sinclair, *Keeping the Peace*, pp. 143–4.
93 CGS remarks, 24 June 1968, p. 43, AHU.
94 Military Board minute 385/1969, 7 November 1969, Military Board Proceedings 1969/7, AHU.
95 Military Board minute 402/1969, 21 November 1969, Military Board Proceedings 1969/7, AHU.
96 Daly, letter to Bland, 15 August 1969, NAA A6835, 2.
97 Daly, letter to Minister for the Army, 6 June 1969, NAA A6835, 2.
98 Defence Committee minute 153/1958, 3 December 1958, AWM122, 71/6020.
99 Sinclair, *Keeping the Peace*, pp. 210–13.
100 CGS remarks, 9 June 1966, p. 45, AHU.
101 Brief to Chief of Air Staff from Air Commodore, DGOR, 30 May 1966, NAA A7941, J6 part 1.
102 Howson, *The Life of Politics*, pp. 199–200.
103 Ibid., p. 214. 'RGM and Scherger and Paltridge procrastinated. Allen [Fairhall] is worried that so many matters reach his desk needing almost immediate decision, with no time to think of future policy. I told him this was the result of the pile-up of work due to Shane's illness.'
104 Military Board minute 256/1967, 21 July 1967, Military Board Proceedings, 1967/3, AHU. The army–RAAF agreement, signed by the two chiefs of service and dated 8 May 1967, is at AWM121, 32/A/3.
105 Howson, *The Life of Politics*, p. 242. Earlier he minuted that he had 'argued the case for taking over the lot'.
106 Daly, 'The Army Aviation Corps'. Howson noted that 'we now have a clear delimitation of our responsibilities and army responsibilities. I am pleased that, after so many months of talk, we appear at last to have a decision', even if it went against his own position as Minister. Howson, *The Life of Politics*, p. 248. See also minutes and memoranda at AWM121, 32/A/3 and NAA 7941, J6 part 1.
107 Daly, letter to Wilton, 7 November 1968, NAA A7941, J6 part 1.
108 DMOP, minute to DCGS, 13 December 1968; Secretary, Department of the Army, letter to secretary, Department of Air, 20 June 1969, AWM121, 32/A/3.
109 Tolson, *Airmobility*, pp. 108–13.
110 Military Board minute 256/1967, 21 July 1967, Military Board Proceedings, 1967/3, AHU. The classification of this minute was upgraded from Restricted to Confidential in line with the Minister's direction that 'caution should be exercised in the timing and promulgation of any decision so as not to prejudice Cabinet consideration of the submission concerning the Oakey project'. Distribution was accordingly restricted to members of the board. The RAAF would continue to snipe at the army over the issue of enlistment of pilots after Daly's retirement.

Minute, Director Aviation to CGS, 22 August 1972, NAA A7941, J6 part 1.
111 Howson, *The Life of Politics*, p. 367.
112 Daly, 'Army Aviation Corps'.
113 In early 2011 it was decided to rename Oakey in honour of Swartz, an announcement that caused some angst among former members of the army aviation community, some of whom argued that Swartz had acted through personal and electoral interests and that there were more deserving candidates. *Fourays* (website of the Australian Army Aviation Association), http://www.fourays.org/history.
114 Howson, *The Life of Politics*, p. 186.
115 Horner, *Strategic Command*, p. 303.
116 Daly, 'Army Aviation Corps'.
117 Horner, *Strategic Command*, p. 304.
118 Daly, letter to AVM C.T. Hannah, 21 August 1968, NAA A6876/1, 3.

6 Daly, the army and the war in Vietnam, 1966–71

1 Daly, letter to Colonel A.G. Rangaraj, 26 February 1968, NAA A6835, 1. Rangaraj had commanded the Indian field ambulance that was part of the 28th Brigade.
2 Lieutenant-General Sir Thomas Daly, interview with Ian McNeill, Sydney, 22 November 1974, Army Historical Program, AWM 107, 707/R2/38 (5), p. 2.
3 Horner, *Australian Higher Command in the Vietnam War*, p. 7.
4 Daly, interview with McNeill, 22 November 1974, p. 4.
5 Ibid., p. 5.
6 Horner, *Strategic Command*, p. 242.
7 Daly, interview with McNeill, 22 November 1974, pp. 5–6.
8 Ibid., p. 20.
9 Howson, *The Life of Politics*, p. 210.
10 Horner, *Australian Higher Command*, p. 17.
11 Daly, interview with Breen, 22 April 1994, pp. 3–4.
12 Horner, *Australian Higher Command*, p. 17.
13 Chiefs of Staff Committee minute 62/1967, 10 May 1967, NAA A1976, 67/1531.
14 Ibid.
15 Wilton, Minute to Minister for Defence, 15 May 1967, NAA A1976, 67/1531.
16 Horner, *Australian Higher Command*, pp. 48–9.
17 Daly, interview with McNeill, 22 November 1974, p. 24.
18 Daly, minute CGS 31/1970, 19 March 1970, NAA A6835, 3.
19 McNeill & Ekins, *On the Offensive*, p. 157.
20 Daly, cable 4198 to COMAFV, 30 January 1968, NAA A6835, 1.
21 McNeill & Ekins, *On the Offensive*, pp. 156–7.
22 Vincent, letter to Daly, 15 July 1967, AWM101, 24.

23 O'Brien, *Conscripts and Regulars*, p. 143. The same thing happened with 2RAR, which returned at around the same time: 'Most of the young officers and junior NCOs and soldiers would leave 2RAR on its return to Australia. The remaining officers would leave by the end of the year' (Church, *Second to None*, p. 1).
24 O'Brien, *Conscripts and Regulars*, pp. 145–6.
25 For a short account of the training process of another battalion, see Wood, *9th Battalion Royal Australian Regiment*, pp. 1–15.
26 Daly, minute, CGS99/1967, to Minister for the Army, 30 May 1967, AWM101, p. 9. In his remarks at the Army Headquarters briefing on 31 March 1969 he reinforced the view that 'the army's first priority was to provide adequately trained troops for units proceeding to Vietnam'.
27 Horner, *Strategic Command*, p. 277.
28 Secretary, Department of the Army, minute to Secretary, Department of Defence, 20 February 1967, NAA A1976/14, 67/573.
29 Daly, interview with McNeill, 22 November 1974, p. 28.
30 COMAFV brief for CGS, appendix 2 to annex B, July 1967. AWM98, 128/1/10.
31 Fraser, letter to Fairhall, 12 May 1967, AWM101, 20.
32 McGibbon, *New Zealand's Vietnam War*, p. 238. The plan originally was to place the two NZ companies in separate battalions.
33 Military Board minute 383/1967, 13 November 1967. Military Board Proceedings 1967/5.
34 Daly, letter to Sir Edwin Hicks, Australian High Commissioner, Wellington, 9 July 1968, NAA A6835, 1.
35 Fraser, letter to Fairhall, copy to Holt, 12 May 1967, AWM101, 20. Consideration was also given to raising 'a tenth battalion, ARA', but nothing seems to have come of this.
36 Daly, letter to Vincent, 21 July 1967, AWM101, 18.
37 Horner, *Strategic Command*, pp. 277–8.
38 Daly, 'Notes for Prime Minister's brief', 26 May 1967. AWM101, 24.
39 Fraser, letters to Fairhall, 20 September 1967, 27 September 1967, AWM101, 17.
40 Mackay, letter to CGS, 30 September 1967, NAA A6836/2.
41 Daly, letter to Mackay, 16 October 1967, NAA A6836/2.
42 'Resume of discussion held in CGS' Office, 17 October 1967', AWM101, 17.
43 Daly, letter to COMAFV, 20 January 1968, NAA, A6835, p. 1.
44 'Resume of discussion held in CGS' Office, 20 October 1967', AWM101, 17.
45 Starry, *Armored Combat in Vietnam*, p. 9. This team comprised a hundred US Army officers, headed by Major-General Arthur L. West, Jr, and produced an extensive study looking at both the deployment of armour and the utility of the armour–cavalry mix on operations in Vietnam.
46 Vincent, letter to Wilton, 22 June 1967, AWM 101, 24.
47 Horner, *Strategic Command*, pp. 279–80.

48 Grey, *Up Top*, pp. 118–21.
49 Lieutenant-Colonel I.J. Wilton, 1st Armoured Regiment to Daly, 28 November 1967, NAA, A6836/2.
50 Daly, letter to I.J. Wilton, 5 December 1967, NAA, A6836/2.
51 Daly, letter to COMAFV, 23 April 1968, NAA, A6835, 1.
52 'Report on the employment of C Sqn 1 Armd Regt South Vietnam – Feb/Oct 1968'; Daly, letter to Minister for the Army, 28 October 1968, NAA, A6835, 1. A series of summary notes on C Squadron operations are found at NAA, A1946, 1968/988.
53 Horner, *Strategic Command*, pp. 246–51.
54 Greville, *The Royal Australian Engineers*, p. 678.
55 Daly, interview with McNeill, 22 November 1974, p. 22.
56 COMAFV, letter to Daly, 15 July 1967, AWM101, 24.
57 Daly, interview with McNeill, 22 November 1974.
58 Ibid.
59 Daly, interview with Breen, 22 April 1994, p. 9.
60 A good first-hand account of the development of airmobility is provided by Howze, *A Cavalryman's Story*. The acquisition and force structure and development issues within the US Army are analysed by Bergerson, *The Army Gets an Air Force*.
61 Grey, *The Australian Army*, p. 216.
62 McNeill, *To Long Tan*, p. 433; NAA, A7941, V16 part 1.
63 Minute, Murdoch to Wilton, 13 September 1965, NAA, 1945, 248/4/128.
64 Daly, interview with McNeill, 22 November 1974, p. 27.
65 Stephens, *Going Solo*, pp. 289, 292.
66 McNeill, *To Long Tan*, p. 431.
67 Daly, interview with McNeill, 22 November 1974, p. 25.
68 Air Commodore DGPP, minute to CAS, 24 August 1965, NAA, A7941, V16 part 1.
69 Howson, *The Life of Politics*, p. 287.
70 Army HQ, cable to HQ AFV, I.0344, 30 March 1967, AWM98 R875/2/36.
71 Daly, interview with McNeill, 22 November 1974, p. 26.
72 Chiefs of Staff Committee minute 69/1968, 29 May 1968, AWM122, 71/6020. See also AWM98, R664/67/3.
73 COMAFV, letter to Daly, 15 July 1967, AWM101, 24.
74 COMAFV, letter to Daly, 4 October 1967, AWM101, 24.
75 Daly, letter to Vincent, 21 July 1967, AWM101, 24.
76 Daly, letter to AOC Support Command, 21 August 1967, NAA A6876/1, 3. Hannah was previously AOC Operational Command and in January 1970 succeeded Murdoch as CAS.
77 Chiefs of Staff Committee minute 65/1968, 4 July 1968.
78 Daly, CGS 57/1969 to CAS, 16 April 1969. NAA A6835, 2.
79 Daly, letter CGS 89/1969 to CAS, 29 May 1969. NAA A6835, 2.
80 Murdoch, handwritten note for file. NAA, A7941, V16 part 1.
81 A/DCAS, minute to CAS, 3 June 1969, ibid.
82 Horner, *Strategic Command*, pp. 305–25.
83 Horner, *Australian Higher Command*, pp. 62–3.

84 Ibid., p. 63.
85 The case for the indictment is made by Lockhart, who sees the construction of the minefield as springing from 'an unspoken imperial impulse to erect barriers against political change in Asia' (Lockhart, *The Minefield*, p. 236). A considered treatment based on an extensive review of the records is McNeill & Ekins, *On the Offensive*, pp. 127–56.
86 Maizey, notes for I.G. McNeill, n.d. (1994?). Copy in author's possession. Hughes later commented that the addition of a third infantry battalion 'made *all* the difference' (McNeill & Ekins, *On the Offensive*, p. 250).
87 COMAFV, letter to Daly, 15 July 1967, AWM101, 24.
88 O'Neill, *Vietnam Task*, p. 230. See as well pp. 184–5 and especially pp. 229–36.
89 Maizey, letter to Bernard Terry, 9 August 2005. Copy in author's possession.
90 Ekins & McNeill, *Fighting to the Finish*, pp. 102–4.
91 Maizey, notes for I.G. McNeill.
92 It is worth noting, however, that mines extracted in this manner were not the only source of explosive ordnance available to the enemy. There had been mine and explosive booby-trap incidents with 5RAR before the minefield was commenced, while there were also large numbers of non-Australian (principally ARVN) minefields in Phuoc Tuy. 1ATF, 'Phuoc Tuy minefields as at 30 Jun 71', copy in the author's possession.
93 Maizey, letter, 9 August 2005.
94 Horner, *Strategic Command*, pp. 329, 331.
95 The official history states, of the decision to deploy armour to Phuoc Tuy, which Graham did not believe necessary, 'Daly maintained that this was the one occasion when the people in the rear (in Army Headquarters) apparently knew more than the person at the front (Brigadier Graham)' (McNeill & Ekins, *On the Offensive*, p. 249).
96 Daly, interview with McNeill, 22 November 1974, pp. 24–5.
97 McNeill & Ekins, *On the Offensive*, p. 145, citing the local communist history of the Long Dat district.
98 DCGS, minute to Secretary, DCGS 335/69, 1 August 1969, AWM98, 776.
99 Horner, *Australian Higher Command*, p. 64.
100 Daly, interview with McNeill, 22 November 1974, p. 25. He commented elsewhere that 'a leader at any level has to be prepared to do unpleasant things' that could, and often did, lead to casualties. See as well Ekins & McNeill, *Fighting to the Finish*, p. 254.
101 Daly, letter to COMAFV, 23 April 1968, NAA A6835, 1.
102 Ibid.
103 Daly, interview with Breen, 22 April 1994, 23.
104 Daly, letter to COMUSMACV, 28 November 1969, NAA A6835, 2.
105 Itinerary contained in AWM98, R875-2–36. See as well letter, Lieutenant-Colonel R.L. Burnard, MA to CGS to Australian Embassy, Saigon, 21 June 1967, AWM98, R875/2/184.
106 Daly, letter to COMAFV, 29 February 1968, NAA, A6835, 1.
107 Daly, cable 4311 to COMAFV, 14 February 1968, NAA A6835, 1.

108 Army HQ, cable to HQ AFV, 38593, 31 October 1967, AWM98, R875/2/184.
109 Ekins & McNeill, *Fighting to the Finish*, p. 522.
110 Military Board minute 1/1966, 21 January 1966, Military Board Proceedings, AHU.
111 Hetherington, letter to CGS, 15 December 1966, NAA, A6836/2.
112 Daly, letter to Hetherington, 23 December 1966, NAA, A6836/2.
113 For example, an article in the *Age* by Creighton Burns (26 October 1967) that queried the force structure implications of deploying the third battalion to 1ATF prompted a two-page note from Fraser to the Prime Minister, NAA, M4249, 2.
114 Daly, interview with Breen, 22 April 1994.
115 Daly, letter to Scherger, 10 April 1968, NAA, A6835, 1.
116 A significant exception, although still partial in its coverage, is Payne, *War and Words*.
117 Ibid., p. 298.
118 Lunn, *Vietnam*, p. 238.
119 Daly, letter to Morrow, 24 April 1970, NAA, A6835, 3.

7 *The civic action crisis, 1971*

1 Daly, interview with Breen, 22 April 1994, pp. 25–6. At the peak strength of 1ATF in May 1969 the force ratio between the USA and Australia was in the order of 68:1.
2 Daly, interview with McNeill, 22 November 1974, p. 23.
3 The subject of Nixon and the war is a large and complex one. An excellent analysis is provided by Kimball, *Nixon's Vietnam War*.
4 Horner, *Strategic Command*, p. 337; Cabinet minute 30, 9 December 1969, NAA, A5873, vol. 1.
5 'Views of Chiefs of Staff Committee on Withdrawals from Vietnam', 5 December 1969. NAA, A1946, 1969/2185 part 1.
6 Daly, interview with McNeill, 4 June 1975, p. 54.
7 Ibid., p. 66.
8 Cabinet minute 218, 17 March 1970. NAA, A5873, vol. 1; Cabinet minute 295, 22 April 1970, NAA, A5873, vol. 2.
9 Cable, *An Independent Command*, p. 78.
10 Secretary, minute to Minister for Defence, 24 November 1969, NAA, A1946, 1969/2185, part 1.
11 Daly minute, CGS 45/1970 to Wilton, 24 April 1970, NAA, A6835, 3.
12 See Smith, *Training the Bodes*.
13 Daly, interview with McNeill, 4 June 1975, pp. 65–6.
14 Laura Tingle, 'Army clash led to Gorton's downfall', *Sydney Morning Herald*, 1 January 2001, p. 6.
15 Cable, *An Independent Command*, p. 72.
16 Wood, *The Division in Battle*, especially chapter 6. For a short account of civic action see Smith, 'The role and impact of civil affairs in South Vietnam, 1965–1971', pp. 229–39. For the reflections of a former

commanding officer of 1ACAU (and subsequent CDF) see Gration, 'Reflections on 1ATF in Vietnam'.
17 Military Board minute 130/1966, 15 April 1966, Military Board Proceedings, AHU.
18 Ayres, *Malcolm Fraser*, p. 175; Fraser with Simons, *Malcolm Fraser*, p. 208. See as well Statement by the Minister for the Army, 'Civic action in Viet Nam', 11 July 1966, AWM101/11.
19 Military Board Minute 248/1968, 12 July 1968, Military Board Proceedings 1968/5, AHU.
20 One of Tange's recurrent themes was that 'the Department of Defence had, with a few outstanding exceptions, a mediocre intellectual level in 1969 when [Fraser] became Minister' (Ayres, *Malcolm Fraser*, p. 163). His views of senior uniformed personnel were even less flattering.
21 Tange, *Defence Policy-making*.
22 Ayres, *Malcolm Fraser*, p. 163. When Tange had been less than three months in the job, he gave his minister what a second biographer has labelled 'a royal ticking off' on the matter: 'I have observed the frequency with which, in extensive conversations with me and other senior officers, you have expressed a sense of urgency about a large number of matters and that you wish to see them brought to fruition. I am convinced that intensive detailed ministerial supervision and requests for explanations and reports, while doubtless seeking to satisfy the requirements that you believe you have, aggravate the delay by distracting senior officers from substantive work. Indeed this is a matter of fact and not opinion. It is a matter of fact and not a matter of ministerial authority' (Fraser with Simons, *Malcolm Fraser*, pp. 192–3).
23 A good summary of the growing animosity towards Gorton on the reactionary wing of conservative politics is provided by Hancock, *John Gorton*, especially pp. 275–81.
24 Ayres, *Malcolm Fraser*, pp. 160–1. Daly believed that Fraser saw Peacock as a rival even at this stage.
25 Tange, *Defence Policy-making*.
26 Daly, letter CGS 80/1970, 16 July 1970. NAA, A6835, 3.
27 Horner, *Strategic Command*, p. 353.
28 Daly, 'The Fraser affair 1971' (typescript), pp. 16–17; original in author's possession. Daly was referring to Confrontation (1962–66) but confusing it with the Malayan Emergency (1948–60).
29 Cabinet submission, no date [late September 1967], NAA, A1945/25, 65/7/1.
30 *London Gazette* (Supplement), no 44327, 10 June 1967, p. 6306.
31 Tange, minute to Fraser, n.d. NAA, A1946/25, 68/1138.
32 Killen, letter 'strictly personal', to Fraser, 29 July 1970. NAA, A1976, 68/1138.
33 Daly, interview with Breen, 22 April 1994, p. 37.
34 Ibid.
35 Fraser with Simons, *Malcolm Fraser*, p. 160.
36 Ibid., p. 209.

37 Holt, 'Mr Y and Mr Gorton'.
38 Daly, interview with McNeill, 4 June 1975, p. 33.
39 Brigadier J.R. Salmon, 'Military civic action, Vietnam 1971: Some personal observations', 16 March 1988. Copy in the author's possession.
40 Ibid., p. 5.
41 The cable traffic between CCOSC and COMAFV concerning this is at AWM101, 21B.
42 Daly, 'The Fraser affair 1971' (typescript), p. 2; McNeill interview, 4 June 1975, pp. 34–5. A background paper on civic action, prepared for Fraser and dated 23 February 1971, is at AWM101, 21B. Further discussion of responsibility for civic action within the Department of Defence is contained in a minute from the Defence Planning Division to Assistant Secretary, 16 March 1971, NAA, A1946/26, 70/1276.
43 Tange, *Defence Policy-making*. Edwards, *Arthur Tange*, p. 188.
44 Hancock notes, however, the convention that the chiefs of the services had the right of direct access to the prime minister and that Gorton, likewise, had tried to contact Fraser in Melbourne, without success (Hancock, *John Gorton*, p. 316).
45 Ibid., pp. 302, 311.
46 Ibid., p. 317; Ayres, *Malcolm Fraser*, pp. 179–80; Daly, 'The Fraser affair 1971' (typescript), pp. 4, 11–12.
47 Routine orders part 1, 6 March 1971, nos 62 and 63, AWM95, 1/4, March 1971 part 3.
48 Daly, 'The Fraser affair 1971' (typescript), p. 20. Daly answered a series of questions concerning his meeting with Gorton, posed by a journalist from the Melbourne *Herald* on 4 January designed as a follow-up piece to the Baudino article. His answers consisted of just five words, and were absolutely characteristic: 'Yes. No. Yes. Yes. Yes.' AWM101, 21A.
49 Ayres makes it clear in several places that Fraser was the original source of some of the stories concerned. *Malcolm Fraser*, p. 178.
50 Ibid., p. 181.
51 Edwards shows as well that Fraser consulted Tange, in whom he placed considerable trust, and that Tange advised him to resign if he lacked confidence in his leader or in the 'patch-up job' on offer between them (Edwards, *Arthur Tange*, p. 189).
52 Ham, *Vietnam*, p. 549.
53 CPD, HofR, 71, 9 March 1971, pp. 679–84.
54 Ramsay had enjoyed good personal relations with Gorton, and apologised within a few minutes (thus avoiding being called before the Bar). Years later he admitted that 'I was a young man and I got carried away . . . I mean, you don't willingly go out and make a clown of yourself' (transcript of interview, Monica Attard with Alan Ramsay, 4 December 2005, http://www.abc.net/sundayprofile).
55 Hancock, *John Gorton*, p. 328.
56 Daly, 'The Fraser affair 1971' (typescript), pp. 33, 37.
57 Ayres, *Malcolm Fraser*, p. 181.
58 Fraser with Simons, *Malcolm Fraser*, p. 216.

59 Horner, *Strategic Command*, p. 361.
60 Fraser with Simons, *Malcolm Fraser*, p. 225.
61 Secretary, Department of the Army, letter to COMAFV, 21 August 1969, AWM98, 776.
62 Daly, interview with McNeill, 4 June 1975, pp. 45, 49, 52.
63 Ibid., p. 45.
64 Ibid., p. 47.
65 Payne, *War and Words*, p. 298.
66 Holt, 'Mr Y and Mr Gorton'. For further confirmation see Howson, *The Life of Politics*, pp. 699, 700, 701, 703; 'I talked with Alan Reid and thanked him for all the help that he'd given us'.
67 Horner, *Australian Higher Command*, p. 71.
68 Ibid., p. 57.
69 Howson, *The Life of Politics*, p. 223.
70 Daly nonetheless believed that 'there would [not] be any real reduction in the size of the Army... the continuing world situation with its tensions and turmoil, especially in the South-East Asian region, would continue to require an effective Australian military capability in the area' (briefing at AHQ, 31 March 1969, 40, AHU).
71 Daly believed that National Service was a national good but that it was 'an expensive exercise as the return of service did not compensate for the expense, in money and manpower, of training'. He was also very alive to the political sensitivities of deploying national servicemen on active service. Susan (Daly) Ryrie, email, to author, 2 March 2012.
72 Palazzo, *The Australian Army*, pp. 282–3.
73 Lynch, letter to Fairhall, 8 August 1969. Copy in author's possession.
74 CGS' remarks, AHQ briefing, 27 October 1969, 73, AHU.
75 Ibid. The letter carries a handwritten annotation at the foot, signed by Bruce White: 'Draft cleared with CGS who agrees.'
76 Major-General S.C. Graham to GOC Northern Command, DCGS 33/69, 14 November 1969. Copy in author's possession.
77 GOC Northern Command to DCGS, 25 November 1969. Copy in author's possession.
78 GOC Northern Command to CGS, 3 January 1970. Copy in author's possession.
79 Minister for Defence, letter to Minister for Army, n.d. (February 1970?). Copy in author's possession.
80 Palazzo, *The Australian Army*, pp. 286–93.
81 CGS' remarks, AHQ briefing, 27 October 1969, AHU.
82 This is not the place for an extended discussion of the Hassett reforms, which continued in implementation phases after Daly's retirement. There is extensive documentation at NAA, A6840, 51; A3688, 581/R1/15 and A6381, 594/2/1. The summary presentation of Hassett's initial report to the Military Board is at Military Board minute 458/1970, appendix 1, 14 August 1970. Military Board Proceedings 1970/6, AHU.
83 Submission to Minister for Defence, January 1971, NAA, A1946/15, 68/1137.

84 Daly, letter to GOC eastern Command, 23 October 1970. NAA, A6835, 3.
85 Military Board minute 172/1971, 14 May 1971. Military Board Proceedings 1971/4.
86 Daly, letter CGS 46/1971 to Director AWM, 15 April 1971. AWM315, 653/001/010 01.
87 Daly, 'The Fraser affair 1971' (typescript), 42.

8 Epilogue

1 Military Board minute 172/1971, 14 May 1971, Proceedings 1971/4.
2 Military Board minute 194/1971, 28 May 1971, Proceedings 1971/4.
3 Signal, Army Pay, Melbourne to DFRBF, Canberra, 14 May 1971; minute, HQ Eastern Command, 4 August 1971. Daly, service dossier. Exactly what was wrong or what treatment he received cannot be ascertained without consulting his service medical records, to which access was denied to the author.
4 Military Board minute 221/1971, 11 June 1971, Proceedings 1971/5.
5 Betty-Ann Daly, email to author, 10 January 2012. The house on Empire Circuit has changed hands only twice since Daly built it (*Canberra Times*, 5 November 2004).
6 CGS, letter to Director, Australian War Memorial, 15 April 1971, CGS 46/1971, AWM315, 653/001/01001. I am grateful to Dr Jean Bou for drawing this to my attention.
7 McKernan, *Here is Their Spirit*, p. 276.
8 Agenda for Board of Trustees, 'Chairman of the Board of Trustees', n.d. (mid-1974), AWM93, 235/2/23, 893.
9 McKernan, *Here is Their Spirit*, p. 276.
10 Michael McKernan, email to author, 20 February 2012.
11 P.S. Evatt, note for file, 17 January 1978, AWM93, 235/2/23, part 2.
12 Gullett, letter to A.J. Sweeting, acting Director, 5 July 1974. AWM93, 235/2/23, part 2. Gullett's father was the wartime correspondent and subsequent official historian, Memorial Director and later wartime Cabinet minister, H.B. Gullett, a personal friend of Bean and many other leading figures from the Great War generation; letter, Daly to Sweeting, 11 July 1974. AWM93, 235/2/23, part 2.
13 Agenda and minutes of 24th meeting of Board of Trustees, 15 August 1974, 893. AWM93, 235/2/23, part 2.
14 Agenda item 13, 'Staffing', AWM93, 784/1/27.
15 Minutes of the first meeting of Council, 17 July 1980, AWM170.
16 Australian War Memorial, *Annual Report 1979–80*.
17 Daly, letter to Sir William Cole, Chairman, Public Service Board, 31 August 1981, AWM93, 745/2/6, part 1.
18 Reproduced in *Newsletter of the Australian War Memorial*, August 1980, AWM93, 745/2/6, part 1.
19 'He was known to the staff of the then much-smaller institution as an approachable and interested figure, remembered warmly by those privileged to have known him.' Peter Stanley, email, 16 February 2004.
20 McKernan, email to author, 20 February 2012.

21 My emphasis. Fairfax digital, 9 January 2004 [reproducing obituary in *Sydney Morning Herald*, 8 January 2004]; *Daily Telegraph*, 15 January 2004; *Canberra Times*, 16 January 2004; *Duty First*, 3:10, Autumn 2004, p. 39. Accounts of the funeral also appeared in the *Sydney Morning Herald* and the *Canberra Times*, both 15 January 2004.
22 Following is drawn from Monsignor Harley's homily, copy in the author's possession and with thanks to Monsignor Harley.
23 Harley, email to author, 19 March 2012.
24 Drawn from family remarks included in Cosgrove eulogy. Copy in author's possession.
25 Lieutenant-General Sir Thomas Daly, 'Major-General Sir James Harrison memorial lecture, 10 November 1982' (Canberra: privately published, 2000), p. 7.
26 Cited in Mallinson, *The Making of the British Army*, p. 473. The reference was prompted by a long and discursive review of Napier's *History of the Peninsular War* (6 vols, 1828–40).

Sources and Bibliography

Daly left few papers, and none of a personal nature. As he was an increasingly senior officer in a paper-based organisation it is possible to recover a great deal of what he thought, said and did through the official record, although there are gaps. This book would not have been possible, however, without the considerable number of interviews that he granted to a number of historians during his long retirement, especially Dr Bob Breen in the early years of the 1990s, and including Colonel David Chinn, Dr Ian McNeill, Dr Garth Pratten and the author. Details of the interviews and, where appropriate, their location, are contained in the notes. Private correspondence is likewise detailed in the notes.

Primary sources
National Archives of Australia

A1945 Correspondence files, multiple number series (Primary numbers 1–300), 1957–74
A1946 Correspondence files, annual single number series, 1967–73
A2653 Volumes of Military Board Proceedings, 1905–76
A3688 Correspondence files, multiple number series with 'R' [Army Headquarters, Canberra] infix, 1946–79
A5873 Third Gorton Ministry – folders of decisions of Cabinet and Cabinet committees, 1969–71
A6059 Correspondence files, multiple number series [class 441] [classified], 1925–66
A6831 Policy and working files of the Adjutant-General (AG)/Personnel Branch of Army Headquarters, 1963–74
A6835 Outward correspondence files of the Chief of the General Staff, 1963–
A6836 Demi-Official (DO) correspondence files of the Chief of the General Staff, 1963–
A6840 Non-file records of the Office of the Chief of the General Staff, 1960–
A7941 Internal CAS files dealing with involvement in DFDC, COSC and COSC SEATO meetings, 1942–82
B883 Second Australian Imperial Force Personnel Dossiers, 1939–47
B2455 First Australian Imperial Force Personnel Dossiers, 1914–20
M4249 Speeches and related papers of Harold Edward Holt as Prime Minister, 1967
MP729/8 Secret correspondence files, multiple number series 1945–55

MP927/1 General and civil staff correspondence files and Army personnel files, multiple number series, 1899–1968

Australian War Memorial
AWM52 2nd AIF (Australian Imperial Force) and CMF (Citizen Military Forces) unit war diaries, 1939–45 War
AWM67 Official History, 1939–45 War: Records of Gavin Long, General Editor
AWM93 Australian War Memorial registry files – First series, 1919–93
AWM95 Australian Army commanders' diaries, 1952–73
AWM98 Records of Headquarters Australian Force Vietnam (Army Component), 1966–72
AWM101 Records of Chief of the General Staff, 1959–72
AWM107 Department of Defence, Army Office, military history transcripts (includes Vietnam period), 1971–80
AWM122 Department of Defence, Joint Planning Committee records from joint military operations and plans, 1959–75
AWM170 Australian War Memorial Council and related committee records, 1918–
AWM315 Australian War Memorial registry files – Second series, 1940–
PR82/119 Wilton papers, 1926–81

National Archives (United Kingdom)
CAB106 Historical Section: Archivist and Librarian Files (AL Series)
WO281 Korean War: War Diaries
WO308 Korean War: Historical Records and Reports

Interviews
All interviews listed were conducted in Sydney, regardless of interviewer.

Interviews with Lieutenant-General Sir Thomas Daly
Bob Breen: 11 March, 8 April, 24 June 1991; 11 May, 15 June, 17 August, 14 September 1992; 12 July, 1 December 1993; 19 January, 22 April 1994
David Chinn: 10 July 2001
Jeffrey Grey: 12 October 1984
Ian McNeill: 22 November 1974; 4 January 1975
Garth Pratten: 26 October 2000

Interviews with Brigadier Sir Frederick Chilton
Bob Breen: 12 May 1992
Garth Pratten: 25 October 2000

SECONDARY SOURCES
Allchin, Lieutenant-Colonel Frank, *Purple and Blue: The History of the 2/10th Battalion, AIF (The Adelaide Rifles) 1939–1945*, Griffin Press, Adelaide, 1958
Andrews, Eric, *The Department of Defence*, Vol. V, *The Australian Centenary History of Defence*, Oxford University Press, Melbourne, 2001

Ayres, Philip, *Malcolm Fraser: A Biography*, Heinemann, Melbourne, 1987
Bacevich, A.J., *The Pentomic Era: The US Army between Korea and Vietnam*, National Defence University Press, Washington DC, 1986
Baker, Kevin, *Paul Cullen: Citizen and Soldier*, Rosenberg, Dural, 2005
Bergerson, Frederic A., *The Army gets an Air Force: Tactics of Insurgent Bureaucratic Politics*, Johns Hopkins University Press, Baltimore, 1978
Blair, Anne, *There to the Bitter End: Ted Serong in Vietnam*, Allen & Unwin, Sydney, 2001
—— *Ted Serong: The Life of an Australian Counter-Insurgency Expert*, Oxford University Press, Melbourne, 2002
Blaxland, J.C., *Organising an Army: The Australian Experience, 1957–1965*, Strategic and Defence Studies Centre, Canberra, 1989
Bolton, Geoffrey, *The Oxford History of Australia*: Vol. 5: *1942–1988: The Middle Way*, Oxford University Press, Melbourne, 1990
Bomford, Janette, *Soldiers of the Queen: Women in the Australian Army*, Oxford University Press, Melbourne, 2001
Bond, Brian, *The Victorian Staff Army and the Staff College, 1854–1914*, Eyre Methuen, London, 1972
Brune, Peter, *A Bastard of a Place: The Australians in Papua*, Allen & Unwin, Sydney, 2003
Cable, R.W., *An Independent Command: Command and Control of the 1st Australian Task Force in Vietnam*, Strategic and Defence Studies Centre, Canberra, 2000
Carver, Michael, *The Seven Ages of the British Army*, Weidenfeld & Nicolson, London, 1984
Church, J.M., *Second to None: 2RAR as the ANZAC Battalion in Vietnam, 1970–71*, Army Doctrine Centre, Mosman, 1995
Cooke, Major-General K.G., 'One army', in Peter Dennis & Jeffrey Grey (eds), *The Second Fifty Years: The Australian Army 1947–1997*, Australian Defence Force Academy, Canberra, 1997
Coombes, David, *Morshead: Hero of Tobruk and El Alamein*, Oxford University Press, Melbourne, 2001
Coulthard-Clark, Chris, *Duntroon: The Royal Military College of Australia, 1911–1986*, Allen & Unwin, Sydney, 1986
Darley, T.H., *With the Ninth Light Horse in the Great War*, Hassell Press, Adelaide, 1924
Dennis, Peter, 'The Duntroon affair', *Queen's Quarterly*, LXXVIII:I, Spring 1971
Donnelly, Roger, *The Scheyville Experience 1965–1973: The Officer Training Unit Scheyville*, University of Queensland Press, St Lucia, 2001
Downs, Ian, *The Australian Trusteeship: Papua New Guinea 1945–1975*, AGPS, Canberra, 1980
Edwards, Peter, *A Nation at War: Australian Politics, Society and Diplomacy during the Vietnam War 1965–1975*, Allen & Unwin, Sydney, 1997
—— *Arthur Tange: Last of the Mandarins*, Allen & Unwin, Sydney, 2006
Ekins, Ashley & Ian McNeill, *Fighting to the Finish: The Australian Army and the Vietnam War, 1968–1975*, Allen & Unwin, Sydney, 2012

Feuchtwanger, Edgar & William J. Philpott, 'Civil–military relations in a period without major wars, 1855–1885' in Paul S. Smith (ed.), *Government and the Armed Forces in Britain 1856–1990*, Hambledon, London, 1996
Frame, Tom, *Where Fate Calls: The HMAS Voyager Tragedy*, Hodder & Stoughton, Sydney, 1992
—— *The Cruel Legacy: The HMAS Voyager Tragedy*, Allen & Unwin, Sydney, 2005
Fraser, Malcolm, with Margaret Simons, *Malcolm Fraser: The Political Memoirs*, Miegunyah Press, Melbourne, 2010
Fruhling, Stephen (ed.), *A History of Australian Strategic Policy since 1945*, Defence Publishing Service, Canberra, 2009
Gration, P.C., 'Reflections on 1ATF in Vietnam', *Journal of the Australian War Memorial*, April 1988
Gray, T.I.G., *The Imperial Defence College and the Royal College of Defence Studies*, Her Majesty's Stationery Office, Edinburgh, 1977
Greville, Brigadier P.J., *The Royal Australian Engineers 1945 to 1972: Paving the Way*, Corps Committee of the RAE, Sydney, 2002
Grey, Jeffrey, *The Commonwealth Armies and the Korean War: An Alliance Study*, Manchester University Press, Manchester, 1988
—— *Up Top: The Royal Australian Navy in Southeast Asian Conflicts 1955–1972*, Allen & Unwin, Sydney, 1998
—— *The Australian Army: A History*, Oxford University Press, Melbourne, 2nd edn, 2006
—— *A Military History of Australia*, Cambridge University Press, Melbourne, 3rd edn, 2008
—— *Australian Brass: The Military Career of Lieutenant-General Sir Horace Robertson*, Cambridge University Press, Melbourne, 2nd edn, 2009
Gullett, Henry 'Jo', *Not as a Duty Only: An Infantryman's War*, Oxford University Press, Melbourne, 1976
Gullett, H.S., *The Australian Imperial Force in Sinai and Palestine, 1914–1918: Official History of Australia in the War of 1914–1918*, Vol. 7, Angus & Robertson, Sydney, 1923
Ham, Paul, *Vietnam: The Australian War*, HarperCollins, Sydney, 2007
Hancock, Ian, *John Gorton: He did It His Way*, Hodder, Sydney, 2002
Hay, D.A., *Nothing Over Us: The Story of the 2/6th Australian Infantry Battalion*, Australian War Memorial, Canberra, 1984
Holt, Stephen, 'Mr Y and Mr Gorton', *Quadrant on-line*, LII:10, October 2008, http://www.quadrant.org.au
Horner, D.M., *Crisis of Command: Australian Generalship and the Japanese Threat, 1941–43*, ANU Press, Canberra, 1978
—— 'Staff Corps versus militia: The Australian experience of World War II', *Defence Force Journal*, 26, January/February 1981
—— *High Command: Australia and Allied Strategy, 1939–1945*, George Allen & Unwin, Sydney, & AWM, Canberra, 1982
—— *Australian Higher Command in the Vietnam War*, Strategic and Defence Studies Centre, Canberra, 1986
—— *General Vasey's War*, Oxford University Press, Melbourne, 1992

Horner, David, *Defence Supremo: Sir Frederick Shedden and the Making of Australian Defence Policy*, Allen & Unwin, Sydney, 2000
—— *Strategic Command: General Sir John Wilton and Australia's Asian Wars*, Oxford University Press, Melbourne, 2005
Howson, Peter, *The Life of Politics: The Howson Diaries*, Viking, Melbourne, 1984
Howze, Hamilton H., *A Cavalryman's Story: Memoirs of a Twentieth-Century Army General*, Smithsonian Institution Press, Washington, 1996
Hyslop, Robert, *Aye Aye, Minister: Australian Naval Administration 1939–1959*, AGPS, Canberra, 1990
Johnston, William, *A War of Patrols: Canadian Army Operations in Korea*, University of British Columbia Press, Vancouver, 2003
Keating, Gavin, *The Right Man for the Right Job: Lieutenant-General Sir Stanley Savige as a Military Commander*, Oxford University Press, Melbourne, 2006
Kimball, Jeffrey, *Nixon's Vietnam War*, University Press of Kansas, Lawrence, 1998
Lee, J.E., *Duntroon: The Royal Military College of Australia 1911–1946*, Australian War Memorial, Canberra, 1952
Lockhart, Greg, *The Minefield: An Australian Tragedy in Vietnam*, Allen & Unwin, Sydney, 2007
Long, Gavin, *To Benghazi, Australia in the War of 1939–1945*, Series 1, Vol. I, Australian War Memorial, Canberra, 1951
—— *The Final Campaigns: Australia in the War of 1939–1945*, Series 1, Vol. VII, Australian War Memorial, Canberra, 1963
—— *The Six Years War: A Concise History of Australia in the 1939–45 War*, Australian War Memorial, Canberra, 1973
Lunn, Hugh, *Vietnam: A Reporter's War*, University of Queensland Press, St Lucia, 1985
Lyman, Robert, *The Longest Siege – Tobruk: The Battle That Saved North Africa*, Macmillan, London, 2009
McCarthy, Dayton, *The Once and Future Army: A History of the Citizen Military Forces, 1947–74*, Oxford University Press, Melbourne, 2003
McGibbon, Ian, *New Zealand's Vietnam War: A History of Combat, Commitment and Controversy*, Exisle, Auckland, 2010
McGregor, Malcolm, 'An army at dusk: The Vietnam-era army comes home', in Peter Dennis & Jeffrey Grey (eds), *Raise, Train and Sustain: Delivering Land Combat Power*, Army History Unit, Canberra, 2010
McKernan, Michael, *Here is Their Spirit: A History of the Australian War Memorial 1917–1990*, University of Queensland Press, St Lucia, 1991
McNeill, Ian, *To Long Tan: The Australian Army and the Vietnam War 1950–1966*, Allen & Unwin, Sydney, in association with the Australian War Memorial, 1993
McNeill, Ian & Ashley Ekins, *On the Offensive: The Australian Army in the Vietnam War 1967–68*, Allen & Unwin, Sydney, 2003
Mallinson, Allan, *The Making of the British Army: From the English Civil War to the War on Terror*, Bantam, London, 2009

Maugham, Barton, *Tobruk and Alamein: Australia in the War of 1939–1945*, Series 1, Vol. III, Australian War Memorial, Canberra, 1966
Moore, Darren, *Duntroon: A History of the Royal Military College of Australia 1911–2001*, RMC, Canberra, 2001
Morrison, James, *Mechanising an Army: Mechanisation Policy and the Conversion of the Light Horse, 1923–1940*, Land Warfare Studies Centre, Canberra, 2006
O'Brien, Michael, *Conscripts and Regulars: With the Seventh Battalion in Vietnam*, Allen & Unwin, Sydney, 1995
Ollif, Lorna, *Colonel Best and Her Soldiers: The Story of the 33 Years of the Women's Royal Australian Army Corps*, self-published, Sydney, 1985
O'Neill, R.J., *Vietnam Task: The 5th Battalion, Royal Australian Regiment 1966/67*, Cassell, Melbourne, 1968
O'Neill, Robert, *Australia in the Korean War 1950–53*, Vol. 2: *Combat Operations*, AGPS, Canberra, 1985
O'Neill, Robert J., *The Army in Papua-New Guinea*, Canberra Papers on Strategy and Defence 10, AGPS, Canberra, 1971
Palazzo, Albert, *The Australian Army: A History of its Organisation, 1901–2001*, Oxford University Press, Melbourne, 2001
Payne, Trish, *War and Words: The Australian Press and the Vietnam War*, Oxford University Press, Melbourne, 2007
Phillips, Peter (ed.), *Heritage Homes of the Australian Defence Force – Queensland*, Defence Housing Authority, Barton, ACT, 1996; http://www.dha.gov.au/publications
Pratten, Garth, *Australian Battalion Commanders in the Second World War*, Melbourne, Cambridge University Press, 2009
Pratten, Garth & Glyn Harper (eds), *Still the Same: Reflections on Active Service from Bardia to Baidoa*, Army Doctrine Centre, Sydney, 1996
Rowell, S.F., *Full Circle*, Melbourne University Press, Melbourne, 1974
Sinclair, James, *To Find a Path: The Life and Times of the Pacific Islands Regiment*, Vol. I: *Yesterday's Heroes, 1885–1950*, Boolarong Publications, Brisbane, 1990
—— *To Find a Path: The Papua New Guinea Defence Force and the Australians to Independence*, Vol. II: *Keeping the Peace 1950–1975*, Crawford House Press, Gold Coast, 1992
Smith, Barry, 'The role and impact of civil affairs in South Vietnam,1965–1971' in Peter Dennis & Jeffrey Grey (eds), *The Australian Army and the Vietnam War 1962–1972*, Army History Unit, Canberra, 2002
Smith, Terry, *Training the Bodes: Australian Army Advisers Training Cambodian Infantry Battalions – A Postscript to the Vietnam War*, Big Sky, Newport, NSW, 2011
Stanley, Peter, *Invading Australia: Japan and the Battle for Australia 1942*, Viking Penguin, Sydney, 2008
Starry, Donn A., *Armored Combat in Vietnam*, US Army Center of Military History, Washington DC, 1978
Stephens, Alan, *Going Solo: The Royal Australian Air Force, 1946–1971*, AGPS, Canberra, 1995

Stockings, Craig A.J., *The Making and Breaking of the Post-Federation Australian Army, 1901–09*, Land Warfare Studies Centre, Canberra, 2007
Strachan, Hew, *The Politics of the British Army*, Clarendon Press, Oxford, 1997
Tange, Sir Arthur (P.G. Edwards, ed.), *Defence Policy-making: A Close-up View, 1950–1980*, ANU e-Press, http://epress.anu.edu
Tolson, John J., *Airmobility 1961–1971: Vietnam Studies*, Department of the Army, Washington DC, 1973
Vamplew (ed.), Wray, *Australians: Historical Statistics*, Fairfax, Syme & Weldon, Melbourne, 1987
Welburn, M.C.J., *The Development of Australian Army Doctrine 1945–1964*, Strategic and Defence Studies Centre, Canberra, 1994
Wilmot, Chester, *Tobruk 1941: Capture—Siege—Relief*, Angus & Robertson, Sydney, 1944
Wood, James, *The Division in Battle*, Pamphlet No. 11: *Counter-Revolutionary Warfare*, Army Headquarters, Canberra, 1965
—— *9th Battalion Royal Australian Regiment: Vietnam Tour of Duty 1968–1969: On Active Service*, 9RAR Association, Enoggera, Qld, 1992
—— *Chiefs of the Australian Army: Higher Command of the Australian Military Forces 1901–1914*, AMHP, Loftus, NSW, 2006

Theses and unpublished papers

Colebatch, P., 'To find a path: The army in Papua New Guinea', PhD, University of Sussex, 1970
Daly, Lieutenant-General Sir Thomas, 'The Army Aviation Corps: The early years', typescript memoir, copy in the author's possession
Horn, Mark, 'Australia's development of the Pacific Islands Regiment from 1951 to 1965', BA (Hons) thesis, UNSW (ADFA), 1994
Lamerton, Matthew, 'An asset to the army: Rotary-wing aviation from the mid-1950s to the mid-1980s', BA (Hons) thesis, UNSW (ADFA), 2005
Murphy, J.E., 'History of the postwar army', unpublished manuscript [prepared at the direction of the Military Board], 1955; http://www.army.gov.au/ahu.
Richardson, Tom, 'The siege of Giarabub, December 1940–March 1941', 2010. http://www.awm.gov.au/research
Vincent, Alison, '"Women have come to stay": The demobilisation and reintroduction of the Australian women's services, 1941–1955', BA (Hons) thesis, UNSW (ADFA), 1992

Index

1st Australian Task Force, 136, 148, 151–2, 156
  base at Nui Dat, 153
  casualties, 169, 170
  expansion of, 158
  helicopter support of, 163, 166, 167
  reduction to two battalions, 178
1st Aviation Regiment, 142
1st Battalion, King's Own Scottish Borderers, 71
1st Battalion, RAR, 70, 72, 92, 158
  B Company, Operation Fauna and, 80
  first tour of Vietnam and, 147
  Operation Trimdon and, 112
1st Battalion, Royal New Zealand Infantry Regiment, 154
1st Infantry Brigade, 100
1st Royal Queensland Regiment, 99
2nd Battalion, 99
2nd Battalion, RAR, 70, 158
2nd Infantry Division, 91
2nd Royal Queensland Regiment, 99
2/1st Machine Gun Battalion, 52
2/2nd Anti-Tank Regiment, 48
2/4th Field Regiment, 51
2/6th Battalion, 38
2/9th Battalion, 47, 51
2/10th Battalion, 82, 127, 152
  A Company, 48, 51
  B Company, 48, 52
  Balikpapan landing plan and, 47
  Balikpapan landings and, 48
  C Company, 48, 51, 52
  casualties, 37, 51, 52, 54
  D Company, 48
  embarkation to Morotai, 43
  'five and two' scheme, implications of, 45
  Hill 87 and, 47, 48
  training, Queensland, 1944, 41–2
2/11th Battalion, 69
2/12th Battalion, 47
2/14th Queensland Mounted Infantry Regiment, 91
3rd Battalion, RAR, 70, 157
  preparation for Vietnam, 158–9
4th Battalion, RAR, 158
5th Battalion, RAR, 148, 159, 160, 168
  casualties, 169
5th Division, 31–2
  deployment to Papua, 33–4
  reduction and capture of Salamua and, 34
6th Battalion, RAR, 148, 159
7th Battalion, RAR, 152–3, 158
7th Division, 17, 31, 41, 46, 54
  landings at Balikpapan and, 47
7th Infantry Brigade, 91
8th Battalion, RAR, 178
9th Battalion, 91
9th Battalion, RAR, 156
  preparation for Vietnam, 159–60
9th (Moreton) Regiment, 99
11th Field Regiment, 91
11th (Independent) Infantry Brigade, 92
18th Infantry Brigade, 15–18, 47
  seige of Tobruk and, 26, 29
  training, Egypt, 21
  transport vehicles, Egypt and, 20
19th Brigade, 39
25th Battalion, 91
25th (Darling Downs) Regiment, 99
28th British Commonwealth Infantry Brigade, 70, 71, 72, 80
29th British Brigade, 80
31st Battalion, 92

31st (Kennedy) Regiment, 99
41st (Byron Scottish) Regiment, 99
42nd Battalion, 92
42nd (Capricornia) Regiment, 99
47th (Wide Bay) Regiment, 99
51st Battalion, 92
51st (Far North Queensland) Regiment, 99
No 16 Army Light Aircraft Squadron, 109

Abrams, Gen Creighton W., 172, 179, 180
Allchin, Capt Frank, 15
Andersen, Brig J. H. ('Hans'), 100
Anderson, Lt-Gen W. A. B., 87
Armstrong, Lt-Gen R. F., 87
Army Review Committee. *See* Hassett Committee
Assisted Migrant scheme, 123
Australian Army
  8th Military District, 90
  appointment to command in, 39–40
  apprenticeships, 108
  Australian Force Vietnam, 119, 173
  average age of command appointments, Second World War, 39–40
  Aviation Corps, 141, 163
  basing in Australia, post Vietnam, 182–3
  Borneo landings, purpose of, 44
  ceiling on strength of, 122
  Chiefs of Staff Committee, 118, 151, 164, 167
  Citizen Military Force and, 91, 92, 98, 101, 104, 105, 106–7, 110, 116, 117–18, 119, 121, 122, 125–6, 127, 182, 193
  demobilisation of, post Second World War, 54
  Eastern Command, 110–13
  education and training and, 107
  Far East Strategic Reserve, committment to, 90
  'five and two' scheme and, 45
  force contribution to Korean War, 70–1
  infantry battalion as unit of, 38–9
  interwar period, 58–9
  management of, 1950s and 1960s, 121–2
  manpower shortfall and, 122–3
  mechanisation of, post–Great War, 14
  military aviation and, 109–10, 140–5, 163–7
  Military Board and. *See* Military Board
  Northern Command, 90–2, 99, 100–1
  Officer Cadet School, Portsea, 67, 70, 108, 138
  organisational change, post Vietnam, 192
  pay and conditions and, 130–2
  Pentropic system and, 91, 98, 101, 103, 105, 106, 110, 112, 119, 125, 148
  Permanent Military Force officers and, 39, 40, 59
  post of Military Operations and Plans, 82–3
  recruitment of ex-British Army members, 123–4
  retention of national servicemen and, 124–5
  service ministers and, 116–17, 120
  Staff College, 137
  strength of, 1960s, 104–7
  Training Team, Vietnam, 111, 128, 147
  Vietnam War 1966–71 and. *See* Vietnam War 1966–71, Australian Army and
  Women's Royal Australian Army Corp, 108–9, 122
  See also Royal Australian Air Force

Balikpapan, Battle of
  battle plans for, 45–6
  Hill 87 and, 51, 53
  landings, 46–7
  Parramatta Ridge and, 46, 47, 48, 53
  second day objectives of, 53
  Tank Farm area and, 53
  third day objectives of, 53
Baudino, Robert, 187
Bennett, Maj-Gen Gordon, 33

Berryman, Maj-Gen Frank, 34, 91
Birse, Lt R. G., 152
Blamey, FM Sir Thomas, 30, 34, 45, 55, 66, 91
Bland, Sir Henry, 139, 168, 181, 182
Bridgeford, Lt-Gen Sir William, 72
British Commonwealth Occupation Force, 55, 66
Brocksopp, Capt W. A., 53
Brogan, Maj-Gen Sir Mervyn, 115, 128, 194–5, 198
Bruche, Maj-Gen Sir J. H., 103
Burnard, Lt-Col Ray, 129

Cape, Maj-Gen T. F., 129
Carver, FM Lord, 1
Cassels, FM Sir James, 77–8, 166
Chilton, Brig Sir Frederick, 38, 40, 42, 46, 56
Churchill, Sir Winston, 85
Cleland, Sir Donald, 97, 98
Combes, Brig B., 66
Cramer, Sir John, 116
Cullen, Maj-Gen Paul, 125, 126–7
Cullen, Simon, 118

Daly, Eileen Mary, 4
Daly, Lt-Gen Sir Thomas Joseph
  1st Australian Task Force and, 151–2
  army exercises 1957–58 and, 99–100
  army recruitment and, 105–6
  as Adjutant-General Military Board, 103–4
  as brigade major of 18th Brigade, 17
  as Brigadier-General Staff, Army Headquarters, 89
  as Chief of the General Staff, 114–45, 146–76
  as commander, 2/10th Battalion. 36, 37, 40–1
  as commander, 28th Brigade, 72–8
  as commander, 28th British Commonwealth Infantry Brigade, 70
  as Director of Infantry, Army Headquarters, Melbourne, 69, 70
  as Director of Military Art, RMC Duntroon, 65
  as Director of Military Operations and Plans, 82, 83–4
  as forward commander, 75
  as GOC Eastern Command, 110–13
  as GOC Northern Command, 89
  as GSO1 (Training), Army Headquarters, Melbourne, 60
  as GSO1 to headquarters of the 5th Division, 31
  as GSO2 to headquarters of the 6th Division, 29
  as Honorary Colonel, Pacific Islands Regiment, 97, 98, 140, 199
  as instructor of the Australian Staff School, 35
  attachment to 3rd Carbineers, 14
  Australian Rules football, RMC Duntroon and, 68
  Australian War Memorial and, 195, 199–204
  awarded CB, 115
  awarded CBE, 82, 184
  awarded DSO, 55
  awarded Legion of Honour, 82
  awarded OBE, 35
  'bastardisation', RMC Duntroon and, 68–9, 133–7
  battalion training and, 32–3, 42
  Battle of Balikpapan and, 48–52
  Battle of Balikpapan battle plans and, 45–7, 48
  birth, 3
  British Army attachment in India and, 13–14
  capture of Giarabub and, 21–4
  'civic action crisis' and, 185–90
  death, 204
  'disturbances', PNG 1957 and, 94, 95–7
  divisional training instruction no. 4 and, 32
  education, RMC Duntroon, 8–11
  establishment of SEATO and, 84
  evaluation of by superior officers, 11, 13, 30, 56, 63, 65, 69
  fall of Salamaua and, 35
  final Military Board meeting, 197–8

Daly, Lt-Gen Sir Thomas (*cont.*)
  guidelines for civic action and, 185–7
  identification with army, 207
  immediate post–Second World War plans, 54–5
  Imperial Defence College and, 85, 114
  importance of family to, 206
  Joint Services Staff College and, 65
  marriage, 59–60
  meeting with Wootten, 18
  mention in dispatches, 35
  Middle East Staff College, Haifa and, 30–1
  military aviation and, 109–10, 140–5, 165, 166–7
  National Service scheme and, 124
  New Zealand commitment to Vietnam War and, 156
  opinion on Korean patrols, 80
  outbreak of Second World War and, 15
  pay and conditions advocacy, 130–2
  possible appointment to 3rd Battalion, RAR, 69
  post retirement positions, 199
  posting as adjutant, 2/10th Battalion, Second AIF, 15
  posting to 3rd Light Horse Regiment, 11
  posting to 4th Light Horse Regiment, 11
  prisoners of war, Korea and, 79–80
  production of ski warfare manual, 29
  professional standards and, 133
  proposal of marriage to Heather Fitzgerald, 42
  recommendations for Pacific Islands Regiment, 97–8
  recruitment of ex-British Army members and, 124
  reform of army education and training and, 107–8
  relationship with enlisted men, 57
  relationship with Fraser, 120–1, 180–1, 182, 183, 184–5, 187
  relationship with immediate subordinates, 56
  relationship with Milford, 33
  relationship with press, 174–5, 191
  relationship with service ministers, 120
  relieved of command, 28th Brigade, 80–2
  religious faith of, 205–6
  retirement, 195–6, 198
  return to Australia, 1941, 31
  review of army organisation and, 193
  service housing and, 61, 62, 99, 111–12, 119, 130, 182
  siege of Tobruk and, 25–9
  Staff College and, 14, 18, 30
  Staff College, Camberley and, 61, 62–4
  'Strategic Basis of Australian Defence Policy, The' and, 98–9
  success as battalion commander, 55–6
  succession to Wilton and, 184
  Vietnam War and, 146–76
  view on Citizen Military Force, 126, 127
  view on Malaya commitment, 85
  view of senior RAAF personnel, Vietnam, 164–5
  view of Vietnam War, 177
  visits to Vietnam, 170–4
  withdrawal from Vietnam and, 178, 179, 185
  WRAAC and, 109
Daly, Thomas Joseph Sr
  death of, 130
  enlistment in Great War, 4–5
  Great War service of, 5–7
  post-war citizen forces service, 7
  Second World War service, 8
Dawson, Maj-Gen R. B., 156
Derrick, Lt T. C. ('Diver'), 45
Dill, FM Sir John, 86
Diro, Maj Ted, 138, 140
Dobbs, Lt-Col J. G., 38
Dodds, Maj-Gen T. H., 103
Dougherty, Maj-Gen Ivan, 40, 57
Duntroon. *See* Royal Military College, Duntroon

Edgar, Lt-Gen H. G., 110
Esher Committee, 102
Ewell, Lt-Gen Julian J., 179

INDEX 247

Fairhall, Sir Allen, 141, 142, 150, 154, 156, 160, 168, 180, 193
Fitzgeorge-Balfour, Gen Sir Victor, 87
Fitzpatrick, Gen Sir Desmond, 87
Forbes, Dr A. J. ('Jim'), 116
Foster, Brig-Gen H. J. F., 68
Fox Committee, 134, 135, 136
Fraser, Maj-Gen C. A. E., 136, 185
Fraser, Malcolm, 114, 117, 120–1, 126, 130, 131, 156, 158, 174, 180–1, 182, 183, 185–90, 194
Frost, Lt-Col John, 64

Garrett, Lt-Gen Sir [Alwyn] Ragnar, 12, 18, 100, 101, 116
Geard, Lt-Col C. J., 38
Giarabub, capture of, 21–4
Goble, AVM S. J., 86
Gorton, Sir John, 116, 138, 180, 181, 185–90
Graham, Maj-Gen Stuart, 128, 129, 168, 169, 192
Grandy, AM Sir John, 64
Green, Lt-Col C. H., 69
Gwynn, Maj-Gen Sir Charles, 68

Hackett, Lance-Sgt C. G., 52
Hancock, AM Sir Valston, 164
Hannah, AVM Sir Colin, 166
Harrison, Maj-Gen J. W., 87, 110, 118
Hassett Committee, 136
  problems addressed by, 194
Hassett, Gen Sir Francis, 115, 193–4
Hay, Maj-Gen R. A., 136
Heritage, Brig F. B., 9
Herring, Lt-Gen Sir Edmund ('Ned'), 29, 34
Hetherington, John, 174
Holt, Harold, 148, 156, 181, 190
Hopkins, Maj-Gen R. N. L., 14, 69
Howson, Peter, 141, 165
Hughes, Brig R. L., 159, 169
Hull, FM Sir Richard, 63
Hunter, Brig I. M., 96
Hutton, Maj-Gen E. T. H., 102

Imperial Defence College, 85–7

Jackson, Col O. D., 147
Jess, Lt-Gen Sir Carl, 103
Jolly, Gen Sir Alan, 87

Kahn, Lt-Col C. N., 129
Kendall, Lt-Gen Paul W., 78
Kerr Committee, 130, 132
Kerr, John, 130
Killen, Jim, 184
Korean War
  Commonwealth Division, relationship with US I Corps, 78–9
  fighting patrols and, 79
  first year of, 75–6
  redeployment of brigades and, 80

Lavarack, Col J. D., 11, 17, 68, 86
Lend-Lease scheme, 58
Lowa, Maj Patterson, 138, 140
Lush, AIRCDE John, 151
Lynch, Phillip, 120, 127, 134–5, 193

MacAdie, Brig-Gen T. F. B., 115
MacDonald, Brig J. F. M., 71
MacDonald, Col A. B., 128
MacDonald, Maj-Gen A. L., 152, 161
Mackay, Maj-Gen K., 129, 147, 148, 158
Maizey, Maj S. J., 168
Mann, Maj A. S., 80
Martin, Lt-Col J. E. G., 23
McDonald, Maj-Gen A. L., 129
McGuinn, Lt-Col L., 95, 96, 97
McKnight, Allan, 116
McMahon, Sir William, 182
McNicoll, VADM Sir Alan, 118, 150, 151
Menzies, Sir Robert, 39, 83, 84, 104, 181
Miell, Lt-Col Albert, 4
Miethke, Maj G. R., 40, 52
Milford, Maj-Gen E. J. ('Teddy'), 31, 33, 34, 46
Military Board, 66, 69, 83, 91, 101, 106, 117, 125, 126, 129, 136, 138, 141, 180, 192, 197
  establishment and structure of, 102–3
  promotions and selections and, 114
  role of Adjutant-General on, 103

248 INDEX

Millar Committee, 193
Montgomery, FM B. L., 63
Morrison, Maj-Gen A. L. ('Alby'), 76, 129, 159
Morshead, Brig-Gen L. J., 15, 17, 25, 26, 28, 88
Morshead Committee, 83, 116, 168
Murdoch, AM Sir Alister, 118, 150, 151, 164, 166, 167
Murphy, Lt-Col J. M., 129
Musa, Gen Mohammad, 87

National Service scheme, 67, 91, 98, 103, 111, 119, 121, 122, 125, 126, 148, 192
New Guinea Infantry Battalion, 92
New Zealand, commitment to Vietnam War, 154–6
Nicholls, Lt-Col N. A. M., 61
Northcott, Lt-Gen Sir John, 35, 39

O'Daniel, Lt-Gen John W. ('Iron Mike'), 78
O'Neill, Capt R. J., 169

Pacific Islands Regiment, 92, 94, 97–8, 99, 122
  1st Battalion, 96
  2nd Battalion, 138
  development of indigenous officers, 138
  independence of PNG and, 137–8
  pay and conditions and, 137–40
  relationship with Department of Territories, 138–9
  reraising of, 92–3
  strike in, 131
Paltridge, Shane, 141
Papua New Guinea, 90, 92
  'disturbances', 1957, 94–5
  relations between army and local administration, 93–4
  role of Pacific Islands Regiment in independence of, 137–8
Papua New Guinea Volunteer Rifles, 92
Papuan Infantry Battalion, 92, 94
Patterson, Maj-Gen A. G., 124
Peacock, Andrew, 120, 135, 182, 183, 184, 186, 187, 192, 194, 197
Pearson, Maj-Gen C. M. I., 130, 136

Pollard, Lt-Gen Sir Reginald, 36, 127–8
Pope, Comr C. J., 86

Ramsay, Alan, 186, 187, 188, 189
Reid, Alan, 191
Richmond, VADM Sir Herbert, 86
Robertson, Lt-Gen Sir H. C. H., 39, 40, 66, 91
Rowell, Lt-Gen Sir Sydney, 66, 71, 72, 82, 86, 129
Royal Australian Air Force, 45, 84, 99, 109–10, 121, 131, 132, 140–2, 143–5, 148, 150, 156, 164, 183
  cooperation with Australian Army, 163
  See also Australian Army, military aviation
Royal Australian Navy, 84, 113, 118, 130, 132, 133, 156, 165, 166, 183, 194
Royal Military College, Duntroon, 65–7
  'bastardisation' and, 68–9, 133–7
  degree-level education and, 134, 136
  entry to, 108
  Four Corners program and, 135
  position of Director of Military Art at, 68

Salmon, Col John, 185
Samuel, Peter, 187, 191
Savige, Lt-Gen Sir Stanley, 29, 34
Scherger, ACM Sir Frederick, 118, 148, 175
Scott, Lt-Col W. H., 5
Sellheim, Maj-Gen Victor, 103
Serong, Brig F. P. ('Ted'), 128–9
Sharp, Lt-Col Derek, 99
Shedden, Sir Frederick, 83, 84, 86, 116
Shelton, Lt-Col Jim, 158–9
Sinclair, Frank, 116
Smith, Lt-Col Eric, 152
Smith, VADM Sir Victor, 183, 184, 191, 197
Squires, Lt-Gen E. K., 91
Stantke, Lt-Gen Victor, 103
Sturdee, Lt-Gen Sir Vernon, 39, 91
Swartz, Sir Reginald, 143

Tange, Sir Arthur, 116, 168, 181, 182, 183, 185, 187
Taylor, Brig George, 72
Tharpar, Gen P. N., 87
Tobruk, siege of, 25–6

Vasey, Maj-Gen G. A., 29, 39, 41, 66
Verrier, Lt-Col A. D., 15
Vickery, Maj-Gen N. A., 126, 127
Vietnam War 1966–71, Australian Army and, 146–76
  1st Australian Civil Affairs Unit, 180
  1st Australian Logistic Support Group, 162, 172
  1st Australian Task Force. *See* Task Force, 1st Australian
  armed warfare and, 160–2
  barrier minefield in Phuoc Tuy and, 168–70
  'Bushranger' helicopter and, 167
  civic action and, 180, 185–6, 187
  command relationships and, 167
  containment of activity to Phuoc Tuy, 179, 192
  cooperation with RAAF, 163, 166
  'gunship kits', purchase of, 167
  Iroquois ('Huey') helicopter and, 164, 165, 167
  Joint Intelligence Organisation and, 187–8
  manpower shortage and, 154
  military aviation and, 163–7
  Nui Dat base and, 154, 162–3, 179
  press relations and, 191
  press reportage in Australia and, 175
  raising of manpower ceiling, 156–7
  soldier preparation, 152–3
  Vung Tau base and, 162–3, 179
  withdrawal from, 178–80
Vietnamisation, 178, 179
Vincent, Maj-Gen D., 129, 151, 152, 154, 160, 166, 168
Vowles, Brig E. L., 66

Wade, Maj-Gen R. E., 102
Warfe, Lt-Col George, 128
Weir, Brig S. P., 151
Wells, Lt-Gen Sir Henry, 67, 89, 109, 140
West, Maj-Gen M. M. A. R. ('Mike'), 78, 79
Westmoreland, Gen William, 147, 148, 150
White, Bruce, 116, 170, 174, 186
White, Gen Sir Cyril Brudenell, 39, 61
Whitlam, Gough, 182
Wilton, Brig J. G. N., 34, 81, 82, 86, 88, 116, 118, 131, 147, 148, 150, 151, 161, 162, 163, 164, 169, 174, 178, 180, 198
Wootten, Maj-Gen Sir George, 18
  capture of Giarabub and, 21–3
Wynter, Lt-Gen H. D., 39, 103